Expensive Habits

Simon Garfield is a 26-year-old journalist living and working in London. While at the London School of Economics in 1981 he was named *Guardian/NUS Student Journalist of the Year, and has since written for numerous newspapers and magazines. He is currently employed at *Time Out*.

EXPENSIVE HABITS

The Dark Side of
The Music Industry

Simon Garfield

ff

faber and faber
LONDON · BOSTON

First published in Great Britain in 1986
by Faber and Faber Limited
3 Queen Square London WC1N 3AU
and in the United States of America
by Faber Inc Boston
as *Money for Nothing: Greed and Exploitation
in the Music Industry*
Phototypeset by Wilmaset Birkenhead Wirral
Printed in Great Britain by
Butler and Tanner Frome Somerset

British Library Cataloguing in Publication Data

Garfield, Simon
Expensive habits: the dark side of the
music industry.
1. Music trade   2. Music, Popular
(Songs, etc.)
I. Title
338.4'778042   ML3790
ISBN 0–571–13720–2
ISBN 0–571–13721–0 Pbk

Library of Congress Cataloging-in-Publication Data

Garfield, Simon.
Expensive habits.
1. Rock musicians—Economic conditions. 2. Rock
musicians—Legal status, laws, etc. 3. Rock musicians—
Salaries, pensions, etc. I. Title.
ML3795.G26 1986   338.4'778   86–6386
ISBN 0–571–13720–2
ISBN 0–571–13721–0 (Pbk.)

For Diane and my family

Acknowledgements

My warmest thanks to all those who offered guidance, time, enthusiasm and friendship. Some who helped directly are revealed in the text, but many others remain of their own volition in the shadows.

Others still are mentioned below. This book would have been incomplete without them.

Laura Flanders, Lucy Benjamin, Julian & Mandy Weinberg, Andrew Bud, Elissa Van Poznak, Andrew White, Pauline Kent, Carolyn Hill, Pam Esterson, Lesley White, Bob Rothenberg, Pat Kavanagh, Mark Hustwitt, Jonathon Green, Jim Evans & *Music Week*, James Henke, John Gill, Deborah Steels, Don Perretta, Geoff Brown, Richard Rayner, Tony Elliott, Don Atyeo, Jerome Burne, David Thomas, Annie Collie, Clare Pogson, Tony Fletcher, Rena & Leon Gamsa, Dave Wilson, Lee Leschasin, Alex Wynter, Dina Rabinovitch, Jane Rackham, Erika Revell, Ian Agnew & Sidekicks, Janet Dawson at Lexis, Jon Savage, Paul Phillips, Carey Labovitch, Simon Tesler, Tim Hulse, Catherine Yass, Brian Eagles, Paul Craig, Chrissie Cremore, Lee Ellen Newman.

Contents

Prologue

'At the end of the day,
it's not the end of the world.'

Three floors up at 64 South Molton Street, that most fashionable of carless shopping walks behind London's Bond Street, Innervision Records was home to a two-foot-square glass frame holding three metal discs commemorating the stunning success of Wham!. It was March 1984, and the discs had been presented to Innervision as reward for having discovered and nurtured the young pop duo's talents for the last couple of years. They were ordinary, seven-inch singles – possibly real Wham! records, but conceivably anybody's – each coated with metallic shine; one was gold-coloured, two silver-coloured, respectively marking sales of 500,000 and 250,000.

Fairly tasteless, opulent things, in fact, but they were symbols of success – a sure sign that the money had rolled in, or was about to roll in, in six figures. Most record companies would have stuck them on their walls with delight. Walk in, say, to the CBS office in Soho Square and you can hardly move for the star fragments in the reception area. Michael Jackson's success is there on the wall – as if we needed to be told – right next to a Paul Young album – CBS's biggest selling UK act, and don't you forget it – stuck beside a Bruce Springsteen album, which was near the shimmering Billy Joel disc, which was adjacent to . . . The cold, harsher way of putting it would be to gum five million pound cheques to the back of a glass case and hammer that to the wall instead, but that would be telling.

Anyway, a mile away at Innervision Records, a company, incidentally, financed by CBS, the Wham! discs lay scratched and dusty in a shattered glass case that was propped up between thinly carpeted floor and whitewashed wall. It looked as though they were set for the next refuse collection. It would only be speculation to say how they got in that state, but a lot easier to guess why they hadn't been fixed and polished and restored to a wall in the previous six months.

Wham! were in exhaustive litigation with Innervision, a small new and independent company, over money and the terms of their contract. The gold and silver discs were there OK, but the band hadn't seen much cash from them. Four huge hit singles and a number one album, and they even had to borrow money for their bus fare home. So their idea was to get out of their contract for good, and Innervision wasn't having any of it. The struggle had been in and out of the courts for half a year, and there was still no end in sight.

The band claimed they didn't know what they were doing when they signed their complicated contract – too young, not enough advice, that sort of thing. Mark Dean, the 23-year-old managing director of Innervision, a powerfully built, curly-black-haired shooting star himself, was not one to let his hit possessions skip off elsewhere without a good fight, and he reckoned he had a strong case. In fact, Mark Dean said that he was just itching to talk about the whole sordid affair. There were some rotten beans, he said, and he swore he was going to spill them – he liked talking in mock melodramatic terms like that.

He wanted to talk about how he had set up the Innervision label with CBS cash, about how he'd been friendly with the Wham! boys since early youth, about just how he signed them to a possible ten-year deal, about how they fell out, and about how, one October day, he received a letter from their new heavyweight music business solicitors stating that his contract with the band was no longer valid – just like that. He was willing to talk about how he fought the present court case, about how he fell out with CBS, about how he issued counter claims against Wham!'s new manager and solicitor, and about how he suffered generally at the hands of the big biz machinery.

'It really should be told,' he said. 'People ought to know about these sorts of things, about the real monies involved. You get bitten a lot and you can only learn from it. Have you read *Indecent Exposure*, about the Columbia film company? That's a great book – so many guilty people in that cover-up. You can't tell me that sort of thing doesn't go on somewhere in the music industry. Come back to me and I'll tell you *my* story.'

Dean was showing me around his offices and sounded as if he

meant to keep his word. I was up there to talk to Girltalk, a more recent Dean signing he always found difficult to over-praise. 'So much talent! They'll be everywhere this summer!' He slammed on one of their early rehearsal tapes, the one that convinced him that he ought to sign them. He turned the volume to Ridiculously Loud, a nasty Dean habit, and the distortion bled out something like a latterday Ronettes. A song about marvellous young love, and how lucky she was that he was all hers, blah, blah. The band sounded very young.

Three agonizing plays and Girltalk still hadn't arrived, but they were late in part just because they were so young; they got caught in the traffic on the way back from school. When they came, there were just two of them, both singers.

Karen Wright was 13, Leigh Pearce 14. They both had expensive leather jackets and layered, partially dyed and uncommonly well-cut hair, but the rest was just as you'd expect – jumpy, giggly, cocky – all the clichés. Most of their behaviour was just beguilingly childish. They bickered a lot amongst themselves; they squabbled about how long they'd been together ('Two years, no three years'); about how many copies of their independently pressed single 'Can The Rhythm' they flogged for 50p each to their schoolfriends ('Just say "loads" '); and about the way they liked to pose for their press photos. 'We don't want to look silly or childish,' said Karen. 'But we want to look energetic,' stressed Leigh.

Karen was the daughter of stockbroker Edward Wright, the man who used to employ the Innervision company secretary before he moved into records – and that, of course, had helped Girltalk get the deal.

In September 1983 they had signed a contract that might tie them to Innervision for up to eight years. More than six months later they were getting restless that the label still hadn't released any of their songs. 'It gets a bit frustrating, this waiting,' said Karen, 'because originally we thought that we'd be in the charts at Christmas. Our friends at school are beginning to doubt whether we even have a record label.'

The first single, 'Marvellous Guy', was scheduled for release in a couple of months, the exact date depending on the developments in the ever-clouding Wham! case. There was a chance that Mark Dean and Innervision might have to sever all ties with CBS and seek a new distribution outlet for future releases, and if that happened, the

Girltalk single might well get delayed even more. 'You've just got to accept things like that and take them in your stride,' said Dean with a little sigh. 'I'm not going to lose this, you know.' And if you do? 'Well, I'm not going to, but if things don't work out so well . . . well, then, I'll just have to pick up and carry on. At the end of the day, it's not the end of the world. These cases are common.' But there are hundreds of thousands of pounds at stake here, maybe millions . . . 'Yeah well, you know what they say about this industry? You'll love it! They say, "Where there's a hit, there's a writ!" Besides, I've got Girltalk and Baby Go Boom and Space Monkey and Jimmy The Hoover, and . . . and they should be enormous!'

Girltalk themselves confessed to being fairly blind to the workings of the music industry, but they felt they at least knew more than they used to. 'Before, we always looked at the good side – you know, travelling and TV. But now we understand more about the studio and the hard work and how boring it is sometimes.' Karen's father handles all their business affairs, and the girls said they knew nothing about their contract. 'We know we're signed up for eight years. But oh, it's so confusing!'

For the present they were just happy being labelmates with Wham!. 'We think Wham! are great, but we haven't met them yet,' they said in unison, nodding approval. Yes, they did know that Wham! were flat broke and involved in a horrendous court battle. 'But we'll be OK – my father's looking after it all,' said the 13-year-old, emphasizing that there was nothing more important than their first big hit single and obligatory appearance on 'Top Of The Pops'. That would really make their classmates sit up and take them seriously, they suggested.

I told them that Wham! almost certainly said the same things when they were signed to Innervision. 'You see?' they said with delight. 'And they're going GREAT!!'

In other words, Girltalk were already bitten. They'd seen the dusty old metal discs and wanted one for themselves.

I

Shaking hands
with the machine

Most nights in London's Dean Street, a heavily littered place that runs
between Oxford Street and Shaftesbury Avenue, and has as good a
claim as any to being the geographical centre of the UK music
industry, the pub conversations invariably turn to pop gossip. Much of
it centres on fashion, style and the charts – the transients that make
the pop world so profitable. What *was* George Michael wearing on the
cover of *Smash Hits* last week? How *could* Elton John's hair transplant
go so horribly wrong? Are The Who *really* re-forming for that Live Aid
concert?

   Money comes into the chat a lot as well. Is George Michael *really*
worth £15 million, as the *Daily Express* estimated? Just how could Elton
John's transplant cost so much? Just how much of the £8.5 million
raised by the Band Aid record has so far reached Ethiopia?

   But the best Dean Street talk covers the *hidden* money – the deals,
the contracts, the rip-offs – most of it keenly shaded from public
view. How much did George Michael lose out on his costly recording
deal with Innervision? Did Elton John really get paid only £15 a week
while writing 'Rocket Man' and 'Daniel', and why had he waited
eighteen years to sue his publisher in an attempt to get his copyrights
back – he wasn't really thinking of shelling out more on a new
transplant, was he? And was it true that Bob Geldof and Band Aid had
threatened to take a handful of street vendors to court in a multi-
million-pound suit over the sale of unofficial Band Aid T-shirts?

   The last area, that fabled fun-zone of *dirty* industry gossip, is
invariably the best – best because unlike the other tattle it's always
more than just thinly disguised public relations hand-outs. It's more
like that old definition of news – the stuff that someone, somewhere,

wants suppressed. And the really juicy stories are always in too short supply.

In other words, the rock and pop industry loves dumb chatter about what it affectionately calls its 'product', because it knows that it can't help but increase sales. What it likes less, understandably, is any public knowledge of its own internal operations – turnover, profits, payments to artists, and the true nature of the company–artist and artist–management relationship. And, of course, it's even less keen to talk about industry scandals – the accusations of chart fixing, the artist rip-offs, the many weeks spent in the law courts each year.

Artists don't talk about their industry dealings much either, for two reasons. First, it doesn't do much for their street credibility if their fans get wind that their chart-topping dole-queue dirges have in fact earned them millions. And second, even the most experienced artists seldom claim to grasp all the industry complexities. Ask them how their recording royalties will be reduced by TV advertising or what the Black Box in Germany is, and they probably won't know.

Enter the biz solicitors, who still won't tell you much about their clients' affairs, but will tell you, with marked delight, that lawyers are now an indispensable part of the industry. For not only have the courts made it clear that a contract signed without independent legal advice is now virtually unenforceable, but the deals themselves have become so complex and riddled with the wackiest of legalesed sub-sub clauses, that only the legal profession could hope to penetrate them. They'll say too that although a large part of their work consists of structuring and okaying contracts, much time may also be spent each year in litigation. For as the industry has expanded over the last twenty-five years, so has the push for profit, so inevitably has the greed, and so increasingly has the viability of court action to settle disagreements.

The bigger the money at stake, the more crucial it is to win the case; the bigger the legal guns, the more devious the methods. It's hard to name one internationally successful long-term British act that hasn't spent at least some time at one end or the other of a writ. And the biggest – The Beatles, The Stones, The Who – have found themselves decidedly writ-happy.

But why, despite the increasing number of specialist music business solicitors, and their increased knowledge of many legal disputes of the past, do so many artists, managers and companies still seem to end up in court? Will the rip-off epidemic ever let up? Answer to the last question: absolutely not. The answers to the first question range from the fact that there's not enough artist awareness, that there's still an over-eagerness to sign *now* no matter what that might entail for the future, and that there are always any number of disagreements that they couldn't have hoped to have foreseen perhaps five years earlier – not only bad deals, but also things like mismanagement and non-payment of royalties.

Few of the disputes produce winners. Most reach unhappy, grinding settlements that inevitably revolve around cash and rarely around anything remotely connected with creativity. Which is just about the harshest, most accurate summation of the whole rock industry that you'll find.

There are notably few decision makers in record companies of any size at all who would release a single that had little sales potential rather than one that had masses, simply because that person preferred the tune. That's not to say nobody releases any good records (it's all subjective anyway), just that successful artists make money for their company by shifting millions of units, not by releasing what a critics' circle might consider to be aesthetically great discs. Besides, ask any company executive for their definition of a good record and they'll say, one that makes number one. That's the neatest, wholly general, definition of the industry beast: sign the tightest deal, fight the court cases worth fighting, and make number one. The same as most commercial concerns, in fact.

And once we understand that, we're already shaking hands with the machine.

And a big beast it is too. The UK record industry of 1984 enjoyed a sales value of £329 million – 14 per cent up on the previous year (breaking down to £141.2 million of album sales, £78.8 million of single sales, £104 million of cassettes and £5 million of compact discs).* The real value of sales in the 1980–4 period actually decreased by 2 per cent, and there's a 27 per cent drop in real terms if you

---

*Source British Phonographic Industry.

contrast the 1984 performance with that of ten years earlier. Total retail sales of records and tapes in 1984 stood at just under £550 million, compared to £491 million the year before. On cinema, theatre and concerts we spent almost double – £1,070 million in 1984. On alcohol we spent over twenty-five times as much: £14,850 million.

Although the UK remains arguably the major musical talent source throughout the world and certainly enjoys an artistic influence quite disproportionate to its size, domestic retail sales in 1984 only accounted for 6.3 per cent of the world market, lagging behind West Germany's 6.9 per cent, the USSR's 8.1 per cent, Japan's 10.4 per cent and the USA's 33.6 per cent.

In 1984 there were seventeen major or mini-major record companies in the UK (defined here simply as any company with at least a 1 per cent share in either the singles or albums market), and perhaps 800 independents (ranging from the well-established and innovative Factory and Rough Trade organizations, to tiny front-room hobbies that spring up and fold each weekend).

Also in 1984, the majors and mini-majors accounted for all but 11.7 per cent of the singles market and all but 13.4 per cent of the albums market. Companies can own, distribute or license more than one *label* of course, and most of the majors and mini-majors have several. (At the last count EMI owned twenty-five labels, including such fabled wonders as Blue Note, Columbia, HMV, Parlophone and Regal Zonophone.)

Here's how the market share for albums broke down in 1984, compared with ten years earlier:

	1984	1974*
CBS	17.2	10.1
EMI	12.9	25.3
WEA	9.8	7.6
RCA	8.4	7.6
Virgin	7.4	2.2
Island	5.4	5.8
Polydor	5.2	10.4
Phonogram	5.0	6.3
Chrysalis	3.0	–
Ariola/Arista	2.6	–
London	2.1	6.3

	1984	1974*
MCA	2.1	–
A&M	1.8	4.9
K-Tel	1.8	–
Telstar	1.8	–

The singles market is dominated by the same companies, although WEA, Island and Phonogram fared considerably better, while EMI, Virgin and Polydor fared a little worse. As with the albums, the lion's share was grabbed by the mighty CBS with 16 per cent.

Profit ratios clearly vary enormously too. The most reliable source has CBS making a pre-tax profit of £11.9 million in 1982–3 and £27 million over the 1980–3 period. The 1984–5 pre-tax profit has been estimated to stand at around £12.5 million. Its nearest rival in the 1982–3 period, EMI, showed a profit of £7 million, but a 1980–3 profit of just £8 million because of a trading loss of £4.7 million in 1980–1, a financially disastrous year for most sectors of the industry.

As with the book-publishing and film industries, end-of-year profits are mostly made up of massive sales of a tiny few rather than steady sales of all releases. Indeed, talk of each record having a break-even point – that is a set amount of sales that will offset all the costs – has now become virtually obsolete. If every album with an average total cost of £200,000 needed to sell around, say, 40,000 copies to balance the books, then you can bet that a sale of 42,000 copies for each of those albums will please any self-respecting record exec not one bit. It would be great sales news for an independent, but read like financial nonsense for the multinationals. Sure, you need the break-even albums and even some loss makers to test the market and break new acts, but what the people at WEA or CBS or wherever really want are not ten marginal profit makers, but nine flops and one tearaway, world-beating blaster, and that's even if aggregate sales were the same. It means the profit comes in quicker for less work, it

---

*The market survey for 1974 was conducted in terms of full-price and mid-price albums. Only the full-price releases have been used here, and performance should be treated as a rough guide rather than compared directly.

Sources: British Market Research Bureau/Gallup.

means you know where to invest heavily and less heavily next time, and it means growing prestige for your company. (In the world of the multinational, of course, prestige comes not from being the company that produces the adventurous or ground-breaking or 'significant' records that critics like, but rather selling by the crateload. It's another rule of the majors that the quality of the music doesn't come into it at all: if the record stinks but the haircut's popular, then sell the haircut.)

In 1984 there were 5,910 new albums released in the UK. Out of those, only a small fraction saw any success in the top 100, and only 147 became really big hits, going either silver (fifty albums or cassettes selling 60,000 copies) or gold (sixty-five albums selling 100,000) or platinum (thirty-two albums selling 300,000). The basic rule governing the release of the vast majority of the non-hits was based on the shit-against-the-wall theory: throw enough of it up, and somebody somewhere is bound to take some home.

Even the quickest glance at the table on page 14 suggests a sweeping pattern of soar or plummet in the fortunes of the biggies in the last ten years alone. Go back ten years more, and several of the companies didn't even exist. Five years before that, three of the big four that dominated UK output were Pye, Philips and Decca, all of which are now mostly noteworthy either for their absence or despairingly low profile as a result of mergers or takeovers. The fourth, EMI, also lost much ground but remains within shouting distance of the market leaders. Though Island, Virgin and Chrysalis are homegrown independents that have now firmly established themselves in the big league (Island a child of the sixties, Virgin and Chrysalis children of the seventies), the major competition came from overseas: from Germany in the shape of Deutsche Gramophon's Polydor offshoot in the late sixties (all of it owned by Siemens), and particularly from America with the emergence of Columbia's CBS also in the sixties (taking over the already-integrated British Oriole), and the success of the UK offshoots of RCA–Victor and the Warner–Elektra–Atlantic companies in the seventies.*

---

*I am indebted to Charlie Gillett's *The Sound of the City* (Souvenir Press, 1983) and Simon Frith's *Sound Effects* (Constable, 1983) for some of the information contained in this chapter.

But what even the market-share tables and changing fortunes don't reveal is that the nature of the industry is oligarchic, that it's a few multinationals that issue almost all the records, and control almost all the means of issuing them. In one sense, only the majors with their own disc, sleeve and label-pressing plants – only CBS, EMI and PolyGram in the UK – can claim to be truly independent. That is, they're the only companies that can manufacture whatever they want, when they want, and in the massive quantities required for continued chart success. That way too, of course, you cut costs and maximize profit by providing your own empire with work that might otherwise have gone elsewhere. The majors' own comprehensive distribution networks serve the same purpose – they provide freedom and security and, if you're an executive at CBS, they integrate you into a warm cocoon that means in one respect at least your teething days are over. It means that others come to *you*, and that's always a good feeling.

In 1984, CBS, EMI and PolyGram (consisting of Polydor, London and Phonogram) held about 70 per cent of all UK disc-pressing capacity (although only about 35 per cent of its cassette duplication capacity), and the same three could also claim to distribute just a little under 70 per cent of all total output.

Now if you're a small indie label hungry for success just to keep going, you're unlikely to have either a pressing plant or a distribution network of your own. You therefore have a choice between a number of independent set-ups or striking a licensing deal for manufacture and/or distribution with the international big boys. An independent may offer you a more personal, dedicated service and cheaper terms, but a major could offer you more experience, more clout, and perhaps a more effective and efficient service. Your choice is most likely to be determined by the size of your purse first, and your idealism second. But maybe you'll also be aware of the fact that in a top-100 album chart of July 1985, for example, 89 out of 100 successful albums were distributed by the majors.

Two points in particular, made towards the end of 1985, should help to put a broader perspective on the current industry. One: disregarding freak runs, it now costs millions for a company to get a string of hit records. Talent (both of the artist and the company employees) might be one thing, but cash is quite another: nowadays you might need £10,000 to produce each single, £200,000 to produce each album and £25,000 to produce each video. You might have to offer average advances of £100,000 and average royalties of 12 per cent (and that's all real conservatism). Then, maybe, you need an annual budget of £500,000 for marketing and promotion, and then you have the pressing and distribution to worry about.

So if you're an artist, you *can* set up by yourself or operate through a small, established independent label, but your chances of success are slim, chances of sustained success even slimmer (and the chances are you'll get bought out by a major anyway). There are exceptions, but fairly few. And your chances of getting large-scale American success – where the real money is, of course – are strictly less than zero. In other words, you've got to be in to win, and if you want to win, you have to play the big game with the grown-up rules.

Or, put another way, lack of money limits talent. If you haven't got the majors' resources to offer a promising act a whacking advance, then how are you going to get the best bands? And if you're a little gutsy independent, how can you get a record to sound as well produced as most things on the radio – and hence ensure that it might be played alongside them – if you only have a studio budget of £1,000 per album? And that's no good even if you've got a great band and a great-sounding record without the cash to promote it through ads on radio and in the music press, the odd launch party, or taking a radio producer out to lunch. And you can forget about these (very rarely justified) rumours of payola and drug deals. Most companies that have attained any size at all don't really need them any more. All they have to do is just keep investing heavily. Because the guiding rule is that most hits aren't born, they're bought.

The second major point is that having slumped in the mid to late seventies and very early eighties (causing perhaps a 40 per cent contraction in the period), the UK industry is, in 1986, once again in boomtime – that is, Britain is once more big in America, the thirty-second British Invasion or whatever. Which means, generally, that there are more profits around, more competition for the talent, more expenditure on the talent, better deals for the talent. Record advances and royalties are improving and so, too, are publishing splits. Which isn't to say there aren't any rip-offs any more – far from it. It just means that generally speaking (and it's a trend visible through the last ten years), artists are getting a slightly fairer shake – say, 14 per cent instead of 10 per cent on record deals, and 70:30 as opposed to 50:50 or 60:40 on publishing splits, which still isn't much, artists will say, and still tells you too much about the industry's history. 'So good for so long', would seem to sum it up well.

The problem is, of course, that figures and company growth patterns are wholly lifeless affairs. Cynics would probably say, with some justification, that they provide an entirely fitting picture of an industry concerned largely with units, turnover, market shares and profit margins. What they don't show is how the figures are arrived at – the exploitation and the ruthlessness, the artists' chronically bad deals and industry ignorance, the factory ethic and the lack of artistic considerations . . . all the things in fact that make those Dean Street pub conversations so juicy, so well worth overhearing.

That, of course, is how the industry would like things to remain.

2
Management

What The Beatles, The Who, The Kinks and Fleetwood Mac didn't know

The large print giveth –
the small print taketh away

Business life was easy in July 1962. You answered the ambition section of a teen poll by saying, 'to become very, very rich', and then two weeks later you agreed to a deal with EMI that gave you personally one-fifth of a penny for every record you sold, and thus ensured that your ambition wouldn't be fulfilled for a good few years yet.

You then let your manager undersell you throughout the world – irresponsible licensing deals, low concert pay-outs, naïve merchandising contracts, giveaway publishing agreements – and maybe later you install yourself as a director of a few companies of your own, even though you still haven't learnt much from all the previous errors.

And then, if you're The Beatles, you spend a fair whack of the seventies in the courts fighting over what money you *have* made and how it should be split, and how you can dispose of those people you feel haven't split it properly in the past. And after that, in the early eighties, you take up the case of the underpayment of royalties with EMI. In Paul McCartney's case you also spend much of the eighties offering around $40 million to get the copyrights back on those 251 songs that were signed away so rashly in the sixties. (To find at the death that you're outbid by Michael Jackson who grabs them for a few million more.)*

One good thing, hopefully, is that other artists and managers would have learnt from your mistakes. (And the mistakes of The Stones, The Kinks, The Who and all those great sixties' bands that also got ripped off and suffered through naïvety, misplaced trust and greed.) Problem was, it didn't happen. The Stones, The Kinks and The Who continued to make huge errors and be manipulated in the seventies, and other artists didn't seem to learn either. Elton John? In court over publishing contracts in 1985! Gilbert O'Sullivan? In court over his early recording and publishing deals in 1982! Joan Armatrading? In court over her management deal in 1985! Sting? In court over his publishing deal in 1982! Wham!? In court over their record deal in 1984! And these are just a small fraction of all those who pursued justice all the way. God knows how many disputes were settled at the eleventh hour. God knows how many artists' crippling early deals meant that they never had the resources for a stab at court success at all.

If you were McCartney or Jagger, or Townshend or Ray Davies, then the news of these cases made you wonder. If the rock industry was transformed by The Beatles, like everyone says, then how come business awareness seemed to change at half the pace? It's not as if they were *small* errors, after all.

For three main reasons: one, you want to be like The Beatles. That is, you'd *kill* to be like them. Your ego demands the glory, your bank manager demands the money and your friends say you won't do it. And you haven't done it yet, after two years. After two years of cruddy gigs, fuddy demo tapes, and too many people laughing at your loopy trousers and your band's name and the hashed logo sprayed on to the bass drum. You've some topper songs and some burning guitar runs and all that great stuff, but no real job, no security, no respect, no influence and really nothing to show at all. You get offered that dream deal, and the last thing you want after those two years is to wait any longer. You don't wish to discover that the deal's not quite

---

*McCartney reportedly offered $40 million to buy back his Beatles' songs and around 3,500 other songs in the ATV Music catalogue. He was outbid by Jackson's August 1985 offer of $47.5 million.

all it could be, because not only is that a blow to your ego, but it could lead to no deal at all. Worse, you don't want some legal man in a three-piece explaining about things like foreign publishing deals at source, when all you want to do is start trying out those studio Fairlight marvels. And if he says, 'Don't sign this!', you maybe look for a new lawyer and sign while in transition.

Reason two is that you can go too far the other way. It can get that you're so aware of all those chart acts battling away in court and accountants' offices, that you feel, well, that if that guy got stung so badly, and that woman got so crushingly exploited, then what the hell hope have I got anyway? It's not like I could actually beat the monster, so I may as well sign right along. And you might seek that legal advice with all good intentions, but you'll reason that lawyers, no matter how heavy and experienced, perhaps haven't been able to foresee all their clients' problems in the past, and so, you think, even if I go along with all his advice I may still end up with a bagful of writs. Hazel O'Connor, Sting and Wham! originally sought legal advice and *still* had to plead their case before the judge.

The third reason extends that notion further: the fact is that most of those big-name cases spin on a vastly different set of circumstances. So, not only must they be considered on their own terms, but the lessons they learnt might not even be all that useful to lesser mortals. It's all mouthwatering and fascinating stuff – the gleaming Sting in court accompanied by his manager, Miles Copeland, who mysteriously seemed to be a lot unhappier with the low deal that Virgin Music had struck with the artist than Sting was himself; Joan Armatrading's battle with the old manager who demanded new commission even after the expiry of his contract; and Wham!'s lousy deal with a young friend of theirs with whom they used to drink, under age, in their local pub, who in turn felt shabbily treated that he was bullied out of the big cash by CBS. Some, like Gilbert O'Sullivan's eighties' bid to get back his copyrights from the MAM organization after years of unjust dealings, even made new law.

The grand soap opera of Rock In Court could, by definition, only have begun around thirty years ago. In reality, it began about twenty years ago, and a lot of those cases were record companies suing for bootlegging and other forms of piracy. Even now there are relatively few industry precedents. In other words, there are any number of ways to screw up and be screwed. New ones every few months. Ask

McCartney, Townshend and Ray Davies now about the industry's snares and they'll tell you that they still don't know them all. They'll maybe tell you that there are no 'best' companies, only 'worst' ones – and the worst ones are the ones they've had to deal with themselves. They'll tell you to get the best lawyer and the best accountant and to think long term. Good fortune takes over at some point after that.

They'll certainly tell you that the creeping insecurity of how much *they're* skimming, how far *he's* screwing, how much *he's* pocketed, and who the hell slipped *her* a cut, can get worse than the worry of whether the next single's going to go top twenty. And, in fact, now that you're terminally fearful that you'll only get one quarter of what's owing, your chances of creative peak-scooping have probably diminished a good few perfect chords anyway. So maybe you should leave all the financial workings to the specialists and your manager, and do what you're good at: use your lemons purely to make lemonade.

But, after The Beatles, The Who and The Kinks, who the hell actually trusts their manager these days?

The Beatles
The mysterious case of Allen Klein's ego

You can date the death of sixties' idealism, the end of a generation, the time teen died out for good, not just to the year or the month, but to the day and perhaps the hour. It was when Paul McCartney sued The Beatles: 31 December 1970.

The case told you more about the group's financial and artistic demise than you could ever have guessed. The greed, the bitching, the rivalry, the deceit, the embezzlement, the true wheelings of those giant deals, the massive corporate manoeuvres – all a bit worse than you'd thought, I'm afraid. Unless, of course, you guessed something awful was up when you bought the lads' recent group or solo recordings, but even then you only knew for sure that you'd been cheated out of three pounds. You still didn't know much about the claims of the cheated millions.

Up to 1971, things had been going pretty well for Allen Klein. In 1969, say, aged 37, he could rock back in his high-backed, black leather chair over forty floors up at 1700 Broadway, New York, and float his ego into the air like an enormous fart, and take certain delight in the wet vapour that settled around his fat shoulders. He was, he knew, without any doubt, the most feared and loathed rock-business manager the earth had ever seen. Record executives called in sick rather than honour a Klein appointment.

And he was proud of it, even: if it meant more money for the artists he handled, and in turn more money for him, then who cared what anyone else thought? Also, he said, no record company would ever like a manager that found they'd been taking what wasn't theirs to take. And the fact that he was the *most* disliked just proved that he was the best.

It would seem hard to argue with Klein's reasoning. In person you wouldn't want to: he's only five foot six, with close-cropped, oily, crinkled black hair and ghastly white polo-necks that one day will surely come back into vogue, but he's meaty and stocky and shouts and bangs his fist a lot, leaving you in no doubt after even the slightest disagreement that you ought to go fuck yourself. And on paper you just *couldn't* argue. In 1969 he was somehow managing the business affairs not only of The Rolling Stones but of The Beatles, too, and, with one very notable exception, the band members were loving him for it. He was not only straightening out their money problems but he was winning deals and negotiating contracts that seemed to double, triple, quadruple what they'd earned previously. And he was no fly-by-night, either. The man may have been brought up in an orphanage, but he had pedigree. He was a trained accountant who'd been handling acts since the fifties.

His orphanage and early years were dumped in a rough section of post-Depression New Jersey, and they did a lot to instil in him a hard sense of injustice. Even in 1969 he saw himself on a financial quasi-crusade against all the awfulness he'd outgrown – the poverty, the racism, the all-round maltreatment.

And he was dead serious. Weary with emotion, he told ex-Who manager, Chris Stamp, about it one night: about how he was a sole white kid surrounded by black kids, how he'd developed a black sort of outlook and mentality, how he knew he had a very cool mathematical mind, and how his love of black music and his roots in black oppression made him want to do something for all these artists who were being completely fucked over by these companies. And so he took on Sam Cooke with the mind to win something back for them, to win back what was theirs by right anyway.

That's how he tells it, in tears. And he did manage Sam Cooke from 1963 until the singer was shot at the end of 1964, and he netted him a bag more cash (near on $1 million in advances alone), but Cooke was far from his first client. He had already done deep audits for the likes of Bobby Darin, Connie Francis and Steve Lawrence, and each had found their record companies owing them tens and hundreds of thousands. His pick-up lines were cute enough: 'I can get you double!' or 'I can get you a deal for a million!', and how could you refuse?

After Cooke, a British allegiance with Laurence Myers and, in particular, Mickie Most won him large rake-offs from deals for The Animals, The Dave Clark Five and Herman's Hermits, among others. The net grew bigger with his ambition, and after The Stones had been won over in 1967, Klein made no secret of the fact that there were only four more artists he was interested in, and all of them were The Beatles.*

The way he tells it, heavy on the melodrama, he was driving out of New York when he heard that their manager, Brian Epstein, had died, and knew then that there were no further obstacles. In fact, it took longer than he thought.

The original plans for Apple, the company the band formed around the time of Epstein's death, didn't feature Klein at all. The group knew of Klein's reputation and had suggested his muscle might come in useful, but they now wanted more control rather than less, and wished to handle not only their creative output but their finances as well. Besides, there was no shortage of advice from their regular

---

*With regard to The Stones Klein had in fact been 'managing their manager' Andrew Loog Oldham since 1965, and had successfully taken over all the reins by 1967.

lawyers and accountants, and, towards the end of 1968, McCartney's future brother- and father-in-law, John and Lee Eastman, entered the frame by offering their own personal US legal guidance too. The Eastmans had big guns and viewed things with a fresh set of eyes. Together they'd surely provide all the help any young company could need.

But in 1969 Klein read that Lennon felt that Apple was now giving the band more terrible waking nightmares than they'd ever imagined possible. They were losing £20,000 a week to hangers-on. In six months the company and the band would be broke. Klein at last had a lever: he argued that they would be insane to think anyone could reverse the trend better, and faster, and more audaciously than he. And in May 1969, the band, with the exception of McCartney (who now refused to trust Klein and preferred to put his weight purely and firmly behind the advice of the Eastmans), came round and agreed.

Klein had them. Exactly how *good* he had them, and what he did with them and their records, and how he helped split them up, comes shortly, in gory detail, in that horrendous McCartney v. The Beatles court case of 1971. But here it's worth pointing out that Klein was also involved in another massive stretch of litigation in the same year, this one instituted by the US Federal Income Office against Klein's failure to file returns of taxes that had been withheld from his employees' wages some ten years earlier. Ten counts in all. Got fined $15,000. Which isn't all that much to a man on 20 per cent of The Beatles' earnings, but also isn't the sort of action to look too good on your career summary. Being a hard man with crinkled, oily hair and white polo-necks who gets you big bucks by banging fists is one thing, but being found guilty of cash crimes is a bit different. Especially if it makes you wonder how strictly efficient Klein had been with the earnings of his Beatles.

McCartney v. Lennon, Harrison, Starkey and Apple Corps Ltd fell to the High Court and Mr Justice Stamp in early March 1971. Judgment took place on 12 March, some ten weeks after the plaintiff had issued the writ. McCartney admitted later that the decision to litigate was one of the hardest he'd ever taken: it was so symbolic after all, the true end and all that, and despite the disagreements and splits of the last two years he still truly loved those bearded, fiery musicians on the stand. They hadn't played together since the summer of 1969, and in September 1969, the same month as the release of *Abbey Road*, the band's last recorded album, it was Lennon who first said that the band was breaking up. But still . . . did it have to end like *this*?

The split was maybe inevitable, reasoned McCartney; the group had achieved everything and run its natural course. And perhaps some of the critics were right after all – the *Let It Be* film was a terrible document of how things had become, and they didn't owe it even to the diehard fans to extend the agony. But even worse, the court case was mostly about money. 'All You Need Is Love' was almost four years old, and anyway it was written by John. Paul wrote the flipside: 'Baby You're a Rich Man'.

Actually, it was about more than money, it was about independence. Independence above all from Klein, who, if not directly named as a defendant, was really up for trial far more than the band. Unlike the rest of the group, McCartney didn't trust him from the off, was convinced they'd be screwed, and he refused to be swayed by them any longer. Hence the writ was brought to call in an official receiver to wrest all responsibility from Klein, and if he had to battle against Klein's advocates, John, George and Ringo, in the process, then so be it. At this stage, he wasn't talking to them anyway.

Though Klein only took over officially in May 1969, the full impact of his hold on McCartney and The Beatles can only be gauged in the light of a couple of deals made two years earlier.

The Apple organization was formed in April 1967. Epstein was just about still around, but his power and sway had diminished considerably in the last year, and the boys now wanted more say. They also wanted a sort of giant playpen where they could offer seemingly limitless philanthropy to other artists and, as it turned out, to a thousand hangers-on as well. They could open a shop where they could sell apple-shaped ice-buckets; they could turn some of their crazy idealistic mind games into crazy practice; and Paul could record Mary Hopkin. Eight hundred thousand pounds was injected on day one. A partnership was formed by the four Beatles on the same day, and it was agreed that profits and losses from Apple would be shared out as 80 per cent to the partnership and 5 per cent to each Beatle.

The Apple agreement (then just called 'The Beatles & Co') specified the usual things: it required its signatories to devote as much time as was necessary to ensure proper conduct, to honour all deals, to make as much money as possible, that sort of thing. Here are the clauses specifically relevant to our case:

1 Each partner was bound to be 'just and faithful' to the other partners and to inform the others of 'all material matters' affecting the partnership.

2 Apple could appoint any 'agents, distributors and licencees' to carry out its work.

3 'Proper' books and accounts had to be maintained.

4 Any contracts entered into on behalf of the partnership had to be signed by (a) one director of the company and the company secretary and (b) one Beatle who wasn't a director. The directors were Harrison and Lennon. McCartney declined the offer, as did Ringo Starr.

Brian Epstein died four months after the agreement was signed, and the Eastman–Klein battle commenced shortly afterwards. The original plan was to have John Eastman acting as the band's lawyer while Klein operated as their manager but it broke down fairly early on, and the widening rift increasingly reflected and extended the Lennon–McCartney divide too. 'Paul behaved like a spoilt child,' claimed Ringo years later.

Although McCartney refused ever to have anything to do with Klein and sided instead with his new family (he had married Linda Eastman in March 1969), Lennon, by contrast, warmed to him more each day. Klein, like Lennon, had been brought up by relatives other than his parents after his orphanage days, Jagger spoke highly to Lennon of his ball-crushing work for The Stones, and he seemed to Lennon like the only man who could shock the Apple finances back into life.

George and Ringo were egged on by John, and the three of them signed a hastily prepared one-page contract with Klein in May 1969. McCartney didn't sign, and hence refused to recognize this fixer as his manager. (But, as Mr Justice Stamp was to point out, he never refused the fruits of Klein's work.)

That one-page deal in fact confirmed McCartney's worst fears. While eighteen lines detailed Klein's commission, not one listed any obligation on his part. Signed by Klein on behalf of his ABKCO organization (the initials stand for Allen and Betty Klein Company, but the contract misspelt it), it was designed to run for three years, voidable by either party at the end of each year with three months' notice. Klein became 'exclusive business manager' under the following terms:

1 He bagged 20 per cent of gross income received from any source during his term, and 20 per cent of all income received after his term so long as that income was generated by deals struck *during* his term. That held good except for:

(a) any Beatles' royalties resulting from earlier deals. From these he would take nothing, unless he increased the old royalty himself – and then he would take commission only on that increase;

(b) all Apple Records income: he would take only 10 per cent of gross receipts;

(c) all merchandising: he would take 25 per cent net;

(d) all publishing income from George or Ringo: he'd get only 10 per cent.

2 Apple Records Inc would pay for all reasonable expenses for Klein and his staff.

The contract closed with the line: 'The above sets out our general understanding and is subject to formal agreement being prepared by our solicitors.' This, however, was scrubbed out, and in its place, and initialled by Lennon, Harrison and Starkey, was substituted in tight, small handwriting: 'If these terms are agreed to, please sign below and our solicitors will draw up more formal agreements.' They signed, along with Klein, under the closing, 'very truly yours'.

Quite apart from the current Apple chaos, Klein had signed himself into two other ongoing headaches that he hadn't caused but still had to act on at once. The first concerned a dispute between Epstein's management company, NEMS Enterprises Ltd, and the band over a large backlog of unpaid commission (NEMS were due 25 per cent of all earnings). EMI, The Beatles' record company, had declined to pay any royalties until after the dispute had been settled. By the time Klein squared with NEMS, the band was owed some £1,370,000 by EMI, but after the deduction of the unpaid management commission and other expenses, was credited with £258,000. It was a figure that even The Beatles couldn't afford to sniff at, and most in their camp

considered the amount and speed of these settlements as something of
a Klein special, a feat of fancy footwork he had patented as his own.
McCartney would soon have other thoughts on the matter in court.

Klein's second immediate headache concerned the band's existing
recording deal with EMI. Struck in January 1967, The Beatles agreed
to render their exclusive services for nine years in return for basic UK
and European royalties of 10 per cent of wholesale price on all singles
that sold under 100,000 and all albums that sold under 30,000, and 15
per cent on both singles and albums after that. There were even
higher US and Canadian points of $17\frac{1}{2}$ per cent, and the US was by far
The Beatles' largest earner. Nothing intrinsically wrong with that for
either EMI or The Beatles, but you can see Klein's predicament: under
his contract it wouldn't earn *him* anything. Not only could he not
negotiate one of his crashing super-advances and take 20 per cent, but
at the time he took over he faced another seven solid years of the
thing – and even in his most luxurious dream he never believed that
The Beatles would be anything but a great pile of old vinyl in 1976.
Now merchandising cuts were all well and good so long as Beatles'
playing cards and Sgt Pepper uniforms continued to sell, but they'd
earn nothing compared to album income. Some problem indeed.
You'll see it took Klein a full few months to figure it out.

But the real kick of McCartney's 1971 case was concerned first,
with whether Klein should have been appointed against his consent,
second, whether he was right to distrust him, and third, whether a
receiver should be appointed to handle Apple and McCartney's other
Beatles' interests in his place. It wasn't a full trial as such, simply an
interim motion, but it would establish the principles well enough.

In Mr Justice Stamp's view, ABKCO and Klein's appointment was
in direct breach of the band's partnership agreement. While this
arrangement allowed for the majority decision to rule in 'ordinary
matters', this was clearly not such a case – in reality, in fact, it meant
that Apple was to be displaced by ABKCO. Neither could Klein be
taken on board by the clause that read that Apple could appoint
'agents, distributors and licensees', as John, George and Ringo
claimed. Klein *was* an agent, but clearly far more besides.

As to whether Klein, or Klein with the rest of The Beatles, could be
trusted, McCartney pleaded a predictably strong case for the negative.
Take that NEMS settlement for example. Sure, The Beatles received
£258,000 as a result of Klein's dealings, but why should his company

receive 10 per cent – £25,800 – as a result? The entire sum was clearly made up of royalties, and none of them had been earned during the period of Klein's management. For their part, John, George and Ringo claimed that Paul had agreed to the payment, but this he denied.

But the amount was beer money compared to McCartney's claim that, without McCartney's knowledge, Klein had misappropriated commission on The Beatles' existing EMI recording agreement. By September 1969, true to classic form, Klein had engineered a successful negotiation with EMI chairman Sir Joseph Lockwood. In fact, it was the second renegotiation of the deal, the first one being concluded by Epstein a few months before his death. As well as the royalty provisions examined above, the existing Beatles' deal specified that they were obliged to produce seventy tracks in the first five years of their nine-year deal (designed clearly to ensure a regular and sizeable flow of product. It's not just coincidence that 1967 marked the start of the band's studio years and the end of frequent live performances.)

Klein's central claim that another negotiation was due shortly after installing himself in Epstein's place lay in an observation that was simple enough: the obligation to record seventy tracks had been fulfilled in just over two and a half years. If they so wished, the band could now take a two-and-a-half-year vacation; they couldn't record for another company, but Klein could now hold EMI to a sort of ransom (he referred to having them 'over a barrel'). So Klein made it clear to EMI that either they shell out more or he'd see that they didn't make more cash from new recordings. Neither Klein nor the band wanted a period of inactivity of course – they had just recorded the great *Abbey Road* album, after all – but there could be no more powerful weapon. Klein, used to winning, won again.

The new deal, the one that saw the band out, ran like this:

1 The period of the contract remained unchanged (that is, the nine years less the three that had gone).

2 There were to be marginally increased domestic and European royalties, but a US increase of some $7\frac{1}{2}$ per cent to a massive 25 per cent (a figure conceivably never exceeded by any other group). Klein and Apple also got far more control over the band's American releases through Capitol, EMI's US subsidiary, and it was this control which resulted in the increased royalty, as Apple was now receiving the difference between manufacturing costs and sale price with no middle rake-off.

3 There were new obligations which Klein undertook to guarantee personally. The Beatles, either collectively or individually, would produce at least three new albums a year for the first three years, and then two albums and a number of singles for the remainder of the contract. It also permitted EMI to repackage old Beatles' product where this had previously been denied – at the rate of one album a year for three years plus an additional album in the same period.

The Beatles – including McCartney – could afford to be pleased with Klein's work. The US royalties were something of a wonder after years of being sold cheap, and their part of the bargain was, on past evidence, quite within their means. 'If you're screwing us,' McCartney was reported to have said to Klein, 'I can't see how.'

But McCartney's objections would later revolve around the size of Klein's reward. Contractually, he was due 20 per cent of the income from the *increased* royalty – that is 20 per cent of the $7\frac{1}{2}$ per cent rise. Instead he took 20 per cent of the whole lot – on all 25 per cent of the royalty.

So by March 1971, after the renegotiated contract had run for just over eighteen months, Klein charged commission of £852,000, £648,000 of which had been paid by this stage. McCartney claimed that Klein's rake-off was at least £500,000 too high. In addition, and also contrary to his original management agreement, Klein scooped 10 per cent from *all* royalties paid from sales outside North America. This, according to Klein's own accounts, amounted to £124,000. And even if Klein's original contract had been altered to step up his commission so radically – another central nub of dispute – McCartney denied ever being told of such an alteration. As such, he claimed, Klein was unlawfully taking McCartney's own earnings and should be duly prevented from doing so further.

First of all, though, the High Court had to speculate as to whether Klein had taken commission way over the odds without the approval of the other Beatles, too. Although neither Lennon nor Harrison nor Starr made any mention in their affidavits of any agreement signed after Klein's initial appointment that might have increased his commission subsequently, Lennon did contend that, 'So far as I know he has not taken any commission to which he is not entitled'.

Klein's defence of his increased haul came in the form of two documents. The first, a letter dated late in January 1970 was addressed to EMI and Capitol, instructing that certain sums owed to

Apple Records Inc under the renegotiated Capitol contract should be paid directly to ABKCO, the sums being:

1 20 per cent of all earnings on records sold between September 1969 and April 1972, and then again after January 1976.
2 15 per cent of all earnings on records sold between April 1972 and January 1976.

Thus, under this letter Klein would not just receive a cut from any royalty *increase* he negotiated, but on the entire royalty. It was signed by Lennon, Starr and Harrison on behalf of the various Beatles' companies, but it was never implemented by Capitol.

The second document was a minute of the Apple Board dated the same day as the letter. It resolved that an agreement 'relating to the payment of record royalties direct to ABKCO' be approved. But this agreement, a part of which detailed that 'certain variations have now been agreed between Apple and ABKCO concerning the percentages payable to ABKCO on Beatles' royalties', remained unsigned by EMI, even though it was sealed by ABKCO and signed by Harrison. This too, therefore, was never directly implemented and cannot be treated as official approval of Klein's increased commission. What the documents may have shown, according to Mr Justice Stamp, was an *in principle* agreement of some changes in Klein's commission – and in the absence of documentation there was, of course, no way of gauging exactly how much.

But although Klein was cleared of any suspicion of improper action as far as Lennon, Harrison and Starr were concerned, McCartney's claims against him seemed irrefutable. Not only did he not approve the increase, but he remained quite unaware of it until he issued this current writ. Mr Justice Stamp agreed that such an increase was not permissible under The Beatles–Apple partnership deal. Although McCartney was not, by his own choice, an Apple director and here stood in a minority, such a fundamental matter had to be approved by the entire partnership to carry – Apple was not 'a Frankenstein set up to control the individual partners,' said Stamp. Besides, this was hardly what the partnership deal referred to as being 'just and faithful' to all partners, or indeed the rendering of full information as it affected that partnership.

There were further clouds on Klein's character and actions, all arising from his own affidavit. Mr Justice Stamp described certain passages as reading 'like the irresponsible patter of a second-class salesman'. Some, he concluded, had 'the flavour of dishonesty'.

In his defence, Klein countered that rather than overcharging on the terms of his original management agreement, he had in fact *undercharged* by £771,000. He had only claimed 20 per cent on receipts after the deduction of pressing costs and royalties, he argued, and not on the price Apple received from its distributors (that is, Capitol, the US EMI). This observation not only missed the point (in so far as the claim against him was for taking a commission based on total royalties and not just the rise he negotiated – that is, it was a specific point, not one of principle), but also looked wholly spurious when examined in any sort of depth. Had he taken commission on the amount Apple received from Capitol at even 10 per cent, his earnings would have been enormous. It was simply never done. His management contract, though brief, could never have been interpreted legally in this way, and Lennon, Harrison and Starr may have been the first to issue writs if it had been. Besides, if Klein's argument was applied to the new big-control deal he had struck with Capitol, there may well have been a conflict of interest. The surprising thing was, even the defendants' counsel conceded that Klein's line of defence was somewhat 'rotten'.

Between May 1969 and December 1970, ABKCO claimed the right to a total commission of £1,816,000 of which £1,504,000 had been paid. It was the sum of Klein's earnings not only from the band, but also the four individuals and various Beatles' companies carrying on business outside the terms of the partnership, and all of it, Klein insisted, was 'strictly in accordance with the terms on which I insisted from the outset'. His affidavit continued: 'There has never been any possibility of misunderstanding. Apart from personal presents exchanged between individual Beatles and myself, neither ABKCO nor I have received either directly or indirectly any other benefits from our association with The Beatles.'

According to the judge, McCartney's counsel painfully demonstrated 'beyond peradventure' that each of the claims above was flatly untrue. In response, the defendants' counsel conceded that the paragraph was indeed a 'silly' one, drawn up by some weary draughtsman late into the night.

Although Allen Klein had been brought in ostensibly to rescue Apple from what Lennon foresaw as imminent bankruptcy, the accounts of the partnership at the time of McCartney's writ were still confused and highly confusing, and showed little sign of any improvement. By the end of December 1970, for example, McCartney had only received accounts of the partnership for the seven months to March 1968, and those were so rough that three separate audits by three different companies had produced profit estimates of wildly varying amounts – £307,000, £111,000 and £50,000. One of these companies, Arthur Young & Co, suggested in court that Klein 'was more interested in generating income than in the preparation of accounts', and the company not only found a state of chaos, but also that little provision had been made for the payment of taxes. They found too that much vital information was missing. There was uncertainty, for example, as to the origin of a payment by Apple Records Inc to McCartney Productions Ltd of $136,000 for his production work on a Mary Hopkin record. And contractual ambiguities created confusion over which Beatles' company should be credited with the income from the US sales of the *Let It Be* album – a total of £1,442,000 up to December 1970.

Arthur Young & Co also calculated ABKCO's partnership income for two later periods: from May to December 1969 it stood at £68,000 on income received, and for the calendar year 1970 it stood at £835,000, based mostly on a 20 per cent cut of total income in this period of £4,285,000. The defendants argued that this massive increase was due, quite properly, to Klein's fine job in resurrecting and boosting the partnership's earnings, and said that it was therefore clear why they wished to retain his services. They argued too that the new accounting system was better than the old, pre-Klein method, and was now under strict supervision which would surely yield a satisfactory result soon.

Mr Justice Stamp, however, concluded that he was unconvinced 'that there is now in the [Apple] office a staff able to disentangle The Beatles' affairs, or to give the necessary directions to professional men, or make necessary administrative decisions' – not exactly a vote of confidence in the ABKCO administration.

Indeed, Stamp found much sympathy for McCartney's claim that Klein was not a man with whom he could entrust his livelihood. His case was strengthened not only by the complaints above but also indirectly by two quite separate and recent Klein actions that had further enhanced that old shaky reputation.

First, that 1971 tax conviction, still under appeal at that time, but, as before, not the sort of thing to parade as an example of upstanding financial conduct. And, second, Klein's takeover of the Cameo Parkway Record Company around two years prior to the clinching of The Beatles management deal, had resulted in the delisting of the company on the New York Stock Exchange and a full investigation into Klein's business practices. He was accused of grand share hype, of raising expectations (and unit prices from around $3 to $75) by circulating rumours of imminent name takeovers. None ever took place. Klein's defence of the affair in his current affidavit was regarded by Mr Justice Stamp as unconvincing: 'He does not persuade me that he was guilty of no impropriety . . .'

And that summed up well the texture of his final judgment. Klein could not be shown to have embezzled any of the *defendants'* money, but there were ample grounds for McCartney's distrust of the man. Hence a receiver *was* appointed to take over the running of the partnership, if only until a full trial could decide the long-term future of The Beatles and their companies.

Ultimately, it looked like a fairly clear-cut decision. 'The defendants are prepared,' said Mr Justice Stamp, 'in conjunction with or at the instance of Mr Klein, to make the most important decisions without regard to the interest of the plaintiff . . . (they) take upon themselves to exclude the plaintiff from his proper share in the management of the partnership. How can the plaintiff . . . be expected to go on dealing with Mr Klein?'

Mr Justice Stamp concluded that the case would take many months to come to court again. In fact, there never was a full trial. It took another six years for the entire Beatles–Klein affair to be wrapped up for good. (And for the next two, Klein remained the manager of George, John and Ringo.) It was interesting that in December 1973 – nine months after his term as business manager had ended – Klein went on the offensive and lodged complaints in the Supreme Court of New York against all the Beatles and Yoko Ono, and against all their associated companies. There were forty-two counts in all. His claims for commission owing and damages were astounding; even the most embittered hack at his Madison Avenue lawyers' must have reeled at the figures. Klein shot for an award of over $42 million and damages of over $10 million. When John, George and Ringo next spoke to Paul, it was clear that they now shared at least some of their old friend's feelings towards their ex-business manager.

Battle ceased in January 1977 with ABKCO settling for a $4,200,000 net cash receipt from Apple. But even in 1985, The Beatles' and Apple's tax problems had still not been resolved satisfactorily.

In the early eighties Paul McCartney could look back in an interview with the London-based music magazine *Jamming* and suggest that the arrival of Allen Klein at least hastened, if not initiated, The Beatles' split:

'It was the first time in my life I felt I'd been done the dirt with the other guys. I said to them, "This is very weird, this is the first time . . . we've been mates till now".' In reference to the court case, he concludes that 'our side won'.

In another article, Klein merely referred to it as 'a legal nuisance' and considered that the whole action was brought purely to embarrass him. It was a screwy way of looking at it, but in one sense he wasn't wrong.

In 1979 Klein was heavily fined and sentenced to two months in gaol, found guilty of a clumsy tax fraud. From 1970 to 1972 inclusive – that is, the calendar years directly buffering McCartney's court case – Klein declined to declare cash payments he received from the illegal sale of Beatles' promotional records which should have been given away gratis. He and a fellow ABKCO employee were charged with receiving just under $220,000 from the wholesale of records that they received at cost price from Capitol. He had previously instructed the company, contrary to its normal practice, to restrain from marking the records with a promotional stamp. As if to astound the moralists further, a large chunk of the income came from the sale of the *Concert for Bangladesh* recording that Harrison had organized as a benefit.

The man indicted along with Klein, ABKCO promotional manager Pete Bennett (real name: Peter Benedetto), in fact secretly pleaded guilty on one count of tax evasion and twisted his course to become a government witness prosecuting against his former employer. The secret plea was sealed by the courts for six months, and court records indicate that this was not only done to hide his action from Klein, but also to protect him from possible danger.

Bennett's attorney, Martin Schwartz, suggested to the case judge in court that, 'We have some reason to believe that Mr Benedetto's family and his personal safety could be placed in jeopardy.' He continued that there were 'clear indications of threats against the family of the defendant on the part of some people who were perhaps in the employ of Mr Klein'.

Schwartz also pointed out that an unnamed investigator for Klein's attorney was seen in Bennett's neighbourhood in New York asking questions about Bennett's children, such as, 'Where were they? Where do they go to school? What time did they come home from school?'

Klein continues to attract artists with his substantial management charms today.* It seems he has two major regrets. 'I often think it would have been nice to have had a mother when I was a little boy,' he says, 'and yes, sometimes I think it would be quite nice to be considered a good guy.'

The Who
'Won't get fooled again'

In the spring of 1985, around two-and-a-half years after The Who's farewell tour, Pete Townshend has greying, thinning hair pulled and tied back over his forehead, and some days carries a distinctly businesslike briefcase to work. He's working on a very late solo album; inspiring, commissioning and writing assorted works from an

---

*At the end of 1985 he was managing the talented soul artist Bobby Womack.

editorial seat at Faber and Faber; and spending a lot of time raising money for his Double-O anti-heroin charity. His own drug and boozing days have ravaged his face, but no more than you'd expect after around twenty years on the road.

His Who memories are aided by a pack of old diaries and a couple of strong group biographies, and as such are fairly well preserved. In fact, if you get the wheels rolling, he'll talk to you, at you, about it all for hours, and he'll talk about nearly everything. But by far the best bits will be the horror, the disgust, the disbelief he reserves for Allen Klein.

Roger Daltrey, Keith Moon and the short string of Who managers all come in for the anticipated fair roasting, but they're mostly fleeting jibes, seemingly untouched by malice and always tempered someplace with deep love. No love for Klein, though. About Klein he wrote a song, 'Lazy Fat People', and for Klein there's venom, and zipping, mordant hatred and God forbid Klein should ever meet Townshend again.

Invariably, of course, the grudge hovers above two base lines only: money and power. Klein's two flash-fry Who shoot-outs, in 1966 and 1977, scarred Townshend not only through the direct issues at stake at the time, but because the two signalled the culmination of a whole series of dire financial and contractual misadventures that on several occasions had edged into full and heavy litigation. Bringing in Allen Klein, or having him brought in against you, inevitably meant that your past had not been quite as rosy as you'd have liked, and that the future looked grey indeed. Or, in Townshend-ese, it meant you were fucked.

The Who's mess, the basic problem of naïvety-as-trust, wasn't theirs alone of course – The Stones, The Kinks, The Yardbirds and the others didn't have it sussed either – but it did seem to take an inordinate length of time for the band to rectify their own and their management's financial folly. Their penchant for mischief – be it Townshend's auto-destruction or Keith Moon's chronic addiction to championship-style hotel bills – meant that they remained in deep debt, mostly to their managers, for a very large chunk of their early UK success. And only after around six years could any of them claim to be well off, which was one hell of a slog for a band with their huge sales throughout the entire mid and late sixties.

Then again, the vast majority of their big deals *were* a fine example in duff. And their early managerial fumblings provide one of those unnervingly sharkish pictures of the world in which they moved.

Helmut Gorden, the band's first manager, was someone who had previously lived moderately well as a manufacturer of decorative furniture fittings, and had two significant traits that, even to the most idealistic and green Pete Townshend, began to cause nervous concern fairly early on. One, he called the band 'my little diamonds' and talked more of financial ambition than of musical direction, and two, he was a complete novice of little style who dreamt of emulating Brian Epstein. But he did bring with him one benzedrine ideas mod, Pete Meaden, who initially hit a long chord with Townshend, and he arrived at a time when the band were pumped high with that 'find a manager, sign now, worry later' rush that might have had them agreeing terms with a chicken, if only the chicken could bluff.

The medium-term management contract was signed in late 1963 by all the parents of the under-age (21) group except Townshend's. (His father was a jazz musician and doubted Gorden's intentions from the outset.) Townshend remembers now 'feeling it was toilet paper' and knowing that the relationship was going to be short lived. It lasted for one unsuccessful single – and that despite Gorden's and Meaden's stab at early success by buying up one quarter of the total pressing of 1,000 copies themselves (much as Epstein had previously done on a much greater scale for The Beatles' 'Love Me Do').

Peculiarly enough, the two men who ousted him were novices too, although they did at least have experience of the film industry. What sold Kit Lambert (son of classical composer Constant) and Chris Stamp (brother of actor Terence) to the band was money and style and contacts. Their attitude smelt right. Which was fine, argued Townshend, because The Who wasn't about experience, it was about teen identity and tension. And if British Rock turned out not to be the three-year wonder that his father and many others cynically predicted, then the money would surely come in time. 'I don't think any band worth its oats ever picked up a guitar because it wanted wealth . . .' he reflected years later.

Gorden threatened legal action but produced none, and sidekick Meaden was paid off around £500 on advice from entertainment lawyer David Jacobs (then one of the very few industry specialists who handled The Beatles among his many famous and generally older clients.) But the open-ended management deal The Who signed with Lambert and Stamp in 1964, and which held firm, after only slight modification, for just under ten years, was certain evidence that little had been learnt either from previous experience or from the calamities of other bands around them. Once again, the deal should have seemed absurdly unjust even to the most pill-headed musician. The band received no independent advice, and, with the exception of Townshend, their parents knew little of the world into which they had consigned their kids.

They were each guaranteed a minimum annual income of £1,000 – the same as they had been promised by Gorden, and a legal requirement for all under-age signatories. But whereas managers normally took a 15 per cent or 20 per cent slice – and even the fabled Epstein only got 25 per cent – Lambert's and Stamp's company New Action Limited received a massive 40 per cent, and hence was bagging more than the 15 per cent remaining for each member of the band. The figure dropped to 30 per cent some years later and is now partially justified by Townshend on the grounds that it was fair payment for what really was a new breed of management; Kit Lambert especially represented the truly *personal* manager, providing not only day-to-day administrative and financial services, but production work and endless creative ideas too – certainly *Tommy* was partly shaped by Lambert. In one sense, indeed, Townshend was Lambert's creative protégé. Besides, Townshend realized that the group's debts were so high that through the bulk of the sixties, management commissions accounted for zero anyway. Which would have been fine conciliatory reasoning if Lambert and Stamp had taken only a cut from net profits. They didn't, they mostly cut from the top. And it would have been still finer comment if Lambert and Stamp had left their cut at that and secured their band a lucrative record deal, but not a chance.

For one thing they tried on a crippling publishing clause that was to yield them, for no effort at all, a large share of Townshend's writing income. Three years earlier, such a clause would have been almost meaningless to a rock band: before The Beatles you grabbed what

American songs you could get and you sang those as if you really meant them. Even after the likes of 'Love Me Do' and 'Please Please Me', The Stones and The Who belted sets made up almost entirely of US-style rhythm 'n' blues. But The Who had recently been turned down by EMI for *not* writing their own material, and Townshend had just begun to compose. Clearly no one could have anticipated *Tommy* or *Quadrophenia*, but just a small loop of hit singles, such as that begun with 'I Can't Explain' and 'My Generation' in 1965, would pull in large amounts of publishing royalties, and Lambert and Stamp were jostling for a stake.

The clause was struck out on the insistence of Townshend's father. As the alto sax in The Squadronnaires swing band, he had witnessed the growing wealth of its pianist–leader Ronnie Aldrich, and most of it had come from royalties on Aldrich's own arrangements and compositions. 'There's no money in being a musician,' he told his son, 'the money's in the writing.'

Lambert and Stamp took a good few days to figure out a way of side-stepping Cliff Townshend's obstinacy: they told Pete, just turned 21, that he ought to set up his own publishing company. With the exception of the name, Fabulous Music Limited, the enterprise was established virtually entirely on Townshend's manager's terms. There were three beneficiaries: Townshend, Lambert and Stamp, and experienced publisher David Platz, who linked the company into the large Essex Music Group, which in turn enjoyed strong links with the massive Richmond Organization in America. Townshend's split was to be only one-third of all publishing income, with Platz also getting a third, and Lambert and Stamp sharing the final third. This compares, for instance, with The Beatles' first publishing contract for their 'own' Northern Songs, the company formed within the impressive Dick James set-up. James got 50 per cent, Lennon and McCartney 40 per cent between them and Epstein bagged 10 per cent. The norm, however, was a 50:50 writer/publisher split with the manager getting his normal cut from the writer's total income.

The Townshend split remained unchanged until the success of *Tommy* in 1969 resulted in a redistribution on the lines of 70:10:10:10. (In the US, Fabulous only received 80 per cent of all income generated, the rest being retained by the Richmond Organization, and hence Townshend received only one-third of *this* figure. But in one sense he still regards himself as fortunate: his early influence, Ray

Davies of The Kinks, had to suffer a 50 per cent US rake-off before he got his share of his income.) To this day, the non-creative beneficiaries of Townshend's publishing deal still receive a handsome cut every time 'My Generation' stutters on to the radio anywhere in the world. And it's a good song – they had to do next to nothing for it.

Townshend's publishing deals were soon complicated by a remarkable array of sub-publishing, sub-sub-publishing and licensing deals worldwide. 'Half the time I really didn't know what was happening,' says Townshend now. 'To this day I have great difficulty understanding the breakdown of early publishing deals and why they were done in the way they were. Just because somebody is 20 or 21 and fairly much a novice is no reason not to take people properly through agreements that are going to affect them for the rest of their lives.'

On the recording side, The Who's first long-term deal was yet worse. Though their records appeared on the Decca–Brunswick label, their contract was with successful American producer Shel Talmy's own company, and it was Talmy who first received the full Decca pay-out. He got a royalty of around 5 per cent on total retail sales and passed only $2\frac{1}{2}$ per cent on to the band. Forty per cent of this was then taken by Lambert and Stamp, leaving each Who member with less than half a per cent each. Before the details filtered through, Townshend expressed his delight that, 'Shel Talmy done The Kinks (and countless others). And that's good enough for me.' But on hearing the exact terms, Townshend knew he had been signed to a disaster from the off. Why had he trusted these people? This deal was worse than The Beatles'!

The group's royalty rose to 4 per cent after lengthy negotiations and after the first UK single under the Talmy deal rose to number eight. But for a boy like Keith Moon, that still didn't keep you in brandy, let alone a fleet of Rollers to drink it in.

Part of the problem, and one which persisted up to mid 1975, was that The Who employed the same lawyers as their managers, which inevitably meant only one line of advice, even over band–management disputes. And it stayed that way because Townshend was trusting and forgiving to a point where he knew it was damaging progress, and he detested arguing over money. (That in turn was partly due to pride, and partly because money wasn't what this whole thing was supposed to be about anyway.) Also, he liked Ted Oldman, his lawyer at Wright and Webb. But above all, Townshend hated the thought of having his own image of his heroes tarnished. Lambert was hero number one, and even in later years Townshend didn't want to hear how much he'd been pocketing.

'Keith and I actually took great delight in putting our lives in somebody else's hands,' he says. 'It was like we'd say to Ted, "Listen, we trust these guys, and even if they're gonna fuck us, we're still gonna love 'em." ' It was quite a dangerous attitude . . .

> Ted Oldman was in an impossible position and I'm amazed that he survived it. He had full sight of everything, like full sight of all the complex contractual things that Kit and Chris had set up ostensibly for the purpose of avoiding excessive tax. He knew to some extent that nobody would ever understand these arrangements and that was the object of the exercise; he didn't understand them, Kit didn't understand them, the Revenue wouldn't understand them, but most of all the band would never understand them. And although Roger and John were always more sceptical, we always ended up saying 'We trust our management.'

Which, if only for practical reasons, was just as well, because almost all the early Who contracts were signed after shows, when the band were drunk, drugged and exhausted.

> It was bloody difficult to get the four guys in the group together, so this was always the excuse. We set a business meeting, say at 2.00 in the afternoon, and Keith would literally show up at 11.00 at night, by which time everybody else would have gone. And if he did show up early, he would often come in and say, 'I'm not going to sign this contract unless somebody gives me £1,000!' We'd say, 'What *are* you talking about?' And he'd say, 'I just got to! I want to buy a new car!' – sort of terrible playful blackmail. So often our business meetings would just collapse into chaos. Sometimes it was just easier to sign blind.

One such drunken signature would later hasten the final split from Lambert and Stamp in 1974. But despite all Townshend's talk of trust, the first attempt to break free had in fact come eight years earlier.

For in 1966, when 'My Generation' had already charted high and 'Substitute' looked set to emulate it, the band had already established that grand unkickable habit that passes as the rockstar lifestyle, and in order to finance it Townshend tried to rid The Who not only of the Shel Talmy production company straitjacket, but also of Stamp and Lambert at the same time. Talmy had to go not just because the 4 per cent he afforded The Who was quite unmanageable for a shocking four-piece (shocks cost cash), but also because Talmy had engineered a blanket production deal with America that would bring in a royalty even lower than their UK deal – less than $1\frac{1}{2}$ per cent for the whole band. So far, no real problem, because The Who enjoyed relatively little success in the States. But America was high on the band's agenda, and they reckoned that sales could only improve with breakneck touring; in other words, if they were going to kill themselves on the road they may as well get some proper money for doing it.

A significant side issue concerned Talmy's production work itself. It was getting too formula, a lot of Talmy records were beginning to sound very similar, and both Townshend and Lambert thought the future Who sound would benefit without him. And Townshend's desire to ditch Lambert and Stamp? That was simple – they were the ones who got the band into this hole in the first place.

The solution proved a little harder. A solo trip by Townshend to Allen Klein in New York – his first meeting with the man – was soon followed by another in which they were joined by Lambert and Stamp as well as Keith Moon and lawyer Ted Oldman, and both centred on ways of easing out Shel Talmy. Unknown to Lambert and Stamp, the second meeting was held in tandem with Townshend's clandestine sessions with Andrew Loog Oldham, The Rolling Stones' manager, and Chris Blackwell, the record producer and owner of the fledgling Island Records – both about the possibility of managing The Who. According to Townshend, Klein said there'd be no problem about ditching Talmy: 'I can do it, sure,' he said. 'But go with Andrew Oldham, or at least *add* Oldham to Lambert and Stamp.'

It was probably Ted Oldman who saw the danger in Klein's machinations first. Klein had been The Stones' business manager since August 1965, had already had his hands on much of their publishing output, and was gradually easing Andrew Loog Oldham out of the picture completely. He feared the same would happen to The Who, and he clearly didn't fancy operating for Lambert and Stamp in a lawsuit against Klein. As Townshend put it, 'Oldman turned round to us after hearing what Klein had to say and said, "You brought me here as your adviser, and my advice to you is to get up and walk out now." ' Klein laughed – they were currently on his yacht on the Hudson River. But the English contingent took their solicitor's advice: 'We waited until we came back to shore, listened to a few records – Klein played us a Sam Cooke thing he was so passionate about. Then we got off the boat, and we came back to Britain. Then we fought Shel Talmy in court, and of course we lost.' And how. The funny thing is, for a long time Townshend regarded the settlement with producer and production company as a vague victory – more fuzzing of the picture by Lambert and Stamp, he concludes.* Without the threat of Klein's heavy-handed interference, the weakness of The Who's case against Talmy produced a settlement that even Talmy surely couldn't have hoped for. He received a 5 per cent override on all Who record royalties for the next five years up to 1971. Not only was this more than he received when he was producing the band, but it would all be money for nothing. And contrary to what Townshend was told by Lambert and Stamp at the time, the pay-off was clean – that is, it couldn't be offset by studio or other producer costs. Lambert's and Stamp's new deal with Decca US and Polydor in England secured a 10 per cent royalty with around £70,000 advance, but the 5 per cent override reduced these benefits to a nonsense. The Who's earnings on *Tommy* (1969) should have been at least three times what they received.

Even before Allen Klein's involvement in 1965, Andrew Loog Oldham and The Stones had engineered a deal with Decca for a royalty of some 24 per cent of the wholesale price of each record sold, and although The Who's royalty was calculated on retail price, it was still a great deal less than The Stones got. And once Klein *did* have his oar in, his negotiation of a Stones' record and film advance of around £400,000 made Lambert's and Stamp's £70,000 look distinctly lukewarm.

Inexplicably, the band remained loyal to Lambert and Stamp despite their poor earnings and apparently interminable run of huge errors. There was creeping dissent, voiced most powerfully by Roger Daltrey, over such things as the pair's failure to attend concerts and

---

*Chris Stamp declined to be interviewed. Kit Lambert died in 1981.

studio sessions, but by and large Townshend's and Moon's loyalty to what were still creatively eccentric management methods, as well as growing album success in America (which led to much greater wealth from renegotiated deals with Decca), held sway for the maintenance of the status quo. It was one of the post-gig, post-alcohol signing stints that forced the band's hand.

A new Decca deal, struck on the soaring wings of *Tommy*, brought the band large-scale financial success for the first time. Much tax had yet to be returned, but the debts had disappeared, and by the very early seventies the band could claim to be paper millionaires. They were now on a royalty of around 12 per cent of retail sales, and albums were shipping small millions. Solicitor Ted Oldman enthused, and perhaps saw justice being done at last. Certainly he advised the boys to sign. The boys were pleased with their new market value too, and signed backstage, post-expensive habits. At the same time they signed an agreement that indemnified Lambert and Stamp against the possibility of any future legal claims made against them by the band over the contractual details.

Trouble was, by blindly signing an inducement document they didn't fully understand, they also agreed to provide Kit Lambert with an additional 2 per cent producer's royalty back-related to *Tommy*, and this was in addition to his already high management commission. Daltrey found out months later and went berserk. The amount wasn't the thing, apparently, it was the fact that now, after all these years, The Who were *still* being kept in the dark, *still* falling for it, *still* being done over.

It marked the beginning of a spate of unhappy Daltrey-inspired management-earnings audits, all opposed by Townshend for fear of what they might reveal. Daltrey embarked on something of a personal crusade – to sack Lambert and Stamp and get an independent lawyer to see the band through – and his resolve was strengthened by his management's hard snub of his début solo album and the last-minute refusal to issue a £100,000 royalty cheque to be put towards the band's own recording studio. The issue peaked in 1974, the band eventually suing for mismanagement and gross under-accounting. That Lambert and Stamp had engineered their boldest, most lucrative US record deal with MCA in 1971 (an eight-album monster with guaranteed advances of £750,000 per year and royalties of 15 per cent) was now no longer the point. It was the principle of the thing, argued Daltrey. It was a case of faith and who the hell you could trust. Also, the pair had run out of steam. Rock had already lasted a little while longer than the original three-year estimate, and the flash fires were out, not even smouldering. Money, of course, did indeed enter into it somewhere too.

The band took aboard experienced entertainment lawyer Sam Sylvester of Clintons, the man who indeed eventually negotiated a ridiculously complex settlement with Lambert and Stamp. But Sylvester recalls that Townshend, loyal to the death, begged him to call off the litigation several times. 'He knew he was losing fortunes, but he wanted to write the whole thing off – hundreds of thousands of pounds – as if it were *his* mistake.'

Despite Townshend's fears, Lambert and Stamp came out of it all pretty well. Professionally they parted company, but personally all remained and remain close. The feeling seems to be that there will always be more money, but there will only ever be one rock opera.

The settlement, however, left untouched Pete Townshend's central grievance – an unpaid US publishing royalty of over $1 million. It was to be a thirteen-hour meeting in July 1977 that was to settle both management and publishing disputes for good, with the deals being clinched, far from happily, by the reappearance of the ubiquitous Allen Klein. Brought in by Fabulous Music co-controller David Platz to conduct a publishing audit, the man from New Jersey emerged typically with what looked like the best pay-off of all, but he still seemed to be slipping. He had pulled out all the tricksy stops and it had still taken him a full thirteen hours.

Sam Sylvester remembers Klein turning up in gym shoes and tracksuit, and clearly has cherished memories of 'screwing Klein into the ground where he belonged'. He recalls too that one agreed settlement document had been materially altered by Klein just before Townshend was due to sign. He spotted it just in time, and threw Klein out until the document had been restored to its original. For his part, Klein claimed that the changes were the result of careless typing errors.

Sylvester did a grand job, but Klein still went home smiling. Out of the $1.4 million he found, he insisted on a 20 per cent cut. He also claimed a 20 per cent share of all Townshend's future US publishing royalties on all songs written up to the date of their meeting – and it's a rake-off that holds firm today. (The stake reduces to $13\frac{1}{3}$ per cent in 1986.) The way Townshend tells it, Klein's original proposed rake-off, including cuts to David Platz and Lambert and Stamp, was to have been 40 per cent, but he cut it in half by persuading Platz and Lambert and Stamp that they forfeit their own shares. 'I justified that with Platz because he should never have brought in Allen Klein in the first place, and with Kit and Chris because an audit would never have been necessary if they had paid me the money that they owed me at the beginning.'

> I remember meeting Klein at The Rolling Stones' 'Rock 'n' Roll Circus' (1968) and he asked me how things were going with Kit and Chris [says Townshend today]. I said, they're fine. He said, 'If you ever need a hand or anything, remember I'm there and I'm an ally.' I said to him, 'We'll *never* need your help,' and I remember him looking really hurt. There was a kind of glint in his eye, like, 'One day you'll regret saying that.'
> I felt that when I sat with him in that day in '77, it was like I was dealing with vengeance. It was like a power trip and he was demonstrating to me that it was relatively easy to get me by the balls.
> I found it one of the most humiliating and dirtying experiences of my life because I was fighting for what was already mine, for what I'd already earned. At one point in the meeting I remember saying to Klein, 'On what basis can you justify taking all that amount? You've *just* done a fucking audit!' He said that it was $1.4 million that I wouldn't have had before, and I said that the point is it's my money anyway, not yours.
> He then went all bleary-eyed and said that he always wanted to be a part of my career and always respected me as a writer. He said that right from the start the three groups of writers he always wanted to be involved with were The Beatles, The Stones and The Who. So I said, 'Well, if you care so much about me as an artist and you trust me and what you are interested in is my career, and you feel that you're entitled to 40 per cent on some sort of perverse basis, then give it back to me and I'll invest it in my career and then you'll get double satisfaction . . .'. He said he didn't understand that.

Townshend left the meeting with a cheque for near on $1 million, and headed for Soho's Speakeasy, determined to booze well into the morning. By chance, he stumbled into Steve Jones and Paul Cook, guitarist and drummer with the already infamous Sex Pistols.

I remember thinking, 'OK, the fucking revolution has arrived, and maybe this money is going to be important to me, maybe this is the end. Maybe this is the last money I'm ever going to make.' Part of me of course wanted that to be true, because the more deeply I got involved in it the more I thought how much this business really stinks, and everything attached to it stinks, and I hate it, and I want to get out.

The Kinks
Ray Davies and
the mysterious cigarette-box
management deal

There are a few rather rich and succulent slang insults that have originated and flourished in the rock industry in recent years, but *burn* is not one of them. Or at least some court transcript vaulted deep away years ago will testify that no such word existed in 1968.

It'll read something like this:

'I put it to you, Mr Page (Larry Page, manager of The Kinks), that you called so and so a *burn*.'

'I don't remember that, no.'

'Come, come, I'll ask you again: did you or did you not call so and so a *burn*?'

'No. Definitely not. You don't, by any chance, mean *burke*, as in *Burke's Peerage*, do you?'

The barrister did mean burke, but he had misread the evidence and thought that *burn* was specialist biz slang, and hence a far more serious insult. Apparently even the judge laughed at that one.

That was one of Larry Page's happier memories from two court cases in which he lost the personal management of both The Kinks and The Troggs. Essentially, it's his way of saying the law doesn't understand the industry at all. 'They don't decide by what's right or wrong,' he jibes, 'they only decide on what there is in law ... I think for the Kinks' case the judge cited a case brought by a steamship company . . .'

Though no stranger to midriff paunch and thinning grey hair, Page is still a powerfully built man well into his middle age, kept youthful in part by almost punkish, tinted, wraparound glasses that rest on a considerable, pointed beak. He talks softly with traces of west London, and combines his lines in optimism and cynicism with effortless delight. He enthuses, for example, about his current management roster – everyone from orchestra leader Johnny Pearson to a young disco singer 'who makes Madonna look like a man with a beard'. But he's hotly suspicious about some of the indirect financial rake-offs from the Live Aid efforts, and he's less than nice about the big-swing machine that has succeeded in turning the music industry into an image industry. As above, the legal profession also comes in for a fair thwack. Personally, he hasn't been in court since 1968. He says that that last Kinks' affair gave him enough unwelcome memories of the grim proceedings to last a lifetime.

Page first met The Kinks around Christmas 1963. He had been called in by their two management greenhorns, Robert Wace and Grenville Collins, to advise them on, well, management. The two had seen the band's potential and obtained a verbal agreement from their singer and (later) songwriter, Ray Davies, that they should look after them. Problem and reasons for Page's call-up: Wace was a 21-year-old with no apparent management talents, and young Collins was a stock-broker. Wace had been involved with the band's earlier incarnation, The Ravens, for a few months now and had received little but industry rejection; he and Collins knew neither what strings or stunts to pull nor where and how hard to pull them.

Page had enjoyed success not only as a fifties chart crooner (Larry Page 'The Teenage Rage'), but also as a small-time manager who had strong links with a major US publishing company. Surely he'd be an ideal partner.

Contracts were signed in February 1964, shortly after the conclusion of a typically rotten record deal with Pye (lousy royalties of 1 per cent, long terms, that sort of thing). Strangely, there were two management agreements. The first, between The Kinks and Wace and Collins, specified a commission of 30 per cent for a five-year term extendable to ten. But the second was signed only between Wace and Collins and Page, with no Kinks' involvement, whereby in return for his advice, Page received only 10 per cent commission from the band, but was also granted the right to place The Kinks' publishing with the company of his choice. The last was a big bonus that might make the 10 per cent almost irrelevant; Page's company, Denmark Productions Ltd, was set up and co-owned by massive US old-time publisher Eddie Kassner (the man who held the rights to 'Rock Around The Clock' and a lot of the Bill Haley catalogue), and if Page could slip Kassner all the band's songs, then who knows the fortunes that could be amassed.

Page himself stood to make nothing from this placing, but he would certainly move up a few rungs in the eyes of his boss.

And for a while it all worked like a dream. 'You Really Got Me', the band's third single, smashed and was followed with similar success by 'All Day And All Of The Night', and 'Tired Of Waiting For You'.

On the eve of their first American tour in June 1965, the four-piece could look back over their first roaring eighteen months and consider themselves, with some justification, to be one of the most successful and popular acts of the sixties. Only The Beatles and The Stones could claim more.

And of that success – a gross income of around £90,000 in a year – Larry Page, as a PR and live manager (as opposed to Wace's and Collins's day-to-day admin operation), could himself claim a fair deal. And when the band played the Los Angeles Hollywood Bowl in the first week of July 1965 there surely could have been no greater testimony to his influence; the start of the truly golden dream in the country where it really mattered and all that.

For Page, in fact, it was the start of the end. The Kinks refused to go on. Ray Davies disliked America intensely, had had to be coaxed into going at all, and now he was there all his worst fears were confirmed: he was something of a herded animal performing for people with whom he felt he had absolutely nothing in common. Page did talk him into appearing that night, but left for England the day after, disgusted with the band's brattish attitude.

A week later, Ray Davies returned to London determined to get rid of Page. He was infuriated at what he saw as a desertion, disgusted that Page hadn't informed him of his plans to leave, convinced that the way forward was with Wace and Collins alone. That at least would be the line for the courtroom, if it ever came to it. Beneath it lay Davies's hatred of Page, accountable more to jealousy, greed, distrust and ego than any breach of management. Wace and Collins of course stood to benefit from Page's dismissal, whatever the cause.

First up in Davies's grievances was the question of cash. The old syndrome in fact. After three international hits, The Kinks had still seen relatively little money and certainly not as much as they had learned to expect. Maybe Page should have got them more. At any rate, the sacking would mean a 10 per cent reduction in commission. Secondly, the publishing deal which saw all their material assigned automatically through Page to Edward Kassner would also come to an end if Page went – that might also lead to a more lucrative new deal. And thirdly, Page's US meetings and subsequent management agreement with the fledgling Sonny and Cher had established a rivalry for Page's time and creative talents that an envious Davies found hard to tolerate; weren't The Kinks big enough for him? And despite the direct benefit to his publishing royalties, Ray Davies was doubly insulted that Page had 'stolen his ideas' by instituting the Sonny and Cher recording of his song 'I Go To Sleep'.

Yet however strong his alienation from Page, and however convinced that he had a strong case, Ray Davies faced the problem that Page had signed not directly with The Kinks, but with Wace and Collins, and Wace and Collins had few grounds for Page's dismissal. What the band and Robert Wace needed was some hotfooted legal loop-holing. What they got, courtesy of their solicitor, Michael Simpkins, was just that.

Though normal practice would have seen Ray Davies (as The Kinks' representative) consulting a solicitor other than that used by Wace (it was supposedly the band's grievance after all), the two colluded in a series of meetings with the same lawyer and devised the following plan to rid them both of Page. (During its conception, there is evidence that Davies spoke to Page several times and although they were often heated exchanges, there was never any proof that Davies saw their relationship as having been terminated.) The scheme detailed that:

1 Page's conduct in America had given The Kinks no choice but to terminate all contact with him, contact that . . .

2 was anyway legally invalid because it had been forged by Wace's and Collins's company when the band were still 'infants' (under 21) and without their consent.

3 This meant that The Kinks' deal with Wace and Collins was also invalid because of their age. This too had to be terminated.

4 This in turn also terminated Wace's and Collins's subsequent deal with Page.

5 *But* The Kinks *were* prepared to strike a new deal with Wace and Collins. Unfortunately for Page, this new deal stipulated that Wace and Collins could not farm off any of their management duties. Wace's and Collins's company wrote to Page's solicitors slyly admitting that 'we have decided to accept this fact . . .'

The scheme took form in a rush of solicitors' exchanges and terminated in a court action brought by Page's Denmark Productions Limited against Wace's and Collins's Boscobel Productions Limited in a claim for continued payment of his 10 per cent commission (which had ceased just before the American tour). The case was tried two years later in June 1967. Page lost out, but appealed. One month later Page personally lost the management of The Troggs also in another case of alleged breach of contract.

In The Kinks' appeal in June 1968, Page lost again. The facts, the schemes and the emotions seemed to him almost irrelevant; it was a no-win situation. For even though in the Appeal Court Lord Justice Salmon expressed his own doubt about the validity of the 'left in the lurch' line, if the band no longer wished to work with Page for whatever reason, then that was really it – he couldn't enforce the contract against their wishes. No one likes stories with morals, but here, perhaps was one which few managers could subsequently afford to ignore

The court ruled that Page's claim for commission would only be paid for the few months from the end of that US tour in July until the official repudiation of the management contract in September. And as for the publishing, the Kassner Organization would retain the copyrights it held already, but would relinquish all future claims on new material.

In all, Page received unpaid commission of around £1,500 and still regards it as a harshly unjust pay-off. 'The lesson', he says, 'is that apart from accounting clauses, a detailed management contract is pretty worthless. The whole thing works on mutual goodwill. You may as well sign a contract on the back of a cigarette box.'

Lord Justice Salmon summed it up rather more bluntly: '...Almost anything a manager might do, however harmless or trivial, could induce hatred and distrust in a group of highly temperamental, jealous and spoilt adolescents...'

Three years later, in 1971, Ray Davies had also seemingly learned a lot. He told the *Daily Mirror* of how he dreamed of forming some sort of society which could provide groups with advice on the industry, 'where we set down percentages pop artists should pay and how they should read the small type in the recording contract before they sign'. The problem was there were so many hidden pitfalls on 'the Beat Scene ... so many kids have been taken for a ride.'*

He swore that if, in four years' time, he had still not won 'the game', then he would 'die'. Perhaps there was some irony in the fact that, fourteen years after the pledge, he could be found acting in the film *Absolute Beginners*.

But it was far more ironic that in 1984, almost twenty years after their split, Ray Davies called up Larry Page to ask whether he would agree to manage him again. Page did agree. 'I think we sort of understand each other now,' he said.

Fleetwood Mac
The awful precedent of
which Mac is which?

There is only one thing worse than the process of ditching an old manager, and that's finding that the old manager won't be ditched. In Fleetwood Mac's case it was finding that an ex-manager decided he

---

*It's significant that around two years later, Ray Davies would sign a young Tom Robinson to his own publishing company. Robinson now admits that they were rotten terms.

loved the name Fleetwood Mac so much, that he set up a new band –
comprising quite different artists – and recorded them under the
name of . . . Fleetwood Mac, much to the chagrin of Fleetwood Mac
the First, (the one that had the big hit with 'Albatross' and several
successful albums) and much to the confusion of the fans: which Mac
is which?

The courts would sure have fun with this one.

And as ever, it seems, the battle raged over a couple of contracts, in
this case publishing deals, which two band members signed in haste
with stars in their eyes. Classic error! By all accounts they didn't even
read the things.

Formed in England in 1967 as a moderately soft-blues four-piece, and
named after drummer Mick Fleetwood and bassist John McVie, the
band enjoyed large success with what was only their first album, and
established a strong modern blues set that appealed to a far less pop-
orientated audience than their later middle-of-the-road chartwork.
Following several line-up changes in early 1971, two new members –
vocalist Christine McVie and guitarist Bob Welch – emerged as the
strongest writers and signed the sort of long-term publishing deals
that for the time offered average terms but also the promise of
fabulous, impossible wealth. And it wasn't any old dodgy company,
McVie and Welch reasoned, it was their management company. They
could keep an eye on things; they knew who and what they were
getting.

Clifford Davis (real name: Clifford Adams), already the group's
manager for a fair while before McVie and Welch joined, had
formed himself into a limited company, Clifford Davis Management
Ltd, with Davis and his wife as the sole shareholders. The deal he
offered the new writers set himself up as their publisher under the
usual plethora of complex terms. The first two were fair enough; the
rest were more than remarkable – they were funny, quite
unbelievable and perversely courageous. They were so open to
ridicule and annulment in any courtroom that Clifford Davis must
have had a strange mixture of guts and stupidity even to try them
on. More relevant, perhaps, is the fact that he knew that they'd
agree to them, no problem.

1 The deal was for five years, extendable to ten on the publisher's but not the writer's option, and bound the writers exclusively to a worldwide deal.

2 Davis would pay a royalty of 10 per cent of sheet-music sales and 50 per cent of publishing income through record sales and performance income. As before, a 50:50 split was nothing special, but it looked all right in the light of the times. There were not, however, any provisions for an increased split in the event of runaway success.

Then the thing got carried away:

3 Christine McVie was contracted to write at least one song a month. For any he accepted, Davis would pay her one shilling (and probably the same fee to Bob Welch).

4 Davis could reject the work, but even on acceptance he was not bound to publish or try and promote it in any way. He could simply pay that one shilling for the song, retain its exclusive copyright, and then lock it away in a drawer and just forget about it.

5 Davis could assign the copyright of the work to any third party of his choice, irrespective of whether that assignee knew anything about publishing or was in a position to publish, and this without telling the writers.

Neither writer was under age, and neither writer sought, or was advised to seek, any independent legal advice. Even in 1974, three years after McVie had signed, the deal held firm.

So far so bad, and both McVie and Welch understandably received little for their writing. But there was worse to come: a management split from Davis in early 1974, caused in part by several financial rifts (despite, or perhaps because of, growing success in America), meant two further complications.

First, of course, was the matter of Davis setting up a new Fleetwood Mac in the US with a brand new line-up and an obvious shot at cashing in on a hard-won reputation. Which would have been laughable if Davis didn't hold the copyright on all the old material. Because he did, he could send his new Fleetwoods across the States, and they'd do the old favourites, and they'd raise a few eyebrows among the fans near the front who could see the faces didn't fit, but so long as the songs were the same, then no one rioted. Not exactly playing the game, though, and the original members succeeded in obtaining an injunction against Davis for 'passing off' – that is, for deliberately misleading the public.

Problem number two, and one inextricably caught up with the first, was Davis's stab at courtroom counter-attack. The band's new 1974 album, *Heroes Are Hard To Find*, sold 150,000 copies in a matter of weeks in America and looked set to do as well in the UK: it was just a case of the US label, WEA, licensing the record over here, and teaming up with CBS to ensure smooth pressing and distribution. Davis objected and issued a writ against WEA and CBS in September 1974, just a couple of weeks before the album was due to appear in the UK.

His argument centred on copyright. He claimed he still retained exclusive rights to any work written by McVie or Welch up to 1981, and the eleven-track *Heroes* album, although composed and recorded under new management acquired since his departure, had not received his copyright blessing. Hence he sought an injunction against the sale of the album, the attainment of all pressing plates, as well as damages for copyright infringements to date.

On paper at least, he had a strong case, and an interim injunction was gained less than two weeks after his writ. And despite objections and the plea by WEA and CBS that it be discharged, the injunction was upheld by another judge three days later.

The record company's final course was to appeal officially and take a new line of attack. They would argue not on the specifics of the *Heroes* album, but on the issue of McVie's and Welch's complete copyright deal signed several years back. How could they be held to such a thing? Why should they be made to suffer for early naïvety for a lengthy period that might well turn out to be their most creative?

Their biggest trump was to argue on the grounds of there being a gross inequality of bargaining power. As above, the contract seemed unfair in that it tied creative juices for ten years with no mutual obligations on the side of the publisher, and no promise of acceptable remuneration. Also, McVie's and Welch's positions were impaired simply because Davis was initially their manager as well as their publisher – and hence they needed the exposure and the continued publication of their material, in any circumstances, just to get on. And above all, they received no legal advice – especially important for a contract so onerous.

Master of the Rolls Lord Denning saw little choice but to lift the injunction and come down against Davis and in favour of WEA and CBS. 'As a matter of common fairness,' he said, 'it was not right that the strong should be allowed to push the weak to the wall.'

Denning's findings didn't quite set precedents, but they were some of the first to establish a clutch of highly significant music industry pointers which undoubtedly helped reshape the legal approaches of all connected with the biz.* Number one was the paramount importance of seeking independent legal advice. Number two was that unfair contracts, signed under duress or on terms of inequality of bargaining power, would most likely be undone in the courts.

All this was fine if, as an artist, you had signed a disaster and could afford to fight it. But the Fleetwood Mac case threw up one terrible observation. The form McVie and Welch signed was a lengthy, complex, boggy affair that had been *photocopied* from a pile of contracts. Though a few blanks had been filled in, it was as far from a personalized document as you could imagine. It was almost half an inch thick, packed with indecipherable legalese that few artists without a law degree could understand. And that's a wholly depressing thought: not only did the form – perhaps nicked from another company – make you a part of the machine (the product) from day one, it also meant that if this band didn't understand it, then why should their predecessors? And that applied to recording as well as publishing deals. This was in 1971. By then, the form must have been photocopied hundreds of times. Hundreds of artists must have been treated as badly as this.

---

*The most significant watershed case was perhaps the 1974 Schroeder–Macaulay brawl examined in chapter three.

3
Publishing

The terrible fates
of Tony Macaulay, Gilbert O'Sullivan,
Sting and Elton John

What Paul Young ought to know

Ask Paul Young, CBS UK's biggest selling male act of all time, just what he understands about music publishing and he'll say: 'I know enough to know that although I sold a lot of copies of *No Parlez* (his first solo album) I made half as much as anyone else might have because I didn't write the stuff.' More than that, he says, 'It really doesn't bother me.'

Which might seem strange, because Paul Young is a hugely successful, highly gifted and creatively meticulous white soul singer who only got on to the Wembley stage for Live Aid in July 1985 after many years of hard-graft apprenticeship and distinctly less successful chart stabs. That is, he is no school-leaver.

He's been with several recording and publishing companies, he realizes he hasn't been treated well by most of them, and he will still shrug off that 'not bothered' line about his publishing income. It's true that he doesn't write all his own songs – at the last count it was about 50:50. But if you're selling millions of albums, as Young does, that's still an awful lot of publishing money – certainly hundreds of thousands of pounds worldwide. So if Young's not bothered about his publishing earnings, then you can assume one, or some, or all of the following: he's an airhead; he's got the best management advice in the business; his publishing firm, Bright Music, is the best in the industry; or, he's trusting beyond the bounds of naïvety.

Then again, so what if he doesn't know or doesn't care about publishing? Both the directors of the major CBS publishing arm, CBS Songs, and the publishing wing of the independent Cherry Red company, Complete Music, two fairly typical polar opposites, will tell you that artists just don't *need* to know very much: 'Let them create,' they'll say, 'and let their lawyers sweat the details!'

That's what happened in Paul Young's case. He got independent legal advice, agreed to the terms which his solicitor had wangled on his behalf, made hits, and didn't worry too much about the clauses he didn't understand. And when Gilbert O'Sullivan ended up in court in 1982, Young probably didn't worry too much because O'Sullivan *hadn't* received independent legal advice in the first place and signed a dud; and the same to a certain extent was true of a massive Elton John writ in 1985 – he was green, said Elton, and pressurized into a deal before he even had a chance to consult his watch.

But when Sting issued a writ against Virgin Music and appeared in court in 1982, the facts were different; he even shook a smug industry for a while. Sting *had* received independent legal advice and he still claimed he'd been done. So maybe no one was as secure as they had hoped. Even if CBS Songs or Complete Music or any of the hundreds of other UK publishing houses instruct each new signing to seek out that great ILA (and a lot of the smaller ones still don't), they could still find that angry artists decide to send an angry writ for gross misbehaviour (which artists invariably describe as 'embezzlement' or just plain 'stealing'). It meant too that artists may be justified in so doing; just because you had independent legal advice didn't mean your publishing company was super honest. Solicitors have recognized this for years, and hence the standard inclusion of a contractual clause that entitles an artist's accountant to regular auditing of the publisher's books.

Those audits are generally regular, bi-annual affairs; the big artists are advised by their accountants when the next audit is due – a bit like a dental check-up. But the Sting case was special because it questioned the validity of the contractual terms – the royalty splits – not Virgin's bookkeeping accuracy, and implied that legal advice might not keep you from the predators after all. Which should have worried Paul Young a bit, for one.

But if you were an artist and actively wanted to find out more about publishing, to know more about the sector of the industry that perhaps provided you with about half of your total income (or of course your entire income if you were purely a songwriter), then where could you start? You could ask the firm currently offering you a publishing deal. But why should you trust any set-up that's trying to make a fortune from you? Publishers have been known to hide the truth from an artist before. You could ask your solicitor, but you might get complex legalese and a massive bill – £150 an hour from the top dogs. Or you could crank up the old Flanders and Swann records and slink back to the music-halls for a valuable publishing history lesson.

For one thing you need that sort of forty-year perspective to understand modern-day publishing, and the music-hall option is bound to make you feel great. For no matter how bad your mythical deal is, it won't be one tenth as bad as what you might have got in the decade after the war. In those days, you were lucky to receive any publishing income at all. Or to put it another way, these days you have something and maybe some of it's stolen from you; in those days you barely had it to steal.

Talk to five record company hacks about the changing face of the music industry as a whole, and you'll conclude that publishing is a very lame parasitic relative of the recording business. It's obvious: it generates about a fifth of total industry wealth, seldom takes big-money risks, does next to no work that a trained monkey and a computer couldn't do better, and continually rips off artists. In short, it gives the rest of the industry a bad name.

Some of that's true of course, but it's so *disrespectful*. Videos and compact discs and twelve-inchers are fine, but before all that was the song, or at least the tune, and that's still relatively essential to most branches of a business of music. Besides, the detractors forget: before records, music publishing *was* the industry. And if Dean Street, or Soho Square, or Broadwick Street is the industry hub now, then it used to be Denmark Street, the UK's original Tin Pan Alley a few blocks north.

The golden days of publishing are now the stuff of *Pennies From Heaven*, of those Cole Porter and Jerome Kern tributes, and of those great caricatures that have the man with the cigar barking down the phone with the immortal, 'Boy, have I got a song for you!'

The reality was only a little less twisted. It revolved around the word 'exploitation'.

If you had songwriting talents (which meant the ability to write *popular* songs in an era when the industry had even less time for that obscure thing called quality), then you could sell a copyright to an agent-publisher for a set fee and a small, very small, performance royalty. If your talent was lasting and recognized then you might be patronized and supported, not unlike a latter-day court composer. A publishing house would pay a nominal weekly wage, and you would be expected to come into the basement each day and supply three inspired musical monsters about how you 'eyed the girl with the silvery breeches but she didn't eye me-o' by teatime. But unless you were in the Gershwin or Novello league, then both ways had you done from the start. This was exploitation part one: payments were low, and if you were promised a performance royalty then you could boast to your friends, but you probably still wouldn't actually get any money.

First, how did you tell how many times your work had been performed; secondly, how could you prevent it from being ripped off and delicately mangled within some smoky club; and thirdly, how could you claim that your publisher was underpaying you if he was also your boss and manager? Most publishers' accounting systems were strictly prehistoric and purposely so. Also, they told you that they themselves had enough trouble raking in *their* cut for the performances of your material. Publishing firms of any size had to employ their own thuggy collection societies to claim what was theirs – a musical mafia that got paid by throwing bricks through windows. That indeed was the way you *became* a publishing firm of any size.

Exploitation part two concerned the pluggers. Here, the word was clean enough: the idea was to have your work exploited everywhere, even if the means of doing it were less than kosher. Payola started here. If you wanted the top of the bill at the Mecca Empire to sing your company's song, then as a plugger you would go round to the dressing room before the show and offer the star turn, Tommy 'Trousers' McHenry, some money or some drugs. The honest way was to sit down at the piano with the newly printed sheet music and say, 'Boy, have I got a song for you!' and then sing it, but money and drugs always gave the song that little lift. And singers and band leaders soon got wise, so that at least four pluggers turned up at most live BBC radio broadcasts and took part in the regular auction. Joe Wand, the band leader, would tell the four that his boys would play any tune at all so long as the price was right. Then the bidding began, and the plugger with the most cash would hear his tune played on the wireless that evening.

What happens these days is that a plugger takes the Radio 1 producers out to lunch. No cash or drugs ever change hands, or at least none is ever found. There are rumours that a major disc jockey has a record company chauffeur his kids to school each day, but it truly is just a rumour – companies just aren't that stupid. Yet the fact that the yarn has a *record* company taking the tinies around tells you something about how the industry has changed: thirty years ago it would have been a publishing firm.

But the grip has gone: in the two decades since the Second World War, publishers had a dominant say in what made the music halls, the hit parades and the money. The big houses will tell you that they still break songs and acts, and do more for their artists than you can imagine, but if they do then it's an exception. Most are banks. Many lawyers feel that they could do the same job themselves. And most will tell you that record companies have almost refined publishing companies out of existence. Thirty years ago you talked of a great song, but today we talk of great records.

As with a lot of other watersheds, the massive publishing watershed happened with The Beatles. Before them, you could have had a UK hit parade made up not only of songs the artists hadn't written themselves, but of songs that were simply cover shots of US hits. After them, bands like The Who got a recording contract *only if* they recorded their own material. Simply put, recording your own work meant less dependence and perhaps greater longevity; for a record company it meant that if an act on your label could come up with one classic then it could most likely come up with another. It wouldn't be any cheaper, because a songwriter still expected to be paid songwriting royalties on top of recording royalties, but it did make life more secure; as a record company you had a hit package, an all-in formula that, no matter how derivative, was still in its way 100 per cent original.

But if you could eliminate the creative need for a publisher to that extent, why not try and integrate the whole racket and get your own publishing wing? And so by the early seventies, every major record company had what many didn't ten years earlier – their own publishing firms.

The reality was that the control of music publishing remained largely outside the scope of the record industry, despite these developments. Reason: artists don't need, and perhaps don't want, to be published by the same firm that records them, and in many cases they couldn't if they wanted to. For a start, they may already have signed a long-term publishing deal prior to getting a record contract with another company, or they may have a record deal first and be attracted by another company's publishing offer that their own record company's publishing offshoot wasn't prepared to match.

The fact that the record majors still wanted to retain a publishing set-up of their own could mean but one thing: there were vast amounts of money to be made. The sixties and early seventies was swindle time, and as much if not more in publishing than recording. Even in the mid seventies artists were persuaded that publishing was something that you virtually gave away. It was still as much of a grey area as the rest of the industry, and this suited the publishers just fine. By today's standards, most were sharks by any other name – Tin Pan Alligators will do.

It was the lawyers that subsequently changed things most. Things are now at the point where publishers are squealing that they can hardly make an honest profit any more – the deals, they say, are too tight, too competitive, too favourable to the artists. Whereas once they split their artist's total income 50:50, they now find that it's 75:25 or even 80:20 in the writer's favour. Which is how it should be, say the lawyers – you don't do nothing. Which is unfair, say the publishers – we still do loads.

Richard Thomas, for example, an ex-band manager, ex A and R ('Artist and Repertoire' – a talent developer) man and now the managing director of CBS Songs, spends his publishing week like this: *Monday* He attends his company's morning A and R meeting along with the creative manager and the A and R director to talk about possible new signings and the development of recent ones. After lunch, he legs it from his plush new Rathbone Place offices across Oxford Street to CBS Records in Soho Square for the weekly general staff meeting, attended too by CBS UK chief executive Paul Russell, for a broad discussion on general policy. CBS Songs, formerly April Music, was established in the early seventies principally as an outlet

for the publishing of the CBS Inc. Simon and Garfunkel/Dylan talent
stream, but gradually developed to enjoy a fair amount of autonomy.
Thomas doesn't have to attend CBS Records meetings, but he says he
likes to keep in touch with what they're up to.

Tuesday   A fair whack is consumed by the weekly publishing business
meeting, where contract and other legal matters are discussed with
the CBS law department. Thomas has fifteen people working for him
in all, and acknowledges that none of them would be able to function
efficiently without the legal department; as yet, monkeys with
computers can't touch it.

Wednesday   Professional staff meeting; discussions about the CBS
song catalogue, how they're planning to expand it by buying up old
classics whose copyrights have reverted back to their writer or their
writer's estate (or buying songs that have reverted back to their
author after, say, a three-month period in which they hadn't been
exploited by another publisher); what they're doing to generate action
on their existing titles – what songs can they plug through TV adverts
and films.

Thursday   Thomas goes back to CBS Records and sits in on the
singles and A and R meetings. The new releases are played, staff offer
comments, and press reaction is gauged from the previous week. New
CBS Records signings are also discussed, along with recent news from
those already signed.

Friday   Thomas meets with CBS Songs' general manager to truck
over general administrative matters and discuss changes in copyrights,
royalties and accounting procedures.

The week will also see Thomas talking to perhaps three A and R
reps from other companies (over lunch, most likely) who will want to
discuss the chances of CBS publishing their new signings. He'll have
around three meetings with signed writers to check how things are
going and discuss possible new partnerships and producers. He'll meet
with artists' lawyers and managers to hammer out contractual points.
And two or three nights each week he'll catch a live band.

And people have the nerve to tell him, this vastly experienced,
one-armed, weary-looking industry hack in his late thirties, that large
publishing houses don't *do* anything for their money. He nurtures
talent from embryonic levels, he says, citing his success in signing
publishing terms with Lloyd Cole and The Commotions and then
getting them a major recording deal. He furthers artists' careers in

more ways than he has time to count. And if the lawyers intrude into his patch and his company's profits much more, he feels that that creative push will be lost for good, and it will be their fault.

CBS Songs is perhaps an exception; perhaps it's just not yet large enough to be nothing but a giant of administration. But ask Bob Grace, the publisher who worked for Chrysalis Music and the highly successful Rondor Music and signed David Bowie, Supertramp, Joan Armatrading, Nik Kershaw and even Squeeze and Dire Straits on the same night, and he will tell you the same; large publishers don't do anything. At best they administrate well, at worst they administrate badly.

And then go to Theo Chalmers, the head of the indie Complete Music, and ask him what his company can provide that the majors can't. He'll tell you that Complete will find you gigs, a manager, a record company, equipment – whatever you need. A major, he says as an aside, won't even give you good accounting.

That's some aside though, because for most writers accounting is all there is. It's true that if you're an unknown without a record company or a manager then a caring publisher could do a lot to boost your career, but it can't make you a star. Only record companies can release your first single and get you on 'Top of the Pops'.

For a record company you may have to compromise, to sign a deal you weren't sure of, to go with the company that had the best reputation or the most clout, and never mind your immediate earnings. But why compromise for a publisher? If you already had, or would soon have, record-company backing, then your songs would be released anyway, wouldn't have to be plugged to a waiting world as forty years earlier (because the record company would handle that for you), and the publishing money would presumably come in as a matter of course, irrespective of the company you signed with.

So how do you choose your publisher? And what should you consider a favourable deal? Your solicitor might tell you, with some justification, that your best bet would be to go with the house that offered you the biggest non-returnable advance. This would be an unquestionably important part of the deal, but not the only important part. After all, you have to sign away your work in return, and you may never own it again. Paul Simon likens a publishing contract to giving away your children. So if they're good kids, you ought at least to make sure you get a lot for them. As with recording deals, you had better make sure that *all* the clauses are right on the money.

If you standardize a new band's mid-eighties publishing deal it would look like this:

1 You would get an advance – £25,000, say – against your agreement to hand over the copyright to a certain amount of songs written over a set amount of years, and you would assign them for an agreed period of time. Most likely you'd assign your chosen company all your sweated *oeuvre* for at least one year with four further years at the company's option (although there are probably still some old-time deals that specify you write maybe twelve or twenty songs per year). The length of time that the company owns your work depends very much on your bargaining strength. The old classic would be your lifespan plus fifty years, but you could easily whittle it down to just ten or fifteen years from the day you handed over, and possibly less – three-year copyrights are not unknown. The expiry of this period would then see publishers outbidding each other for the future rights of successful titles. In return for your copyrights, the publisher agrees to exploit your stuff to the best of his or her ability.

2 The wider the territorial scope of the copyright, the more beneficial the deal. Clearly the big advances are likely to come from signing a worldwide copyright and hence permitting your company to license your rights overseas, either with its own offshoots abroad or with whichever unlinked publishing company could offer the most favourable 'sub-publishing' terms. Alternatively, you could offer UK terms only and have your manager or lawyer negotiate deals 'at source' for other overseas territories. If you regard publishers merely as collecting houses, then this line would seem to be as good as any, some argue. But lack of experience and contact would make active song plugging next to impossible, and the administration would be extremely time consuming. The plus would be that you would eliminate the publisher's rake-off and that could almost double your money. You might earn more up-front too – your lawyer could perhaps negotiate large country-by-country advances that wouldn't cross-collateralize.

3 Aside from advances, you receive income through two basic channels. You get a mechanical royalty on each sale of any recorded song, set at $6\frac{1}{4}$ per cent of the retail selling price, and paid for by the record company. This is split equally between the copyright holders of both A- and B-sides, or ten ways in the case of a ten-track LP. Hence on 'mechanicals' you can earn as much by writing an obscure single B-side as the writer of the hit A-side. Sales are logged, and cash distributed by the Mechanical Copyright Protection Society (MCPS). In 1984, the MCPS collected around £14 million worldwide. The other collecting body, the Performing Right Society (PRS), collects around five times as much. Each public performance of each separate copyright is logged and charged worldwide, either on a per-performance rate as with radio and TV (in 1985 BBC Radio 1 paid £33 for every three minutes of broadcast) or by licensing fees charged, for instance, to pubs, supermarkets, dance-halls, hospitals or hotels.* Even piped-music lifts pay a token fee.

PRS income – some £67.7 million in 1984 – is then split proportionately between the thousands of registered society members, who are, essentially, any songwriters or publishers who can prove even the minimum of public performance. Each writer and publisher receives his or her due, plus a small split of licensing receipts. In reality this means that a few make a fortune (Paul McCartney's PRS income is calculated in hundreds of thousands or millions), but that the vast majority make pennies. Nineteen eighty-four money looked like this: out of the total of £67.7 million (an increase of £7.6 million on 1983), £42.2 million came from radio, TV and public performance in Great Britain and Ireland, and £22.3 million came from overseas territories. After cost deductions, £55.1 million was distributed to around 15,500 writers and 2,500 publishers (though most were tiny), and it worked out that 68 per cent received less than £250, 16 per cent got between £250 and £1,000, 10 per cent between £1,000 and £5,000, 3 per cent between £5,000 and £10,000 and 3 per cent £10,000 plus.

4 And then, if you're a writer, your publisher takes a cut.

Up until recently, almost all writers accepted that their company would take half of whatever they earned, irrespective of the actual work done on their catalogue – the 50:50 split was integral to your contract and one of the few basic clauses everyone seemed to understand. It was a classic case of so good for so long; lawyers began questioning it in the late seventies. The question was: why? Why did publishers deserve such a rake-off from the talent? Why did they feel they could continue to get away with it?

---

*The £33 Radio 1 payment is per three-minute song, not per writer.

Hence, the splits changed in the artist's favour. The group Then Jerico, for instance, a new band with a major record deal, landed an 80:20 divide in early 1985 with an offshoot of the massive Dick James organization (Elton John's publishers and one-time controller of The Beatles' Northern Songs), and the very top acts are signed on what is regarded as merely an admin split – 85:15 or 90:10. Some majors will even buy the bigger titles at any cost, that is, a royalty that sees the artist receiving 100 per cent of their earnings. They do it for prestige, to get it out of the market-place, and to swell their market share. If you've got The Stones, then you'll get new acts, no problem. It's something a bit nice for shareholders too. And if The Stones don't actually make you much money direct, then who cares?

The lawyers' auction is the best sign of hit potential that an artist could want. The tighter a publishing house will split, then the more confident it is of your selling and earning ability. Which means the less work it will have to do to reap any rewards.

That at least is the basic contractual equation. What it omits is the risk factor, the factor that dictates that for every success there is a flop, or maybe twenty, for even the most experienced publishing firm. It makes life exciting of course, but it invariably encourages rule and ethic bending.

If you can pay an artist less than the norm, or if you are obliged to do nothing with that artist's work, or if you can illicitly hive off an extra share of a writer's income, then why not do it? Surely it's almost justifiable in such a high-risk, high-cost environment . . . And it's not as if you'd be the first to try it on.

'Love Grows Where My Rosemary Goes'

In January 1972 an advert appeared in the industry trade paper *Record and Tape Retailer* promoting the talents of songwriter Tony Macaulay.

He had written for Presley, Andy Williams, Glen Campbell, The Fifth Dimension and The Hollies, he included 'Build Me Up Buttercup', 'Baby, Now that I've Found You' and Edison Lighthouse's number one 'Love Grows Where My Rosemary Goes' among his hits, and the ad had it that he was looking forward 'to another successful year . . .'

'Successful' may have meant hits, but it certainly didn't mean money. The 28-year-old talent, a dark- and longish-haired man with a goatee beard, a boxer's nose and a passion for silk neckscarves and flowery shirts (as seemed fitting at the time), had been receiving the sort of minor-league rewards that had him having to borrow money to go on holiday. There were few, if any, popular songwriters who could touch him for the number of swirling, big-production love thumpers he could place in the charts. He himself acknowledged they weren't exactly high art, but that wasn't the point; they sold and should have kept him in the sheerest silk for life. Instead, of course, there was this rotten publishing deal he had signed six years earlier . . .

In 1966 he was unknown, eager, gifted and kiddable. He had already written a boxful of songs with friend John McLeod, but none had been published, and he began looking for work as a producer. He approached Mr and Mrs Aaron Schroeder, the sole shareholders in a large American publishing corporation, with this box of songs and production aim in June. In July they came back with the hope of production work in the future, but a definite offer of publishing terms now. Macaulay jumped at it: the Schroeders' company, January Music, had an extensive and valuable catalogue, and the affiliates worldwide promised unlimited contacts and opportunities. He was told that the deal was the standard form on offer to all the best writers of the hour, and that being with the publishers' London-based affiliate would ensure close personal attention.

With no legal advice, the 22-year-old signed a true horror: if this was standard, there could surely have been no safer or more lucrative job in the whole music industry than owning a publishing house.

1   He signed away his entire output on a worldwide deal that was to last for at least five years. The term was extendable to ten if the writer made more than £5,000 in royalties over the first period, and his copyrights were given up for life plus fifty years.

2   The Schroeders had no obligation to promote his work or provide a minimum income or salary. While Macaulay was forbidden to

sell his songs elsewhere, his publishers could merely put his compositions in a box and print or push none of them. Also, the Schroeders could cancel the contract at a month's notice; the writer, by contrast, was locked in for the full term and no get-outs.

3 Macaulay received an advance of £50, recoupable against royalties. Once he had *earned* £50 he received another advance of the same amount and so on through the years, and hence the Schroeders never stood to risk more than a token sum.

4 Royalties were set at 10 per cent of all sheet music receipts and a straight 50:50 split with his publishers over all other mechanical and performance royalties.

Irrespective of the harshness of the other terms, the last clause did indeed seem to be as much of a norm as Macaulay could have hoped for. He was unknown, after all, and he knew that even established writers accepted 50:50. What he hadn't counted on, or what he hadn't understood, was what awful things happened when the Schroeders licensed his songs to their affiliate publishing houses abroad – notably in the US, Germany and Scandinavia. And he only found it out by chance.

In March 1969, Macaulay's songwriting success was decidedly small. He had negotiated his much longed-for production deal with Pye Records, but it yielded only a set wage for his work in producing perhaps twenty singles a year, irrespective of how many they sold, and the large publishing supplement he had anticipated from the Schroeders had not materialized. Foreign royalty statements were particularly poor, and he blamed the Schroeders, claiming they had done little to push his work.

He turned for advice to specialist industry accountant, Laurence Myers (the same man who would later help Hazel O'Connor). Myers arranged for an American accountant to audit the books of Schroeders' central US office. The results were not only astounding, but also suggested the possibility of a major publishing fraud. The Schroeders received a letter from Macaulay's solicitor shortly afterwards: Macaulay considered himself no longer bound by their deal.

The New York audit had exposed a well-honed system of overseas rake-offs that left the writer with a fraction of his expected earnings. Instead of a 50:50 split, the worldwide Schroeder organization could at times have enjoyed an 82.5:17.5 cut, and possibly more.

It worked on the basis of the Schroeders having a number of their own affiliates in various countries which would each take a cut before passing on the small remaining royalties to Macaulay, exactly like this: the Schroeders' publishing wing in Germany received £100 from the local collecting societies accounting on behalf of a Macaulay song. The German company took a £30 cut in return for their admin input, and passed the rest on to the Schroeder head office, January Music in New York. January took a 50 per cent cut of the £70 – just for being the head office – and passed the remaining £35 to the Schroeders in the UK. The Schroeders in London then take their agreed 50:50 split and send what's left, a meagre £17.50, to Macaulay. So the publishers didn't have to lift a finger to make the song a European hit, and they could still claim 82.5 per cent of the royalties. It looked like quite a racket.

What's more, the Schroeders defended it. They refused to let Macaulay go, not least because by the early seventies his talent had finally materialized into large hits. Macaulay was advised to sue. Laurence Myers, by then his manager, had sought counsel's advice and was told his writer didn't have a chance; the contract may have been unfair, but nothing like it had ever been made void in the music industry before. If he didn't lose, he was told, he would be making new law, and that, bucko, was a privilege afforded to the very few.

The case hit the High Court in July 1972, exactly one year into Macaulay's second five-year period with the Schroeders. His recent hits had ensured that he had earned royalties in excess of £5,000, and hence the extension of his contract. Macaulay had also earned £10,000 a year on his Pye production deal, and although this had now ceased through Laurence Myers's insistence (and Pye's refusal) that he should receive a royalty on the sale of each record he produced, he was clearly not on the breadline. His claims of borrowing money to go on holiday may have been valid enough, but probably resulted from the standard delay and cashflow problems. His claim was not that he was poor, but that he was poorer than he should have been. He had signed a deal that was quite one-sided, he argued, and he had been deceived over the accounting of royalties. He not only wanted the contract made void, but he demanded his copyrights back too.

Aaron Schroeder, a successful songwriter himself who was now described in court as 'a shrewd and forceful' businessman, simply defended most of the contractual terms on the grounds that they

were just and standard practice for the times. As to the foreign
royalties claim, he suggested that Macaulay knew of the terms when
he signed – certainly it was there in the contract. And to some
extent Schroeder was right: Macaulay had overlooked, or did not
comprehend – and certainly was not advised on – the clause which
specified that 50 per cent of his overseas earnings would indeed be
retained by Schroeder affiliates abroad. The writer would then
receive a straight 50:50 split on the remaining 50 per cent, equivalent to 25 per cent of initial overseas earnings. That was the
minimum.

The problem for the Schroeders was that Macaulay's audit had
revealed that he had in fact been paid a lot less, and that his
publishers' US office had taken off 50 per cent of earnings only after
the amount had already been diminished by German and Scandina-
vian affiliates, occasionally amounting to another 30 per cent. So the
worldwide Schroeder organization had in fact raked off twice.

On the evidence at least, Macaulay stood strong: the accounts
clearly showed improper receipts. Whether it was fraud or not
depended on the publishers' ability to prove that the additional cut
was a confused error they had attempted to correct before the
disclosure. What should have happened, they said, was that the
deduction made by a Schroeder affiliate, based, say, in Germany, was
compensated for by topping up the remaining income back to 100
per cent in the US, and only *then* detracting the agreed 50 per cent.
That this hadn't happened was down to a New York staff misunderstanding, corrected when the error was realized. The reason this had
been kept from Macaulay's US auditor, leaving him to expose the
gaff himself, was put down to another oversight. In the High Court,
Mr Justice Plowman sided with the publishers: it was a nonsensical
muddle rather than fraud or a fraudulent cover-up. But the most
important question still remained: was the contract enforceable
under such unequal and harsh terms?

One key expert witness was David Platz. A highly regarded
industry figure, Platz headed the massively successful Essex Music
publishing group, controllers or overseers of almost the entire early
Stones and Who copyrights, as well as hits by George Harrison, The
Moody Blues, Donovan and Procol Harum. If anyone could be
expected to provide an accurate view of acceptable and standard
industry practices, then it was he.

His conclusions, however, were remarkably doubleheaded. Yes, he said, Macaulay's contract contained terms that were 'strange, unusual, unheard of and unfair', but they wouldn't necessarily lead to a repudiation of the agreement. A clause that requested the writer to 'use his best endeavours to promote the interests of' the Schroeders, as opposed to vice versa, Platz claimed was 'strange', just as the built-in ten-year deal obligation was 'unusual' at a time when most contracts stood for a maximum of five years and were then renegotiated. He had never heard of a contract which could be terminated by the publishers at will on a month's notice, but which carried no opportunity for the writer to do the same. And he thought it 'unfair' that royalties would be stopped entirely if Macaulay failed to remedy any breach of contract within a month, no matter how insignificant.

Concluding, however, Platz suggested that the contract as a whole was not unfair, or at least not unfair for 1966. He acknowledged that it was now 1972, and Macaulay boomtime.

The Schroeders' own defence revolved principally around Macaulay's success. He had now made it, they claimed, and even if it did take a while, he couldn't have done it without them. Forget the contract details, said Aaron Schroeder, ignore what *might* have happened, and look at the realities. Besides, if anyone should be reprimanded, surely it should be Macaulay: contrary to their exclusive agreement, he had assigned, or had attempted to assign, songs to publishers other than the Schroeders. Harold Waterman, an experienced music business accountant called in as an expert witness by the Schroeders, talks even in the mid eighties of Macaulay pulling 'every stunt in the book' to free himself from the contract, suggesting that 'it wasn't all white by any means'.

The judgment sided with Macaulay. He didn't get his copyrights back (in fact that claim was dropped by his counsel midway), but his contract with the Schroeders was nullified on the grounds of inequality of obligation caused by inequality of bargaining power at the time of signing. In other words, without legal advice, Macaulay had signed a deal which might effectively have killed off his publishing talents and was thereby adjudged to be in restraint of trade.

The Schroeders appealed against the judgement, first through the Court of Appeal, and then, in 1974, to the House of Lords. The sight of four lords and one viscount referring to pop and the principles of

Benthamite *laissez-faire* in the same sentence amused many, but their verdict was the same: Macaulay's existing copyrights would remain with the Schroeders for the period agreed previously and on the same 50:50 split, but the writer was now free to sign new terms with whomever he liked. The Schroeders were bound to pick up the massive costs.

Interestingly enough, the string of hits Macaulay had clocked up with the Schroeders failed to repeat itself in any subsequent publishing deal. But although it was slim consolation, he could at least look back later with Laurence Myers and reflect on his publishing precedent. He had struck fear into writers and publishers countrywide – the former alerted to the threat of overseas royalty frauds, the latter alerted to the consequences of offering unfair terms. Because though modified, the Schroeder contract was a standard deal: it probably varied little from that offered by the other major houses at the time.

The total costs of the case were estimated to have been substantially over £200,000, enough, certainly, to deter a rush of similar cases from hard-done-by writers, irrespective of the strength of their cases. But it is likely that many contracts were subsequently renegotiated and foreign royalty clauses re-examined. Above all, publishers made a firm mental note to instruct all their clients to seek that invaluable independent legal advice.

Publishers, writers and solicitors had clearly all learned a great deal in a short time. For many, however, including Gilbert O'Sullivan, the knowledge still came far too late.

'Clair'

Rules of the game, number fifteen: worldwide rockstars are not made in Swindon. The talent may be made in Swindon, but the stars are made in New York, Los Angeles or London.

Raymond O'Sullivan realized this fairly early, abandoned Swindon art school, moved down to a three-share Ladbroke Grove bedsitter early in 1967, and changed the name to Gilbert. He was a slightly perverse-looking, cripplingly shy, 20-year-old Irishman who considered himself a born songwriter. Certainly his maximum joy seemed to come from these strange, nasal moans about awkward love and crushing loneliness, all hammered out on the nearest piano when there was no one else around.

He recorded a stack of tapes when still in Swindon, shipped them out, and predictably the majors showed little interest. CBS, however, thought he had something. Both publishing and recording wings made offers, and though the company was still relatively unproven in this country, O'Sullivan moved down to the capital at once and clinched the deals within a month. On the publishing side, April Music (CBS) had him for three years with one option for two further years. CBS Records got him for at least one year.

Poor contracts. Very little success. (The same story.) After two disastrous singles, CBS Records declined to take up their options, and permitted Gilbert (no surname at this time) to sign a new deal with the small Major Minor label. No success there either.

The publishing deal held good, but yielded so little income that the writer took a £10-a-week job as a postal clerk. The dream, meanwhile – to hear those anguished nasal moans at the top of the charts – remained grimly intact. And he seemed fiercely idealistic too: it wasn't the money, he told his friends, it was the recognition he craved. Above all, he valued his songs and was convinced of their worth.

When Major Minor cancelled his contract after the failure of another single, the battle just began afresh. Believing that a record/publishing package might attract greater new-company interest than a record deal alone, O'Sullivan tried, unsuccessfully, to get out of the April Music agreement. Failing that, perhaps he'd benefit from new management, and should let a hard man organize the new deals and fight the battles for him. And if O'Sullivan was to be the best, why not get the best manager?

He wrote to Gordon Mills late in 1969. It was a real long-shot, because along with Allen Klein, Lambert and Stamp, and very few others, Mills was that rare industry commodity: a manager–star. He'd been a performer himself, but singing had got him only a fraction of his present biz and media celebrity. He was now the man behind Tom

Jones and Engelbert Humperdinck – some went so far as to say he *was* Jones and Humperdinck. By the time O'Sullivan approached him, the groovy medallioned deep-throats had between them enjoyed twenty-three top twenty UK singles and had sold millions worldwide. The pair seemed rich beyond O'Sullivan's imagination, and Mills appeared to have done just as well. He owned a Surrey mansion with a zoo, and his various recording, publishing and amusement-machine companies (later to be tied under the collective banner of Management Agency and Music (MAM)) reported record share dividends with each annual report. MAM made money and success and seemed unstoppable and O'Sullivan was surely twisted even to try it on.

In fact, Mills, an auburn-haired Welshman, proved remarkably approachable. He liked O'Sullivan's demos, liked the enthusiasm and ambition of the writer himself, and offered him not only a management deal, but an agency deal as well. For five years, extendable to seven if things worked out, Mills would become his exclusive manager and concert agent, and for a 20 per cent cut and an understanding that O'Sullivan would cover all the expenses, the singer-songwriter would get Mills to protect him from unfair exploitation and act solely in the writer's best interests. Above all, he'd get Mills's vast experience and unequalled empire of contacts.

'When I signed [the contract],' O'Sullivan told the *Evening Standard* a few months later, 'I didn't even look at it. If you respect somebody, and they're going to manage you, then you have to trust them. That's the most important thing.'

The management and agency deal was restrictive in the extreme: not only did Mills control O'Sullivan's entire artistic output – live as well as studio work – but also the negotiation of all future professional contracts. One clause stipulated that O'Sullivan could not talk to the media without Mills's written consent.

Within months of the February 1970 signing, O'Sullivan was not only recording with Mills as a producer, but had entered the Wonderful World of Mills, never seemingly to return to normal life again. He moved into a cottage in his manager's grounds, became a protégé to be introduced to Mills's friends and business colleagues, and developed a close, loving relationship with Mills's wife, mother, and one-year-old daughter, Clair. 'I'd lost respect for everyone in the record industry before I met Gordon,' O'Sullivan said at the time.

'Now he's the only person who's had any influence on my life.' Years later he told the *Daily Mail* he felt he had a 'father and son relationship' with Mills. 'I'm not anti-Semitic by any means, but he was the first non-Jewish impresario I met in the business ... and I took to him instantly. There was none of this "my boy" business, no initials on the shirt, no knife in the back.'

And if that wasn't enough, he began to have his first hits as well. The single 'Nothing Rhymed' charted in December 1970, reached number eight, and eventually sold 350,000 copies. It was followed by 'Under The Blanket', 'We Will', 'No Matter How I Try', 'Alone Again (Naturally)' and many more, all similarly successful. All were produced by Mills, later to be named *Music Week*'s top singles producer of 1972.

Unlike Tom Jones or Engelbert Humperdinck, O'Sullivan had signed to Mills's MAM Records direct (the other two were licensed by MAM to Decca). The deal could run to at least five years, and provided a royalty, even when successful, of a low 5 per cent in the UK and only $3\frac{1}{2}$ per cent elsewhere. (Had he had an independent manager, he could have hoped for at least 8 per cent with increments.) Still worse, there was no mention of any advances. He received no legal advice, and was still far too much in awe of Mills to do anything but sign on any dotted line presented to him.

Next up were the publishing agreements. Again, O'Sullivan signed a rotten deal without legal advice. As with the Tony Macaulay contract, it looked as though O'Sullivan promised the moon while Mills promised next to nothing. Mills had negotiated a joint April Music–MAM deal for the remaining two years of O'Sullivan's CBS commitment, but from 1972 had obtained the copyright of his entire output for the maximum period. According to O'Sullivan, Mills offered him joint publishing terms on a 50:50 copyright ownership basis and was told that his wish to own his own songs fully would have to wait a period of some eight or nine years.

But the 50:50 arrangement had not materialized even by May 1974, after nine top-twenty hits and three top-five albums. A board of directors meeting noted in that month that a new 50:50 MAM–O'Sullivan copyright ownership company, into which all MAM's existing copyrights would be placed, would be established 'in recognition of what had always been an obligation of the company (MAM Music Publishing Ltd) to Gilbert O'Sullivan as expressed by ... the chairman [Mills]'. The company was never formed.

One letter, sent by MAM managing director William Smith to Mills in 1970, seemed to sum up their control over their new acquisition best of all:

> Dear Gordon,
> Enclosed is a list of songs written by Raymond Sullivan [sic] from which you will see that nine have had some recordings. The remaining 16 had been assigned to April Music, but as they had not been recorded within the period of three months from the date of assignment, they have reverted back to Raymond. I am enclosing a series of Deeds of Assignment covering these 16 songs, in favour of MAM, and would appreciate it if you would get Raymond to sign each of these documents when you next see him. It will be necessary to sign Raymond to our music publishing company, and enclosed herewith is a composer's agreement to run from the date of expiration of the present agreement with April Music. The term for which this new agreement should run has not been completed, but no doubt you will be able to fill this in yourself.

But what the hell! Why should anyone bother about the terms if you had no troubles and growing wealth and continual hits? And things just got better the more the seventies progressed: babysitting for the Millses had inspired 'Clair', O'Sullivan's first number one at the end of 1972, and his next single 'Get Down' quickly followed it. Better still, O'Sullivan's corny college-kid image (which replaced his earlier northern Bisto Kid look) was huge in America, where 'Alone Again (Naturally)' sold a million at the top of the charts.

At the end of 1972, MAM reported fine 1971–2 pre-tax profits of £2,569,000 (up £158,000 on the last year, boosted largely by O'Sullivan, and soon to be increased further by the sudden success of new signing Lynsey de Paul), and it announced that with a recent takeover it had acquired the UK jukebox monopoly of some 10,000 machines.* In mid 1973 Mills even announced that MAM had bought their own jet plane at a cost of £700,000 to wing O'Sullivan, Jones

---

*Lynsey de Paul's MAM contract provided considerably higher royalties than O'Sullivan's – the result of de Paul's use of independent legal advice. She was on 8 per cent of retail sales worldwide, compared to O'Sullivan's 5 per cent in the UK and 3½ per cent elsewhere. O'Sullivan was alerted to this fact early on, but he chose to accept Gordon Mills's denial that this was so.

and Humperdinck to their concerts. 'He has a bird at last!' screamed the *Daily Express*, spinning on (erroneous) claims that O'Sullivan was gay. 'I feel thoroughly spoilt!' squealed O'Sullivan, 1972's Songwriter of the Year.

O'Sullivan's own purchases were significantly less spectacular. Royalties seemed to take an age to materialize, and he lived day-to-day on what appeared to be a salary provided by MAM. Mills's companies covered all his living expenses (and then detracted them from his earnings) and initially paid him only £10 a week. The figure rose to £150 a month at the peak of his early-seventies' success, but O'Sullivan later recalled how he was reprimanded for spending £1,000 on a brass bed. He was told, too, that he couldn't afford the £95,000 house he planned to buy near Mills's home in Weybridge, and so would have to borrow. O'Sullivan considered it strange: his début album, *Himself*, had sold almost a million and grossed MAM £2 million. He questioned his royalties, but Mills 'like a schoolmaster, gave me a good rollicking for going behind his back'.* And even that was OK for a while. O'Sullivan reasoned that he was still living in luxury unimagined during his comparatively tough Irish childhood with five brothers and sisters, and the royalties, though hardly enormous, did at least seem to come through eventually.

The hits dried up in the mid seventies. The singles came out as before, but airplay was slight and sales small. The songs in themselves didn't change that much, and perhaps that was the problem. After four great years, O'Sullivan was now something of a man out of time.

What began as creative disagreements with Mills turned into copyright and financial disputes as the lean period continued. At the end of 1977, four years after his last top ten hit, he could tell London's *Evening News* that even Paul McCartney had had his fair share of flops and that, 'I'll make it, I'll be back.' It was clear, however, that O'Sullivan had already begun to worry about possible

---

*Though O'Sullivan remained unaware of sales figures and grosses at the time, some sample splits now expose the size of his financial dilemma. The 'Alone Again (Naturally)' single sold over 2 million copies, and grossed around £900,000. Of this, O'Sullivan received only £28,000. His second album, *Back To Front*, sold over 3 million copies, grossed £1,700,000, and netted O'Sullivan just £60,000. And the 'Clair' single sold 1½ million, grossed £600,000, and earned O'Sullivan just £21,000.

contingency plans if the rot continued. His Weybridge house, now valued at almost £200,000, might have to go, he said; he was now living on peas, baked beans and sausages, and was having to fend for himself for the first time since Mills first championed and adopted him eight years earlier. 'I got the biggest fright of my life when they showed me a statement of how much money I need to live as skimpily as I do. The rates for this house are fantastic, and the cost of food – even when you eat as little as I do – is frightening.' Why did he have such huge gates on his house? he was asked. 'I don't trust anybody,' he said.

The main problem was that his relationship with Mills had, by the late seventies, deteriorated into total non-communication, and without his manager and his manager's companies, O'Sullivan simply ceased to function. Bound exclusively to MAM Records, he could demand neither that his work be promoted, nor that he be allowed to record elsewhere; his deal with the MAM agency meant no live performances at all if it so dictated; and his exclusive copyright deal meant that even fine new songs might get no push and zero returns. Above all, all the earlier talk of joint ownership of the early hits now just seemed so much unattainable nonsense. At best, he could hammer out creative tales of love and loneliness on his piano at home. At worst, the contractual and financial worries so upset the creative process that he was prevented from doing even that.

Surely, he figured, there should have been more royalties than *that*. And how could Gordon manage me, and run everything in my best interests, and then sign me to his companies which presumably all have the paramount aim of maximized profits? More for me *and* more for them? Surely there was a severe conflict of interests?

Though loath to sue Mills and MAM, O'Sullivan saw little alternative. Money wasn't the thing – it was the control of his copyrights and his release from any future MAM stranglehold. But there'd be a royalty audit for good measure, and a claim for damages against the lack of promotion of his later career. Counsel advised him that to get his copyrights back he'd have to follow the Macaulay case and make new law, and he was told that even Macaulay's copyright claims were dropped before judgment. His chances were slim in the extreme. He was advised also that the case could take around four years to conclude and that costs would run into hundreds of thousands.

Set in motion in 1978, the case in fact lasted seven years and was financed by the sale of O'Sullivan's house. If he won in part, he'd probably swing a new creative outlet and the chance of success again. If he lost, he'd be out on the streets with debts.

First step: get a new lawyer and manager. The publicists Rogers & Cowan had introduced him to self-employed entertainment solicitor-cum-manager Charles Negus-Fancey, a stocky, boyish-looking man in his mid thirties who had picked up varied experience as managing director of the Robert Stigwood Organization and Alan Carr film company, had acted as a quasi business manager and lawyer for several songwriters, but had never before taken on a case of the stature of O'Sullivan's. He was something of a low-key, no-jazz operator who stood out markedly from the flash associated with Mills and showman-managers like him. The two hit it off at once: Negus-Fancey was an old fan eager to help O'Sullivan shoot for the legal history books, and O'Sullivan himself believed the guy might just pull it off. He became his personal and business manager, working closely with the recently appointed legal firepower of solicitors Amhurst Brown Martin & Nicholson.

Priority one was to get back to recording as soon as possible. O'Sullivan wrote almost every day, had amassed a pile of songs he believed were on an easy par with anything he'd done earlier, and had busted a gut and a half trying to prevent himself from breaking his MAM deal by signing with another company. In truth, O'Sullivan had signed more than one recording agreement with MAM, and was uncertain exactly how long his old commitments had yet to run, but now sided with Negus-Fancey to force MAM's hand: with litigation already more than a year old, they chose to risk the threat of injunction and seek a deal elsewhere. If an injunction came through, then at least it had been worth a try. With any luck, though, MAM wouldn't bother, preferring perhaps to seek damages instead or just add the incident to their ammunition for the court showdown that was now surely only a few months away.

He was signed by the head of CBS A and R, Muff Winwood (himself no stranger to crippling deals since his bass-playing days with The Spencer Davis Group), who took a similarly opportunist line on the injunction threat and expressed more concern over the extent to which O'Sullivan's creative output might have been affected by the previous years of dispute. The early pointers, however, were encouraging enough: an upbeat single, 'What's In A Kiss?', just entered the top twenty, and the album *Off Centre* did only average UK business but reached number one in Spain and sold well throughout Europe. And despite early threats, MAM declined to go for an injunction. But the follow-up album, *Life In Rhymes* produced by 10cc's Graham Gouldman, received a critical mashing, no airplay and very few sales. He left CBS, the company noting that the legal twistings had indeed taken their creative toll at last.

It was hardly surprising. A High Court date was now set for April 1982, and the gathering of evidence, affidavits and witnesses was now occupying much of O'Sullivan's time and certainly all of his thoughts. Increasingly he found that what had started as a claim for copyrights and a release from his MAM commitments had now also turned into a ferociously complex and bitter wrangling over money and the accuracy of accounting procedures – O'Sullivan's weakest hand, it transpired.

At trial, expert witness Harold Waterman popped up again, ten years after the Schroeder–Macaulay affair, but this time called for his opinions by the plaintiff songwriter. O'Sullivan also called ex-solicitor and managing director of WEA UK Charles Levison to advise on what constituted a fair contract, and accountants Stoy Hayward were called in for the massive audit. No one, however, was able (or was principally called) to produce sufficient evidence to prove deceitful accounting or other financial mistransactions on MAM's part. Instead, the claim switched to the world of subjectivity: what could or could not be considered fair earnings or a fair deal?

In his judgment, Mr Justice Mars-Jones quoted evidence showing that between 1970 and 1978 five O'Sullivan singles and seven O'Sullivan albums had produced a rough gross income of £14,500,000. Of this, O'Sullivan and his company received a pre-tax figure of only £500,000. Though he confused the amount of albums with singles, he concluded that, 'These figures give some indication of the scale of the exploitation of this young man's talents.'

Earnings aside, O'Sullivan's case centred on the circumstances surrounding his contract signings, not least the great unquestioning awe in which he held Mills at the time, as well as the conflict of interests and the never fulfilled promises of joint copyright ownership. Mars-Jones seemed impressed with O'Sullivan as a witness, but he regretted that he 'cannot say the same thing about Mr Gordon Mills or (MAM managing director) Mr William Smith, the chief witnesses for the defendant. In so far as their evidence conflicts in any respect with that of the plaintiff, I prefer the plaintiff's testimony.'

By 1982, the MAM set-up had changed considerably from the organization O'Sullivan had entered more than a decade earlier: Mills had moved to Los Angeles to promote Tom Jones, having lost Engelbert Humperdinck in a series of ego rows in which the singer claimed he had always been treated as 'number two' by Mills; pre-tax profits levelled out at around £2 million at the end of 1982, with shares of 95 pence, compared to over £2½ million and a rough share average of 180 pence from ten years earlier; and almost two-thirds of MAM income now came from around 16,000 amusement machines and jukeboxes.

But along with expert witness Dick Rowe (the Decca A and R man who had resigned himself to the fact that he would probably never live down the ignominy of turning down The Beatles), Mills and Smith claimed that, irrespective of subsequent personal or industry changes, their O'Sullivan contracts had been just and normal for the times, and that without MAM's huge efforts and resources he might still be employed as a postal clerk today. Besides, they said, the man was hardly poor, and if the talent for hits had dried up, then it wasn't their fault – they'd done all they could.

Mars-Jones not only differed from MAM in his reading of the events, but he differed so dramatically that even some of O'Sullivan's supporters expressed surprise at the totality of his victory. There had been no independent legal advice and hence severe inequality of bargaining power and a resultant restraint of trade, he said. There was an insuperable conflict of interest. And the copyright documents examined above had shown that the songwriter was like putty in a craftsman's hands.

He was released from all MAM ties. He got his master recordings back. He got all his costs. And he received an astounding award of publishing and recording profits, estimated by MAM's counsel to stand, after interest, as high as £7 million pre-tax. The amount and copyright award had never been seen in the industry before. To many in the game, it came as a great shock: the artist had scooped the pool.

MAM lodged an immediate appeal, heard in December 1983, judged initially in November 1984, and finally settled out of court in March 1985. As expected, it repeated its claim that there was nothing in the least illegal about MAM's actions, that the court decision over copyrights and profits had been entirely unjustified, and that MAM should at least receive adequate remuneration for its tireless efforts in promotional star-making. And it resulted in some joy at least; O'Sullivan would still win back his copyrights and masters, would still receive a generous profit award, but would have the exact amount of payment reduced by an adequate reward to MAM. The out-of-court deal set O'Sullivan's final award at £1,983,520.

Add to that an annual publishing copyright income of at least six figures, and even after tax deductions you're looking at an extremely wealthy songwriter. 'It gave him a pension for the rest of his life,' says a beaming Charles Negus-Fancey. 'He can own his own songs for ever now – he will publish himself over here and grant finite sub-publishing rights overseas - and they are evergreens, and they will always produce money. But he never went into this for the money, and it doesn't really change what he's most interested in, which is success with what he's doing now.'

Accordingly, the same spring week in 1985 that saw MAM merging with the Chrysalis Group to form a record–management–amusement-machine–jukebox complex, found O'Sullivan and Charles Negus-Fancey discussing the possibilities of new recording deals with several majors. The negotiating methods would be different from the ones of fifteen years earlier, but the aim was the same. Sign the deal, sell the product, and make number one.

'Roxanne'

By July 1982 Virgin Group founder and chief executive Richard Branson had established a small empire with a 1981–2 turnover of around £39 million and a profit of a modest £1.5 million. Both Virgin and Branson personally had appeared in the courts numerous times – artists suing over mean royalties, Customs and Excise suing over irregular export returns – but it was all in a day's empire building, and a sure sign in the record world that business was ticking over as usual.

Miles Copeland Jr, the son of an ex-CIA Middle East bureau chief, manager of The Police, and similarly impressive label-owning entrepreneur, had also fended off many writs with a notably stoic, cool-headed realism.

In the case of Gordon Sumner (Sting) v. Virgin Music the two of them met at last. It was a rather romantic grudge match, not unlike two top seeds meeting at Wimbledon. Industry staffers in the know began to place side bets.

Both sides claimed victory. Neither in fact won. As so often, the only beneficiary seemed to be the legal profession. Sting himself certainly emerged far from happy.

The Police's singer-songwriter had signed to Virgin Music in 1976, aged 24. He was still based in his native Newcastle, then in a jazz band called Last Exit, and had received scant interest from several other companies who had also heard his demo tapes. Carol Wilson, Virgin Music's general manager, enthused against the run of play, and signed him to a 50:50 split on a five-year deal. 'I thought the man was a star and I loved his songs,' Wilson remembers. 'We became great friends – he used to do his demos in my loft.'

Even in 1985 Wilson considered the terms to have been quite fair in the circumstances, not least because she claims she spent much Virgin time and money in an effort to get him a recording deal.

Sting joined The Police and signed a short-term contract with manager Miles Copeland's Illegal Records some eighteen months later. 'Fall Out', the band's first single, sold well for an independent but pulled in relatively little publishing money, and it was only after the first A&M single 'Roxanne' began charting high in America that the details of the split first came under close scrutiny. Terms improved to 60:40 after the UK success of 'Roxanne' some months later, and in early 1982 stood at 75:25.

According to Carol Wilson, 'Copeland was 100 per cent unhappy with the deal. Sting was perfectly happy. Copeland kept telling Sting from the first day that he should get out of Virgin. Sting only said OK once I had left (in 1979).'*

---

*Copeland was not available for interview, and it's likely that he was anyway bound to silence over the details of the case by the terms of the settlement. His own interest in Sting's departure from Virgin Music may have been twofold: he may have received a greater management slice of improved royalties offered by another company; and he may have got an even larger cut had he also partly owned that new company.

The eleven-day July 1982 trial centred on Sting's inequality of bargaining power at the signing, with the singer claiming damages and a reversion of his copyrights. But it emerged that Sting did receive independent legal advice, albeit from a non-music specialist, and that the contract was subsequently amended considerably from the original. Sting's counsel also claimed that Virgin Music had done little to further his career, a point hotly contested by Carol Wilson. It was a peculiar irony of the proceedings that for much of the time Wilson and Sting sat next to each other and chatted happily. They remain good friends to this day.

The details of the out-of-court settlement have been disclosed by neither party, though the compromise seems to have granted Virgin Music the copyright of one further album (*Synchronicity*) in return for a much higher artist royalty (possibly 90:10). Copyright ownership is also likely to revert back to Sting before 1990.

It was a messy, expensive affair, with Sting's share of the costs alone estimated at £150,000. But it didn't stop there: the week after the trial saw Copeland and Branson in a splendid public row. Copeland told the *Daily Mirror* that Sting had earned Virgin £5 million for only a £200 outlay. He claimed too that Virgin had always refused to renegotiate the contract.

Branson retaliated in the *New Musical Express*: 'He signed Squeeze to a far worse deal than Sting got from us a year earlier. They got no money and did not take legal advice . . . we spent over £2,000 on recording demos for Sting's first band . . . the total money we collected on his behalf was only £1,500,000 . . . I'm boiling mad with the hypocrisy of the situation . . .'

It was one of the very few times when a detailed industry dispute has turned public. Many in the business considered this a development not to be encouraged.

'Rocket Man'

In April 1985 Elton John caused around £5,000 worth of damage at the Savoy. He ran a bath in his suite, called his wife Renata in New

York, and left it running. And running. The water reached composer
Marvin Hamlisch in the room below within minutes. It reached Mary
Parkinson in the room below that shortly afterwards.

A month earlier, a criminal court had heard how John had lost a
£6,000 limited edition diamond-studded gold Cartier watch. The
police found it by raiding the home of a suspect who claimed he'd
been given it by a friend who had himself been given it by John. The
cops discovered it in the elasticated turn-ups of his pyjama bottoms.

Great dining-out stories both of them, and if one was to cost John a
few grand, well, it probably wouldn't break the bank. John, needless
to say, is a multi-millionaire getting richer by the hour. At the last
glance at the PR hyperbole he's sold over 80 million records
worldwide, and has earned over £20 million from record sales alone.
By the time you've read this page, some DJ somewhere will have
made him wealthier still. He has invested heavily in property and his
darling Watford FC and has his own flourishing record label –
seemingly all a 37-year-old performer could want, not least because
he's still one of the most prolific, and most successful, most naturally
bald artists to have survived almost twenty years in the business with
a good measure of sanity.

But in June 1985 in the High Court his sanity was cast in severe
doubt. Greed, a feature rarely associated with John in the past, had
now apparently assumed grim control: he was suing his publishers and
former record label Dick James Music (DJM) for the return of his
copyrights and master recordings, and he sought damages for the
improper diversion of his royalties. Along with lyricist Bernie Taupin
he was claiming back 136 songs written between 1967 and 1973,
including 'Rocket Man', 'Crocodile Rock' and the rest of his early hits
– songs that have already reputedly grossed £200 million.

He claimed that he was impossibly naïve when he signed with
DJM, that he trusted Dick James implicitly and hence sought no
independent legal advice, that both his recording and publishing
royalties were cripplingly mean, and that DJM had consciously
concealed the workings of a network of overseas publishing affiliates
which greatly diminished his earnings.

If John lost, he might face costs of up to £1½ million. But if he won,
he might gain assets estimated at £30 million. More significantly, an
outright John victory might well turn the entire music-publishing
industry inside out and unleash a pack of major-artist writs all

straining for a similar prize. Many industry staffers saw it as potentially the most important biz court case ever, and Dick James's son Stephen went so far as to predict that if John won, 'The music business is finished.' The case ended in November 1985, after more than fifty court days. It was quite a battle; it's likely that some publishers are still quaking at the outcome.

John first met Dick James when he was still the 20-year-old Reg Dwight, an unsuccessful keyboard thumper with a weight problem. Three early singles with his former band Bluesology had sold poorly, and his greatest achievement had been a tour backing Long John Baldry. He had begun writing with the 17-year-old Bernie Taupin in 1967, first by post (Taupin mailed the lyrics to which John added the music), and later in person when the producer who had first matched them up brought them together to demo in DJM's tiny recording studios in New Oxford Street. Their output was both prolific and embarrassing – John took fifteen to thirty minutes to write most tunes, and it showed.

But the two were hooked: songwriting *was* the life, not least because an ex-Bluesology guitarist was now a DJM house engineer and let the duo record after hours and free of charge. What happened when Dick James heard of the studio abuse is still the subject of bitter quarrelling. John claims he was summoned to James's office and waited outside 'like a schoolboy waiting for his O Level results'. His counsel, Mark Littman, argued in court that while they 'were waiting in reception quaking in their boots, a sound engineer told Dick James that he was impressed with what he had heard, and that James ought to sign them up ... when they came out of the office they were absolutely delighted, breathing sighs of relief'.

Dick James contends that it was John who first approached him, eager for a DJM publishing contract and a weekly retainer. He recalls having 'a minute or two to spare' to hear John's request, and on hearing some tapes a few days later, offered the pair what he considered to be a fair and standard contract.

'I was very young – it was a very exciting period,' John recalled in court. 'The basic points of the contract had been pointed out, and in all good faith I just signed it. I was very green behind the ears [sic] . . .'

John and Taupin both obtained parental consent before signing. But neither sought independent legal advice, and neither could claim to have full grasp of all their contractual obligations. 'I did not think about going to a solicitor,' said John. 'I just trusted Mr James. Their terms seemed very fair to us at the time . . . Anything anyone told me I believed.'

John, in fact, had good reason to trust James. As the publisher of The Beatles and the man who established Northern Songs in partnership with Lennon, McCartney and Brian Epstein, he was not only one of the most successful and respected publishers in a distinctly venal world, but undoubtedly one of the wealthiest: DJM received 50 per cent of all Northern Songs' worldwide income (excluding sheet music) – an asset valued at £10 million when he sold the catalogue to Lew Grade's ATV in 1969.

Aged 65, James resembled a striking vision of what Elton John himself might look like in thirty years' time – and what John's detractors would claim he looks like now: plump, bulbous-nosed, wrinkled, bespectacled, amiable and very bald. James also began as a singer, but it's a measure of his success that he's still best remembered for his 'Robin Hood' theme on the TV series that starred Richard Greene. He established DJM in 1961, and signed The Beatles exactly a year later. In 1967, after endless number ones and countless millions, he had new offices, a small recording studio, and had expanded from publishing into records and management. Elton John, meanwhile, had only recently left his job as a £15-a-week post- and tea-boy.

Judged by today's standards, not always a great idea, John's first DJM publishing and recording contracts were a disaster: a classic case of low royalties and savagely prohibitive terms. Again, these were standard, or marginally below standard, deals for the time; hundreds of artists must have been stung like this.

John and Taupin each received a £50 publishing advance and a weekly retainer of £15 and £10 respectively ('For jeans,' said Dick James), and were required to produce at least eighteen songs per year for three years, with a DJM option to extend it for a further three. All income, excluding sheet music, would be split 50:50. The contract, however, made no provision for an increased cut if successful. In theory, John could have written 'Rocket Man' and all the rest and still be paid an unknown's royalty.

The 1968 five-year record deal, signed with a DJM subsidiary that saw his work licensed at first through Philips and then through Pye, looked mean even measured against the terms offered by DJM's contemporaries. John received around 2 per cent of the retail selling price of each record bought, and again the chances of upping it with success looked bleak.

John also signed a five-year management deal with DJM in 1968, a move that would now be seen as posing a gross conflict of interest, not least because the contract specified the provision of advice on *all* matters affecting his career. John did not see an independent lawyer until 1970. The deal yielded DJM a 30 per cent commission, declining to 20 per cent after two years.

'Look at Elton John,' Dick James implored in a *Sunday Times* interview of 1973. 'I take 20 per cent of his personal earnings, excluding his music writing and records, because I publish his compositions and make his records, and it would not be ethical to have two bites of the cherry, though some people would do it . . .' Up until 1970, however, there was nothing in his contract with John to prevent him from doing the same.

John's disillusion set in early, though it was more to do with his continued lack of success than with his lack of royalties. The fame he believed to be synonymous with DJM writers eluded him throughout 1968 – his first single, 'I've Been Loving You', sold disastrously and necessitated a dramatic change of style – and by the end of his first year with James he had already consulted another publisher who advised him to seek help from a lawyer. John declined, preferring instead the guidance of Island Records founder Chris Blackwell, a keen admirer who suggested there may be certain 'holes' in his existing deals. 'Most of my contracts void!' John scribbled in his diary after their meeting. But he took no action.

And slowly things began to improve. His next single, 'Lady Samantha', enjoyed large-scale radio play, and his *Empty Sky* album sold well for a début. The breakthrough arrived with the appearance of new producer Gus Dudgeon in 1970, and early tapes of that year's *Elton John* album suggested to Dick James that the potential of three years ago had now materialized into a unique, high-quality and highly commercial product: it looked as though he was going to sell by the crateload. Accordingly, James offered him another recording contract.

This one led to the retention of John for a further five years, but now on an increased royalty of around 4 per cent of retail selling price up to February 1972 and around 6 per cent from March 1972 onwards. For one of the most successful acts in the world the cut was still low – 8 or 10 per cent might have been more realistic – but John appeared more than happy with it at the time. He was, after all, in boomtime. The glasses, the heels, the hats and the costumes had never been so outrageous.

'Your Song' was followed high in the charts by 'Rocket Man', 'Honky Cat', 'Crocodile Rock', 'Daniel', 'Saturday Night's Alright For Fighting', 'Goodbye Yellow Brick Road', 'Candle In The Wind', and many more. The albums *Honky Chateau*, *Don't Shoot Me, I'm Only The Piano Player* and *Goodbye Yellow Brick Road* were selling in many millions.

The quantity, and arguably the quality of the advice John took increased with his success. In 1970 he had met both his first lawyer and his current manager John Reid (the former sought out on Dick James's suggestion, the latter initially involved in John's career as a liaison staffer at DJM), and with the negotiation of what they saw as steadily improving publishing, management and taxation-easing terms, the two began to steer John away from complete DJM control.

They expressed unease at what might be happening to John's publishing income in America – they suspected that DJM's US subsidiaries were siphoning off larger than normal amounts before returning his earnings to be split at home – but decided to hold any possibility of litigation until the termination of his contracts. John himself remained on close terms with Dick James even after his final commitments to his DJM companies ended in 1975. By then he had written 136 songs and recorded 169.

His subsequent output for his own Rocket Records proved less prolific and, with the exception of 'Don't Go Breaking My Heart', significantly less successful until the early eighties, but his royalty rates for new work were now high, and his interests had diversified into the worlds of Watford FC and hair transplants. His memories of DJM were seemingly confined to interviews, boozy nostalgia and regular royalty cheques.

And then, in 1982, the writ. He claimed he'd been cheated over royalties. He claimed Dick James had taken dreadful advantage of him. He wanted to own his entire written and recorded DJM output. He wanted back his past.

Even after the success of Macaulay and O'Sullivan, John could not afford to be confident that the courts would see things his way.

Although present for several days of the trial, he was not present for the judgment, probably because he was playing live in Edinburgh that night, but possibly because he feared the worst. Bernie Taupin, now back writing with John after a long gap, had flown in from his Beverly Hills home to attend, and sat tense and grim-faced throughout, his earring and purple-streaked hair raising the odd eyebrow in the packed benches of legal advisers and sober industry observers.

Dick James and son Stephen (the current DJM managing director) sat a few feet away on the same benches, the former occasionally shaking his head at a turn in the judgment, the latter seemingly hooked on the taste of his fingernails.

And no wonder: the conflicting evidence was massive. John's counsel accused Dick James of 'undue influence'; James denied it. John's counsel claimed that John and Taupin had lost royalties of around £1 million that had been deliberately siphoned off in an overseas publishing scam that saw 'shell' subsidiaries, which may have had neither staff nor offices, rake off as much as 50 per cent of the writers' income before returning it to be split in the UK. DJM's counsel denied this, claiming it was normal business practice in return for the services provided. DJM's counsel suggested that John and Taupin had only brought the case at all on the advice of John's new lawyer; the writers' counsel maintained that a third of their songs were as yet unpublished and that their concern was less with the past than the future. John's counsel claimed there had been excessive fees and unfairly low royalties; DJM countered that while John had earned £13.4 million on his records and £1.14 million on his publishing up to December 1982, the DJM record labels made profits of only £8.5 million, and the entire DJM publishing group worldwide had profits of only £2.6 million.

In a four-hour judgment in December 1985, Mr Justice Nicholls agreed that John had suffered under the 'dominating influence' of James, but reasoned that the gap between the signing and the writ had been too long, not least because he had never previously voiced any complaint against James. There was no doubt either that DJM had invested large sums of time and money in breaking John worldwide, and that there should be certain reward for the risk-taking. His manager John Reid was also seen to have benefited from Dick James's continued goodwill between the termination of the contracts and this action. In the light, too, of his subsequent and continued success, Mr

Justice Nicholls failed to set aside the contracts, and declined to order the return of the copyrights or master recordings.

Taupin's main claims also failed, in part because he took no action 'until stirred up by others'. The judge did, however, find DJM guilty of the 'deliberate concealment' of those overseas sub-publishing negotiations (excluding those in the US) which substantially decreased John and Taupin's income.

The extent of their award was not specified, and at the time of the judgment it looked as though it may well take months of audits, interest calculations and hair-tugging to agree on a figure. But the respective PR machines began grinding into overdrive just hours after the verdict: the John and Taupin camp claim it may be around £5 million; DJM estimate that it won't exceed £500,000. The division of the action's costs also remained undecided at the time of judgment. The industry consensus is that John won a battle, and perhaps several moral victories, but he ultimately lost the war.

Outside the court, Dick James expressed 'relief after a marathon' and looked set for around four days' sleep.* Bernie Taupin looked disappointed that he hadn't gained more, but claimed he was delighted with the outcome.

Elton John, caught before another live show in Scotland, professed to be happy enough. As to his present-day contracts, he admitted that, 'I still don't read them.'

A little deceit between friends
The magnificent scandal of Allen Klein, David Platz and the publishers of The Rolling Stones

A new Performing Right Society yearbook – handsome, glossy, and painstakingly proper – came out in July 1985, proud as ever. It

---

*Dick James died of a heart attack two months later.

reviewed the year, catalogued its massive income and resultant massive distribution, explained about copyrights and how the whole PRS system operated, and backslapped with news of scholarships and songwriting awards. Sting picked up a 1984 Ivor Novello Award for 'Every Breath You Take', another glob of achievement went to Annie Lennox, and both of them had their pictures in the yearbook.

There was also a list of the PRS General Council, detailing directors and honorary members, and listing one of the publisher-directors as David Platz, the man we've met previously in connection with The Who and Tony Macaulay. There were forty names in all, the list being approved as correct as at 3 April 1985.

Platz was a strange inclusion, even though he'd built up wide respect in well over thirty years in the trade. Four months earlier, he had emerged from a seventy-seven-day High Court trial with a judge's verdict that he could not be trusted. It was ruled that he had asserted facts which turned out to be nothing remotely like the truth, and that 'even when he did tell the truth, he often did not tell the whole truth or anything like it . . . He will write anything at all which he thinks will assist his case, without any regard whatsoever to its accuracy.' One Platz letter to emerge during the trial was described as a 'simple tissue of falsehoods ending up . . . with the last paragraph which can only be described as a particularly nasty piece of nauseating hypocrisy'.

The trial involved not PRS, but Platz's conduct as the managing director of Westminster Music Ltd, one of the largest independent UK publishers which, with its affiliates and sister companies, controls huge hits by The Rolling Stones, The Moody Blues, George Harrison, The Who, Procul Harum and many more. It forms part of the Richmond Organization, a huge international network of publishers that together makes up one of the largest independent houses in the world.

Platz, in his mid-fifties, had been found guilty of dishonesty, ruthless self-interest, greed and devious plotting against the man who had brought him into the organization, and yet here he still was, a director of the PRS, the society that in 1984 handled a royalty income in excess of £64 million.

There may be a number of explanations for this: one, the PRS doesn't know about it, which is unlikely considering what a close-knit industry publishing is; two, it doesn't care about it – also unlikely considering what a conscientious and upright organization it is; three, it regards it as 'just one of those things' and sees fit to honour the old-boy network and protect its own; or four, it doesn't regard the trial's findings in any way relevant to Platz's involvement with the PRS. This last comes nearest to the truth: Platz was elected in 1983 by fellow members, and, unless he resigns, will probably only cease to be on the general council if he fails to be voted in again at the next election. If it does come to a vote, the outcome may well depend on how much is known about the details of this 1984 case.

And a lot of them are pretty shocking. It's an elaborate tale, but, as Woody Allen's fond of saying, 'Keep with this, 'cos it's great.'

By 1954, the ambitious and highly successful American publisher Howard Richmond began to look for additional footholds and income overseas. It seemed a natural progression: the Richmond Organization had begun small and had grown to control many major single and stage musical copyrights, and the plan was to establish a fibrous spread of affiliates that may one day girdle the globe. Accordingly, Essex Music Ltd was set up in London and Richmond came over to look for new staff.

He met David Platz in 1955, and each seemed to have something the other wanted. At 26, Platz was a brash and highly motivated self-made shooting star. He had thick, black prescription glasses to match his dense black hair, he often dressed flamboyantly but seldom touched alcohol, and as a German refugee who had fled from the Nazis in 1939, aged ten, he had graduated from office boy at the major Southern Music to the post of general manager of a Southern subsidiary. He was told that he was far too young to become managing director and by his mid-twenties was already looking round for more challenging work.

Howard Richmond could offer it. He'd heard of Platz's reputation, wanted a young gun, and signed him up for one year as general manager of Essex Music. When the year was up, Platz signed on for a further ten. He got a fat salary, a share of the profits, and 10 per cent of company and subsidiary-company shares. Essex prospered, Platz signed hit copyrights, Platz did well, Howard Richmond smiled, *everyone* smiled.

At the end of the ten-year term, both Platz and Richmond wanted to extend their relationship further, and Platz naturally looked for, and was happily granted, further reward. So in 1967 Platz became the managing director of an entirely new company, later to be known as Westminster Music Ltd. Half of the shares in the company were owned by Platz's interests, the other half by Richmond's interests, and because Platz was also managing director he became, in practical terms, the half with the most influence in the event of any dispute.

Westminster was governed by four central agreements signed in 1968 and 1975. The first, the Songways Agreement, set up a new wholly-owned subsidiary to provide services (personnel etc) to Westminster, and Platz became MD of that too. One important clause bound Platz to secrecy over all Westminster affairs.

The second agreement, the 'Essex 20 per cent Agreement', related to the transfer of copyrights from Platz's old company Essex Music, to his new one, Westminster. Platz agreed to draw up ten lists of equal value comprising Essex's most important English copyrights, and of these Howard Richmond would choose any two and agree to transfer all the rights to them to Westminster. It was agreed too that all songs newly registered with Essex between January 1966 and June 1967 should also be shifted to Westminster with all their rights. In other words, a lot of valuable songs.

The third of the agreements is irrelevant here, but the fourth, the Separation Agreement, is important. It was a grand ambition of Platz's one day actually to own his own song copyrights, and to assist the dream two subsidiary companies were established – Wildwood and Bucks – the first to be controlled entirely by Richmond's interests, the second controlled entirely by Platz's interests. In short, the new agreement determined what happened to Westminster assets if, after five years or more, either Platz or the Richmond Organization decided that they'd had enough of each other. Assets would be split 50:50 between Wildwood (Richmond) and Bucks (Platz), and two copyright lists of equal value would be drawn up so that Wildwood could take one list and Bucks the other. That was the broad theory.

It's not hard to figure that Platz did remarkably well out of the agreements – but Richmond clearly thought his talents were worth it. By the time of the new deal, Platz had already signed The Rolling Stones (one of the few deals which he celebrated with alcohol), and his name was now one of the most highly regarded in the industry. In radiospeak, the hits just kept on coming. Frank Richmond, one of Howard's five kids, aged fifteen in 1968 when the agreements were signed, regarded him as 'Uncle David – my mom always looked at David as being her security blanket. If anything ever happened to my father, David was going to be the family's protector and benefactor.'

Thus, when Howard Richmond did fall ill around the time of the new contracts, with a bleeding ulcer which demanded hospitalization and the removal of half of his stomach, then thank heavens Platz was there to mind the shop. And since the ulcer and all-round stress necessitated that Richmond move into semi-retirement in California, Platz was invaluable not only in emergencies, but now year in, year out, perhaps for all time. He began controlling more and more – in the early seventies he accepted a very large salary to take charge of all the Richmond Organization affiliates outside the USA and Canada – and throughout the decade he accepted more rewards for more responsibility. Richmond's trust grew yet deeper, and the golden period of Westminster and many other reaches of his network continued against all the odds well into the mid seventies. It was a remarkable partnership whichever way you looked at it; most people in the industry had a maximum golden run of five years – these two had two decades each.

But in June 1979, when success levels had waned markedly, Platz again approached Richmond for increased remuneration, including a deal whereby he would manage Richmond Organization affiliates for life. Richmond objected, claiming he'd already given him enough, but Platz reasoned that without his work in London, Richmond would be nothing like as wealthy as he now was and hence owed him more. The dispute was one of the most severe clashes in their twenty-four years together. At the end of one particularly bitter argument, Platz says he rushed to see an old friend and burst into tears.

No big thing had his friend not been Allen Klein.

The two had known each other for well over a decade, had had frequent dealings over The Stones' copyrights in the years since Klein had become their business manager, and in 1969 their names had been closely linked in The Beatles' unsuccessful £2 million takeover bid for Northern Songs (the company that held their golden copyrights). Had it come off, it was likely that Platz would have taken management control of Northern Songs at John Lennon's request, and would also have advised on the management of Apple.

It's not known what solace Klein offered Platz over his disagreements with Richmond in 1979, but it is known that Platz put Klein forward as an arbitrator and adviser in the dispute. Richmond considered Klein a strange choice, not least because Klein's ABKCO Music Inc, the owners of The Stones' copyrights, were currently pressing claims that Westminster and the Richmond Organization affiliates had recently underpaid royalties. Richmond later swore in court that he had no idea how close Platz and Klein were, and hence agreed that Klein should act as an intermediary. He also had no knowledge that, after December 1979, Platz was paying Klein huge amounts for his supposedly impartial 'advisory' services. The payment was originally to be 20 per cent of Bucks' income from the assets due from Westminster under the Separation Agreement, but was later commuted to a cash payment of around $500,000.

The huge sum posed one sensible question, asked in the 1984 trial by Mr Justice Walton: 'What on earth could Mr Klein have been doing on behalf of Mr Platz that would be worth that sum?' He concluded that he must refrain from speculation 'however great the temptation'. He noted, however, that 'virtually every one of the many self-serving letters which were sent by Mr Platz to Mr Richmond after 1979 was drafted or approved by Mr Klein and a great many were actually typed in his offices in London'. The judge would find later that Platz and Klein had in fact been plotting against Richmond from the outset. 'Thick as thieves' was his exact phrase.

In the five months that followed the commencement of the Platz–Richmond dispute, Platz acted contrary to an earlier agreement in an attempt to terminate some of Westminster's sub-licensing arrangements with the Richmond affiliates without proper consultation, and it was clear that the trust between the parties had completely dissolved. Inevitably, the Separation Agreement was invoked, but the intended simple division of Westminster assets proved fraught with problems. Platz and Klein drew up two lists of Westminster copyrights together, but Richmond complained that not only were they unequal in value but that they omitted master tapes and songs that had so far not yielded any income but might do so in the future. It was found also that the two lists – called simply A and B – contained one song that was common to both. There were additional unforeseen tax problems – much greater amounts would be lost to tax than was originally envisaged when the agreement was drawn up – and these too caused delays.

Platz become restless, and in June 1980 issued a writ against Richmond that ordered that the Separation Agreement be enforced as stated without further delay. 'What on earth was the purpose of issuing this writ at this particular time?' asked Mr Justice Walton in 1984. Richmond was doing all he could, he said, and

> It is as plain as a pikestaff that the writ was not issued for its main ostensible purpose.
>
> It is here that one detects the fine italic hand of Mr Klein, who, even if he had [as he said in the witness box] ceased to use writs as negotiating tactics on his own behalf, certainly retained the trick on behalf of his clients. For, after some attempt at evading the issue, Mr Platz in the witness box had to concede that he had been 'strongly advised' to issue the writ . . . and that, although he could not remember from whom that advice came, it might have come from Mr Klein. Since Mr Platz at no stage suggested that he had any other advisers than the highly paid Mr Klein, it scarcely needs a Sherlock Holmes to deduce whence the 'strong advice' came.

It was more than coincidence, too, that the day after the Platz writ, Klein's ABKCO company issued its own previously threatened writ against Westminster, Richmond and Platz regarding what he saw as underpaid royalties.

Before looking at the claim itself, here are three intriguing sidelines:

1 Klein issued the writ only days before he entered gaol on tax offences.

2 The writ made a direct charge of fraud not only against Richmond but also against his old friend Platz even though, in Mr Justice Walton's words, 'he did not for one moment really believe that Mr Richmond or Mr Platz had indeed been fraudulent'. It was, however, peculiar that although Richmond immediately refuted all Klein's accusations, Platz refused to join him. In fact, after the writ against him had been served, Platz even sent Klein a flattering birthday telegram: 'To Allen Klein . . . I scoured the country in search of the most appropriate and witty greeting, held competitions among the staff without avail, so I guess you'll just have to settle for an old fashioned Many Happy Returns. Lesley and David.' Which leads on to point

3 that Platz and Klein were hand in glove throughout these actions.

To a large extent their objectives coincided [suggested Mr
Justice Walton]. Mr Klein wanted Mr Platz to continue to
manage the ABKCO catalogue, which was not at all certain if
the Separation Agreement was carried out literally, and also
more money from Westminster. Mr Platz desperately wanted
to continue to manage the ABKCO catalogue. The object of
their collaboration was to put pressure on Mr Richmond with
a view to softening him up so that he would agree to both
their demands. It must be remembered that Mr Richmond
was a citizen of the USA and not all that frequently in the
United Kingdom. The conduct of litigation by him . . . is by no
means easy and certainly a far from inexpensive matter. The
double blow of the receipt of the two writs virtually
simultaneously was, I think, calculated to cause even the
stoutest heart to quail.

And Richmond indeed almost buckled. Klein's claims revolved
around 'black-box' income, which consisted of payments received by
publishers from collecting societies abroad (foreign equivalents of the
PRS) that were additional sums not directly related to specific
royalty earnings. In essence, it was a share-out of all unregistered
copyrights and/or income from other society property and/or the
repayment of overcharges made to members of the society. The
black box was shared out to member publishers partly with regard
to how much they earned in straight royalties from that society and
partly with regard for how long that publisher had been a member –
that is, the more the publisher earned in bona fide registered
royalties and the longer that publisher's membership, the greater the
share of the black-box income. Klein claimed that a large share of
Westminster's black-box income should revert to ABKCO, and in
the days prior to the writ being served, Platz typically advised
Richmond that he should settle in terms advantageous to Klein.*

When the writ came, coupled with that from Platz, Richmond
thought seriously about settling out of court and meeting Klein's
demands.

---

*Klein claimed a share of the black-box income on the grounds that the
Westminster affiliates wouldn't have received it at all had it not been for
ABKCO's Stones' copyrights.

My father was always of the opinion, 'Well, look, it will avoid three years of litigation . . .' [says Frank Richmond, the son who by 1980 had been sent to London to deal with the situation]. But I think every once in a while you have gut reactions about things, and his demands were so big . . . I knew early on that this was a bunch of shit and he was just after some money.

My father was ready to settle but in the end their demands just kept on coming. That's Klein's tactic – he gets to a certain point and you think you have a deal and then three more demands come through. And then you agree to two of those and you reject one and you think you're there, and then some more come through. My father said, 'They stole my underwear and that's when I put my hand up.' He always drew the analogy that he was sitting there screaming and he was getting raped by these guys and there wasn't a policeman and nobody believed that he was getting raped.'

It was Frank Richmond who had to deal personally with 'Uncle David'. He says he felt sadness as opposed to anger: 'I felt like shaking him sometimes and saying "David, what's the matter?" ' For Klein he has only contempt, but says he understands how so many had fallen under his spell. With regard to the A and B lists under the Separation Agreement, 'He once challenged me to a game of tennis for the ownership of the A list'. He refused, but learnt subsequently that Klein's a rotten tennis player.

But between 1980 and 1982 both Frank Richmond in London and his father in Los Angeles grew increasingly worried about many of Platz's activities, not least because of the adverse effects they were having on Westminster and other Richmond interests. At the end of 1980 for example, Platz transferred the contents of the A and B lists to Bucks and Wildwood without any authorization from the directors of Westminster, and he executed all the necessary documents on behalf of Wildwood without the slightest right.

Platz also acted against the Richmonds' wishes in transferring the majority of the personnel of the Songways Service Company into his own company, Platz Holdings Ltd, leaving Westminster without the necessary staff to carry on its own operations. He moved his Bucks firm and its subsidiary into offices of another Westminster subsidiary in Soho's Poland Street – also without approval from Westminster or Howard Richmond, and also without any contractual right to do so.

Platz did not pay a realistic rent, nor did he pay for the use of Westminster's rates, telex and electricity facilities. But worse was that Platz began to set himself up in direct competition to Westminster, despite the irony that he remained Westminster's managing director. There were attempts by Platz to dispose of the lease of the Poland Street premises, deliberately designed, in Mr Justice Walton's words, 'so as to put himself in a position in which he could, without Mr Richmond being in any way able to prevent him, place a large amount of the assets and business of Westminster in his own pocket . . .'

At the end of 1982, combined Richmond interests served a writ seeking to remove Platz from the post of managing director of Westminster, claiming that he had grossly misused his position, had deprived Westminster of many of its assets and was attempting to deprive it of many more with the intention of benefiting himself. Platz agreed to many temporary restricting clauses in court until the full judgment could be heard, and shortly after was confronted with another action, this one from the Richmond Organization affiliates, claiming that Platz's attempt to terminate their licensing deals was invalid.

These two actions, along with the 1980 writ served by Platz against Howard Richmond regarding the Separation Agreement, were now, at the end of 1984, on trial together.

Needless to say, the Richmonds shone while Platz and Klein came out of it disastrously. And as if to pile on the agony, Mr Justice Walton spoke caustically on the trustworthiness and conviction of the witnesses: again Platz and Klein emerged far from unscathed. Platz was regarded as 'not a witness upon whose written or spoken word I could possibly rely without corroborative evidence. Certainly, as compared with Mr Richmond, he fell far short of any acceptable standard of evidence.'

Midway through the trial it emerged that as well as the rough figure of $500,000 that Platz was paying Allen Klein for his assistance, he had also been paying him £1,500 per week since the beginning of May 1984 for services rendered during the trial. Klein denied vehemently that this fee included payment for any evidence he gave in court, though Mr Justice Walton commented that he was 'in no means certain that that in fact was the case'.

Walton described Klein as a partisan witness who had 'master-minded most of Mr Platz's campaign against Mr Richmond . . . so far as he was concerned, quite properly, in return for the promise of handsome remuneration'. The bulk of his evidence was adjudged to have been perfectly accurate, but on the second day in the witness box he complained of having a 'mental block' the day earlier and proceeded to change chunks of his evidence quite dramatically. Walton refused to accept that there was any such block: 'His original answers were just untrue.'

In summation, Walton ruled that Platz's 1980 action regarding the performance of the Separation Agreement was doomed from the outset. Its only purpose, he said, was as a negotiating ploy, arranged with Klein to weaken Howard Richmond for their own benefit. Regarding the Richmond interests' action against Platz, Walton fired for the plaintiffs with alarming power and direction: Platz was in direct and wrongful competition with Westminster through his own companies; he had not used his best endeavours to obtain or retain the business for Westminster that he should have done; he disclosed to Allen Klein much information regarding Westminster that he was bound to keep confidential; and he had blatantly used the assets of Westminster, especially the Poland Street premises, to conduct his own competing business. In short, Platz 'has simply shown himself utterly regardless of the interests of Westminster, save where those interests happen to coincide with his own. Putting it as kindly as I can, he simply cannot be trusted.'

The final action also found against Platz: his cancellation of sub-publishing licences was judged to be without effect, new licences were ordered, and Westminster was also ordered to pay at once a sum owing in excess of £68,000 that had been withheld on Platz's instructions.

The hardest question remained: what happened to Westminster and its assets now? The immediate solution, souped up at the tail end of 1984, was to restrain Platz in his conduct as managing director of Westminster and to demand an inquiry into damages. An order the following May detailed the removal of Platz and his nominees from the head of all Richmond companies and ordered that he should pay costs and damages well in excess of £1 million. He was, however, retained and paid by Westminster on a consultancy basis. Platz moved on to control his own Bucks Music Ltd and Standard Music Ltd and Frank Richmond accordingly installed himself in the Poland Street offices.

The final settlement was still many months away as this book was being finished – much of it in the hands of accountants – but Frank Richmond feels that the major battle is over: Platz has been branded the villain, the Richmond defence vindicated. The Separation Agreement was ruled to be unenforceable, and, pending appeals, Platz's outstanding Westminster assets should have been sold to the Richmond interests by mid 1987.*

But the relief in victory is clearly mingled with a sadness that it should come to this – that it should come to him testifying against 'Uncle David'. Along with Mr Justice Walton, Frank Richmond puts Platz's actions primarily down to greed and the belief that his father would go on giving, whatever the cost. 'I don't think that until almost the very end he [Platz] could have believed that we were going to go through with this, because it was out of character for my father to fight on this level. My old man's position was always, "If it's a question of money, let's settle".'

It wasn't just a question of money, of course. It concerned a large part of the Richmond family's future security and over thirty years of hard graft, reputation and respect.

Not that the fun is over: Frank Richmond knows well that there may yet be further ulcer-busters ahead. There's Allen Klein, for instance, and probably many years of dealings over that early Rolling Stones catalogue. Frank Richmond realizes that 'probably Klein looks at the Richmonds with anger and hate in his heart'.

'Yeah,' he says, 'he'll probably try and do something someplace along the line . . .'

---

*In mid October 1985, Platz summed up the position thus: 'The settlement which Howie Richmond and I are discussing is a separation by way of de-merging my share of Westminster's assets into my own companies, which is what I have long sought. Part of the settlement will involve my not proceeding with my (already lodged) appeal.

'. . . the litigation has affected me personally in that it has cost me dearly both emotionally and financially. However I am comforted by the fact that the loyalty of those members of the profession who have known me best has not been affected in the slightest by the adverse judgement which the court, in its wisdom, thought fit to pass.'

4
The problem of A and R

Just why does EMI dislike
Ray Jackson so much these days?

Muff Winwood, the ex-bass player with The Spencer Davis Group, was worth more in 1985 to CBS UK than any other bass player alive. Sade's young bass player's pretty hot, but he could be replaced if need be, and probably with no apparent decrease in sales. And the same with Springsteen's, and Billy Joel's, and Alison Moyet's: good bassists are hard to find, but Winwood is in a different league entirely. Now in his early forties, he's still completely denim-clad, still speaks with the fruitiest of Birmingham twangs, and is assuredly more filmstar-handsome now than when he bassed on 'Keep On Running' in the mid sixties. But he's currently senior director of A and R for both CBS and Epic, and vice president of CBS International, and as such is utterly invaluable.

He's the person who helped sign Sade when RCA and Virgin failed to, the one who saw the potential of Paul Young as a solo artist, the one who gambled fortunes on the Alison Moyet auction, and the one with the courage to sign longer shots like Dead Or Alive and King and get them to number one as well. He takes home a huge pay packet, and justifies it with the knowledge that without him CBS and Epic wouldn't hog the market shares and would perhaps make only a fraction of their profit. What's more, in an industry where knife-sharpening is a certain art-form, this guy is actually highly and widely respected. In biz jargon, he has ears.

Not all A and R employees are so lucky. Some are only interested in getting drunk in the early afternoon, getting coked out of their tree in the early evening, signing bands only through personal favours, living their lives like someone going over the trenches in the First

World War. Winwood's been with CBS since 1977. A lot of A and R staffers would have been sacked before hitting the eighties.

That at least is the picture unblurred. In reality, Winwood's fouled up many times too, signed turkeys, invested hundreds of thousands of pounds on artists who made records even their grandmothers refused to buy. His rivals, meanwhile, those swaggering coke fiends, have signed gems that have made millions. But the important part is that these are the people (again mostly men, but there are a few successful A and R women) who effectively push the 'go' button on what we hear, what we read about, what we buy. And the best way to insult them is to call them 'just a measly old talent scout', because at their best they're by far the most artistically creative people in the industry.

In itself, of course, the title Artist and Repertoire tells you nothing. Fairer, in fact, to call it F and C and D and A and S and P and D – Finding and Convincing and Demoing and Auctioning and Signing and Producing and Developing – but even those are only the edited highlights. No room left on the calling card for the pressuring, the deceiving, the neglecting, the damaging, and the shambles.

The theory
Let's make a lot of money

Muff Winwood's judgement on whether an act is good or not comes primarily from seeing it live: 'It's got to have flair, imagination, a determination to get itself and its identity across the footlights to the audience; it's got to *deliver* itself. Plus it's got to have some great songs and some great ideas for the arrangements of the songs.' But the chances are he'll only check on these things after his scout has seen it, and told either the CBS or Epic A and R people working below Winwood about how fascinating or talented or just plain great the act is. This scout's a true talent spotter and nothing but, usually someone in his late teens with unflagging energy and an unhealthy line in rabbit, who'll spend perhaps four nights a week going to gigs throughout the country and much of his remaining time on the hunt for promising indie records with an aim to a buy-out or buy-after. He'll report back at the weekly A and R meeting, suggest what ought to be followed up and repeat the whole affair the week after. His obvious promotion route will be either to one of the CBS or Epic A and R desk jobs, now occupied by the person he's reporting back to. He'll only get it if one of them dies of ulcers, gets sacked, headhunted by another company, or takes over from Muff Winwood.

Once there, he'll do a number of things. He'll follow up tips from the newly appointed scout below him, he'll talk to an artist he's interested in about their history, their plans, and the possibility of striking a recording deal, and he'll then refer the matters to Winwood for further approval.* He'll also assist in making demo tapes and selecting suitable producers, and he'll spend time selecting the act's best material and possibly suggesting cover versions. Hence his company will probably be spending small cash even before signature, but it all helps to hold that act – to withdraw it from the market place for a while. At the same time he'll have a load of already signed acts to look after: the process of discussing material, demoing with various producers, arranging recording time, and suggesting single cuts from albums.

If the demos of that unsigned act go well, then Winwood and the CBS legal affairs and business departments start talking deals. Advances and royalties depend on temperature: the hotter the act, and the more other companies have shown interest, then the bigger the money, the deeper the commitment and the more the act becomes a priority. An average CBS advance would be in the region of £20,000 for a solo artist and £60,000 for a band of promising but not blinding sales potential. This would be a per-year advance rising with each album, and list royalties between 10 and 15 per cent. All the usual claw-backs might be in there too.

If the money's bigger for a surer, more in-demand act, then CBS boss Paul Russell will probably see it as well: if you're going to guarantee hundreds of thousands in advances for between five and eight albums, then you may as well be sure you've got blessing from somewhere on high. Then again, if the big-money acts keep on failing, you're probably the first to be sacked anyway. For 'big money' read £250,000 annual

---

*Clearly, there are other people involved in A and R too, such as A and R managers. This is only the basic plot.

advances and royalties in the mid-teens, and from that draw two main conclusions: one, if an act is in enough demand, then the major with the most conviction combined with the most money will usually get it; and two, at lay-outs of £250,000 per year (plus marketing on top of that), mistakes as to wrong single releases, or the wrong producer for an album, are costly.

Even with the best talents, even with Muff Winwood at your helm, and even with the vast resources of a market leader, A and R is a risky business, and an awful lot of money disappears down the toilet. That's one of the reasons market leaders don't usually remain market leaders for more than a few years. All you can do is limit your risks by shrewdness and skill, and often by cunning cost-cutting. And *if* you uphold all your commitments to your artists and don't break any rules, then you're doing your job as best you can and must leave the rest to good fortune. Some, however, inevitably find the temptation to rule-bend – to intervene with good fortune – too strong to resist.

The practice
How to cut a lot of losses

By the beginning of 1973, Newcastle band Lindisfarne had enjoyed two top-five singles and three top-ten albums – hummable and swaying singalongs mostly – and could reflect that in the last year they had sold more albums in the UK than any other act. A monster thumping live band too.

When they split, some months later, singer-songwriter Ray Jackson joined several new groups but achieved little. In the mid seventies, with the boomtime still fairly fresh in his mind, he decided to try for success again and go solo. He signed a one-year deal with EMI.

In 1985, exactly nine years after his signing, Ray Jackson appeared in court claiming EMI had ruined his career. The A and R department had failed to promote him, he said, its organization was a mess, and it had failed to honour its agreement. They had signed him up, secured his talents exclusively, and then had declined to do what they had promised – namely, to treat him as a top priority act. They had even declined to release more than one Jackson single in over eighteen months, despite the contractual obligation to release at least three in the first year.

Ray Jackson and manager Barry McKay first approached EMI in late 1975. McKay was only 21, still fairly green to the ways of the industry despite operating a handful of record and instrument shops and promoting concerts in his native Newcastle, but he'd been surprisingly impressed by six Jackson demo songs and had agreed to do what he could to get him a new deal. EMI was an obvious choice: McKay liked the idea that it was British and had promoted The Beatles, and he was convinced that the company had a sufficiently professional set-up to know what they were doing. The deal was struck: Jackson was signed to EMI through McKay's own management company, International Music (UK) Ltd, on (then) pretty average and certainly not generous terms. The contract would be for a minimum of one year, in which time both Jackson and EMI guaranteed to record a minimum of three singles at a royalty of 6 per cent of 90 per cent of retail sales. He received an advance of £1,800, but was guaranteed a further £10,000 if the first option period for one album was taken 'up, and the same for the second and final album options. The normal clauses regarding exclusive artist availability and the approval of selecting material were also there, and the first-term dates were set from 1 February 1976 to 31 January 1977.

Hardly a spectacular deal, but it could have set Jackson up again, and surely it would only lead to better things. The first single, 'Take Some Time', came out in mid 1976 and did abysmally, selling under 300 copies. Jackson was upset at the lack of the priority promotion that he believed he'd been promised, but the EMI A and R and promotions departments largely blamed the lack of Radio 1 airplay. The next single would just have to do better. Only there wasn't another single.

Although only established acts could hope for a contractual clause guaranteeing the release of their recordings, all, including Jackson, were guaranteed that the agreed minimum requirement at least be recorded. In Jackson's case, they weren't. Further songs were only recorded more than six months after the first year had lapsed, in the period previously assigned to be the first-album option period. This being the case, argued Jackson and McKay, then a £10,000 advance should be paid. It wasn't. Nor were any further records ever released by EMI.

The legal flak – between Barry McKay's management company and the EMI legal department – began in 1978, only culminating in the Newcastle and London High Courts seven years later. 'Breach of contract on two counts!' screamed Jackson and McKay, referring to the unfulfilled three-single commitment and the non-payment of the accepted album option advance. 'Not so!' yelped EMI's chief defence, Nick Mobbs, A and R general manager from 1977 to 1978, insisting that Jackson and McKay had misinterpreted the small print. It was to be some scrap.

Jackson and McKay's claims were simple enough: they demanded damages for holding the singer with insufficient promotion up to the point when the likelihood of solo success had passed. They pointed out that another deal signed in 1980 with Phonogram resulted in album sales of only 1,680: by then, Jackson's material was quite out of step with the market. If EMI had tried and failed, if they had pushed the records out and nobody had bought them, then that would have been different. As it was, they said, they signed him and didn't even try, and as such rendered him impotent at a crucial stage in his career. 'Just think of the repercussions if any company could sign an artist and then lock that artist away,' said McKay.

The plaintiffs wheeled on the witnesses with delight. Steve Weltman, managing director of Charisma Records, the company that enjoyed the massive early seventies' Lindisfarne success, described Jackson's initial chances of success with EMI as 'strong', and famed record producer Gus Dudgeon, who had worked with Elton John, Gilbert O'Sullivan and many others, told the court that 'This has always been a chancy business, but with the right promotion I think he could have made it.' McKay's and Jackson's counsel, Jeffrey Gruder, summed it all up sweetly: 'The conduct of EMI . . . is absolutely appalling. They did, by their complete neglect of Jackson, stifle any chance of a solo career. They had him on their books for two years and did absolutely nothing for him.'

EMI's defence hinged on rather more technical contractual matters. Nick Mobbs was joined by another member of the A and R department, John Darnley, in EMI's claim that they did the best they possibly could for Jackson, but were hindered by lack of suitable material. They pointed to a clause specifying that the artist committed himself to be 'ready, willing and able' to record as agreed, contending that because of a failure to come up with the right material, Jackson was neither ready nor able to fulfil his side of the arrangement. The contract specified that recording material should be 'satisfactory' to EMI, and the company now claimed that this was not the case. They further contended that Jackson was 'signed as a singer–songwriter', and that there had been an unwillingness on his or his manager's part for him to record other writers' material. His own material, said EMI, was so unlikely to succeed commercially that to record and release it could only have damaged his career. And this they were unwilling to do. They claimed that their actions were also quite within their contractual rights by virtue of an exemption clause which ruled that if Jackson fell ill or was involved in an accident or 'for any other reason beyond (McKay's) control' was unable to fulfil the agreement, then EMI could either terminate the whole thing or extend it for the same length of time as the previous inability to perform. It was clear, they said, that Jackson's failure to come up with the satisfactory material qualified in the 'or for any other reason' category.

Nick Mobbs asserted further that 'making an album was totally out of the question' and that no album option had ever been taken up. It was true that the original first-year period had been extended, he said, and that more tracks had been recorded in the autumn of 1977, but only as a result of notice given to Jackson and McKay that they had failed in their part of the bargain. He claimed that the notice was given 'either orally or impliedly'.

In short, EMI turned the matter on its head: they alleged it was McKay and Jackson who had fouled up in their failure to produce the goods. Nick Mobbs and John Darnley were therefore hardly the villains; they claimed they had done all they could.

Ultimately, however, it was EMI's own witnesses that let them down. Whereas Mr Justice Michael Davies found Ray Jackson to be 'a very impressive and fair witness with a strong, indeed burning, conviction that he had been let down by a great company which he trusted', he found Nick Mobbs to be altogether less convincing in both 'demeanour and manner of giving evidence'. Moreover, a fair proportion of EMI's most potent evidence conflicted to the point where the company's own counsel pleaded despairingly that some of it be forgotten or rejected. For example, although Nick Mobbs had claimed that an agreement for an extension of the three-singles obligation had been attained, and that this extension lasted well into 1977, a letter sent in the autumn of 1978 from EMI's group legal department showed that the agreement with Jackson terminated on 31 January 1977. In court, EMI's defence of the contradiction was that the person responsible for the letter, Mr Roger Drage, had simply done insufficient research on the matter. Mr Justice Michael Davies found this argument 'as airy as it is unconvincing'.

Another conflict of evidence arose from the work of the then EMI contracts manager, Chris John. A central plank of EMI's defence ran like this: one, we did our best; two, the initial one-year period was lengthened so that the minimum requirement of three singles could be recorded, thus making both parties fulfil their side of the agreement; and three, that this was in fact done – in October 1977 it cost them around £7,000 to record additional tracks with an aim to releasing them as the two final singles.

Chris John, however, rocked the boat. Part of his job at EMI was to inform Nick Mobbs and others about the upcoming expiry of artists' contracts, to enable them to decide whether to take up an option or not. With Mobbs, he attended regular option meetings. Some time before the intended first-year expiry of Jackson's contract in January 1977, John wrote 'hold' on the right-hand side of the memo detailing the upcoming expiry. The minimum three-single commitment had not yet been fulfilled and the 'hold' signified that an option decision could not yet be taken.

But John then gave evidence that at an option meeting of 5 August 1977, he was instructed by Nick Mobbs that Jackson's contract was to lapse. Hence on the same memo on which he had previous written 'hold', he wrote 'NM drop 5/8/77'. Six days later John sent another memo to Mobbs and Paul Watts, the general manager of EMI's pop division, confirming the situation as follows:

> This will confirm our discussion regarding options which took place on the morning of Friday 5th instant . . . You advised me that the contract with International Music for Ray Jackson which had been in a 'hold' situation should be considered as having lapsed. We have rights in perpetuity for any product recorded under the aforementioned agreement.

Nick Mobbs and Paul Watts both said that they either did not receive this memo or could not have read it properly. Not surprising, because Chris John, 'a careful and convincing witness', had clashed severely with Mobbs's own defence. Whereas Mobbs had contended that they had recorded in October 1977 because of an extended period caused by Jackson's and McKay's failure to produce satisfactory material, and/or that such an extension had been mutually agreed, there was now evidence that Mobbs had already decided to drop Ray Jackson two months earlier in August 1977. Mr Justice Michael Davies concluded that the recording of the extra tracks was little more than an afterthought, the obligatory face-saving measure. 'I strongly suspect that it was realized that the minimum commitment had not been fulfilled and accordingly [EMI] might be in difficulties in escaping from it and so they decided that they had no alternative but to record further tracks.' He credited Nick Mobbs with the hope that some of these tracks might yield something of which he could approve, but noted also that the recordings were never completed to final single-release quality.

And, point by point, the judge sided against the bulk of Mobbs's and EMI's other defence claims too. He concluded that there was sufficient evidence to show that Jackson and McKay were at all times 'ready, willing and able' to fulfil their part of the deal. If Jackson hadn't come up with the material himself, then it was up to the A and R department to find it for him – there was nothing in the deal that even hinted that he had to write his own songs. Once that was clear, the whole subjective question of what was or was not satisfactory material became superfluous. Besides, there had never been any suggestion from anyone in A and R that the first single wasn't any good; all they said against it was that it didn't sell.

The 'or for any other reason beyond its control' argument also could not be applied to this particular case. This was more than a 'broken leg' clause, but it still didn't go so far as to cover what EMI regarded as the production of unsatisfactory product. With regard to the oral or implied extension of the first three-single term, and with regard to the gaping conflicts in their own evidence, the judge found no acceptable foundation to suggest that either form of notice was given by EMI nor accepted by McKay and Jackson. Notice of such an extension should be in writing, and in so far as EMI claimed that under the circumstances a 'gentleman's agreement' was in order, Mr

Justice Michael Davies observed that 'in the course of the case I was not sure what a gentleman's agreement was . . .'

But if agreements had to be in writing, then that too would apply to the taking up of an option. Hence McKay's and Jackson's claim to the unpaid £10,000, for what they interpreted as a clear acceptance of the first album option, was similarly thrown out by the court.

For the plaintiffs, however, one breach of contract victory was clearly enough. They had proved their case: EMI had failed to honour their contract. As for the damages, they were calculated on the understanding that even in such a high-risk business (where over 100 singles are released each week, of which perhaps four get into the top fifty and three of these would be by established artists), even then Ray Jackson should be compensated for not receiving a 'fair crack of the whip', for the loss of possible success, and for the loss of royalties as a singer, a writer, and perhaps even loss of income as a live performer.

> If [EMI] had played fair . . . there was a real and substantial probability . . . that Ray Jackson would have succeeded – [the judge concluded]. Not that he would have become what is referred to as a megastar, but that he would have achieved such a success as a solo recording artist as would have brought in for him and his manager substantial sums of money.

EMI's counsel disagreed, of course, claiming that Jackson's chances of success were virtually nil. Strange then, that EMI's A and R department should bother to sign him up.

EMI were ordered to pay damages of £12,500 plus interest, which by 1985 almost doubled the award. Joint costs came to nearly £80,000.

Barry McKay later claimed that the case had set a thumping and crucial precedent. Henceforth, no record company could afford to mistreat and neglect their artists in a similar way. However, EMI's business affairs executive, Gareth Hopkins, countered that this was not in fact a general precedent but an isolated and dated case.

It is one of those differences we can only judge in ten years' time. Yet it was perhaps more than coincidence that in the same month the case came to trial, chart toppers Spandau Ballet announced that they were suing their record company, Chrysalis, for breach of contract. The band claimed neglect and inadequate promotion, and the dashing teen idols believed they had a very strong case.

5
Hype

The Sex Pistols, Bucks Fizz and
how to get to number one

As a 13-year-old schoolboy, I was never remotely interested in the record industry. Like most kids, I didn't care about sales figures, profit margins or rip-offs – but I cared desperately about the singles chart. Every Tuesday lunchbreak I crowded around the radio with a few friends for the first public airing of the new top thirty. The music wasn't important, it was the climbers, the non-movers and the number ones that used to grip.

I used to like all records that came in straight at number one, irrespective of the artist or artistry; that it had achieved this remarkable feat was entertainment enough. Also, music didn't really exist *outside* the top thirty; if it wasn't high in the charts, then it must have been awful. I had no need to know how a record had got there, how much money had been used to promote it, or which label it was on. I was happy in the knowledge that if a record came in at number one, then that was showbiz, and as showbiz was rare at my school I usually spent Tuesday afternoon in a state of smug and boundless wisdom. Screw the maths: Slade had come straight in at the top spot, and most people didn't even *know*!

Looking back, a decade and a bit later, I suppose I had the right idea but for all the wrong reasons. From the industry's point of view, I understated and oversimplified. The charts are entertainment, but more in the sense that they *control* entertainment than reflect it. And the top-thirty placings are still what matter more than anything, but only because of the income generated. In other words: I was never interested in the charts for aesthetic reasons, and nor are the major companies today. Then again, I was never interested in the charts because of money either, and to the majors, of course, money is all.

It is impossible to imagine the music business without charts, just as it would be impossible to imagine a railway without tracks. They provide power, direction and security, and, to the music industry, a record in the charts also provides a gauge of taste, a streamline of sales and marketing resources, an abundance of media exposure, huge marketing and live spin-offs, the sales-from-success spiral, the feeling that someone out there likes you, pleasant telegrams from America.

Whatever happened to showbiz? Nothing much: these days we just know it as hype. Hype itself has two meanings. One is known, tongue-in-cheek, by the record companies as 'aggressive marketing', and includes hard-sell TV ad campaigns, the offer of free gifts with record purchases, and target-selling promotions in those shops that you just happen to know file sales returns to the chart computers. And the other is just plain cheating: contravening the British Phonographic Industry (BPI) code of conduct by bribery, filing incorrect returns, or the mass purchase of your own records.

Both forms of hype still exist, though the latter has now been contained to the level of a minor irritant. Gallup, the chart compilers since early 1983, will tell you that the only way you get into the top forty these days is by selling a lot of records *legally*. You can still fix a record into number 147 or so, but you'd only be fooling yourself and might soon be picked up by the BPI or Scotland Yard. Before Gallup (Gallup will tell you with veiled pride), the British Market Research Bureau (BMRB) let 'corrupt' records slip much higher – number eight in one case – and had far less satisfactory methods of fraud detection. Gallup now boasts a highly efficient computer system, foolproof checking methods and a supremely balanced chart. And the vast majority of the large record companies would agree with it; it's now practically impossible to swindle with any effect. But the fact remains that the chart is *so* important, and the problem remains that there are few who won't still try it on.

Take these prime fix revelations since 1980, and take them as you should the chart itself: a sample drawn to represent the whole.

In August 1980 a Granada TV 'World In Action' programme interviewed two ex-WEA promotions men, Ian Mallett and Andrew
Ferguson. Mallett told how he often went to record shops in the
north-west and provided owners with free records. In return, they
would allow him to enter the sales figures of his choice in their
chart-return diary. Ferguson described seeing a WEA executive at
head office filling in four of the record shop returns himself. WEA
memoranda revealed a list of free gifts being offered by other record
companies, including satin jackets and bottles of whisky, and another
former WEA rep, Avis Lingard, estimated that such gifts could be
worth £10,000 a year to owners of chart-return shops. Records
supposedly hyped included releases by Elvis Costello, Dusty Spring-
field and Gary Numan.

WEA managing director John Fruin refused to answer the specific
allegations, but said: 'I think it is morally wrong for a record to be
shown at a chart position which is not an accurate reflection of its
sales.' A few weeks later, Fruin was managing director no more.

Charles Levison, the man who replaced him, speaks now of how
'WEA got in such a mess – they were selling loads of records, but
not making any money.'

It was the biz's mini Watergate. John Fruin was even chairman of
the BPI, the body that had campaigned to eradicate hyping more
vociferously than any. The BPI refuted the allegations on the
grounds of insufficient evidence, at which point Rod Stewart's manager, Billy Gaff, cancelled his Riva Records' BPI membership. Gaff
claimed that the industry was being ruined by 'fixers, cheats, con-
men and hypocrites', and that 6,000 copies of *Rod's Greatest Hits*,
which appeared on Riva but was distributed by WEA, had been
used for 'promotional purposes' by WEA. He claimed too that over
100,000 copies of two other Stewart albums, *Atlantic Crossing* and
Night On The Town had been 'mislaid' by WEA and CBS.

It is likely that the WEA allegations only scratched the surface.
And with the BPI failing to recognize publicly the scale of the
problem, the fiddling continued, even at the heavily indicted WEA:
book-cooking resulted in a sacking from the sales-force not very
long after Charles Levison's appointment.

Godfrey Rust, the Gallup manager responsible for the smooth
running of the current, largely hype-proof charts, and a former BPI
employee, now suggests that the old system was there to be

exploited, and was mistreated because not to do so meant falling behind.

> When you're so competitive and have to pick up any chance you can, you abuse it. Some companies might be worse than others, but they'd all do it. Most of the reps out there have probably worked for at least five different companies.
>
> Everyone had their hyping year – I remember RCA had their year, and it included the most outrageous single entry: Gerard Kenny's 'New York, New York'. It came in at number 41 from nowhere one week and there was absolutely no way.... It had been getting airplay for seven weeks and the airplay had just about completely ceased and it had sold nothing. Then the record flew in and then of course the airplay took off when it charted, and the sales collapsed! By no stretch of the imagination ... and the reasons that we heard ... I remember talking to the guy who was promoting it who said: 'Oh, he was in a car crash the week before, and there was a lot of sympathy for him ...'!
>
> There were a lot of presents to dealers in return for favours. The Gerard Kenny album made the top twenty in its week of release, and again, 'Gerard *who*?' That was the gold watches ... But every company had their period – RCA, CBS, WEA and EMI. And it would depend on how much pressure they were getting from America or which person was in the hot seat at that stage. It was just a case of an MD saying to the sales people 'We have to get this record in the top seventy-five and I don't care how you do it ...'

One way you can do it is by bribing the shop owners as above, but another is by bribing the customers. It's mild bribery – it says if you buy this record in this week in this shop, you'll also get a free T-shirt – but it seems to work because up until November 1983 most of the heavyweights did it with regularity.

The basic thinking is simple: any survey, whether conducted by the BMRB or Gallup, depends for its findings on a sample. Under the current system, Gallup compiles any one week's chart with returns from around only 275 shops (there are roughly 5,000 UK record outlets and the sample is around 1:18). Hence the obvious possibility of every sales team's ultimate wet dream: dynamic target marketing. If you can sell in those 275 shops, then you don't have to sell one single copy in the remaining 4,725. On its head, this means that if you sell a million in the 4,725 and nothing in the 275, you won't get into the charts at all. (This is simplified, and it will become clear later that Gallup isn't actually as archaic as this all suggests, but we're dealing with a great wet dream here, and a recurring one.)

Then, if you're a rep or a marketing person, all you have to do is get hold of a secret list of chart-return shops. This is easy. I got hold of a fifteen-page photocopied list, providing me with names, addresses and account numbers, just by calling someone I knew on a Fleet Street paper who said he got it from an independent record company. If I can get one with one phone call, you can bet that the people who want them at CBS, EMI, WEA and everywhere else can get one in embossed gold leaf with just *half* a phone call. And once you have the list, you know exactly to which dealers you offer your free albums or gold watches or bottles of whisky.

But if that's playing it too crude, then the list is also great for that mild customer bribery. Why print enough free T-shirts for every shop in the country when all you have to do is print enough for the demands of 275 shops? More crucially, if you *just* print enough for the 275, then you can train the customers to use those shops more often; if you sometimes get a free T-shirt with a single in *this* (chart-return) shop, but never do in the (non-chart-return) shop across the road, then you may as well always go to the goodies shop and hope you're lucky. (And if the customers can't work it out for themselves, then you go so far as to tell them where to go, as happened with Epic's Nolan Sisters. In July 1983, Nolan fan club members each received details of where they could get a free Nolans' poster with all purchases of their new 'Dressed to Kill' single. Gallup determined that of the 100 shops listed, an 'unacceptably high proportion' were chart-return shops. The single was withdrawn from the charts.)

Once the customers are there, you ensure they buy your label's records as opposed to another's by bigger and better inducement – that is, not just a T-shirt but an Adidas T-shirt, and not just any old free baseball cap but a foam-padded baseball cap with easy-adjust poppers at the back. It would be worth giving away a limited number of gifts valued at many times the profit returns of its accompanying single if they were to launch an unknown artist or help spiral sales of an established one; once a record enters the top forty, bona fide sales take over and dispense with the need for further hype.

There was nothing to stop sales reps loading the free goodies into the chart-return shops (Gallup in fact tacitly acknowledged that 'we know that you know . . .'), but telling the customers about their whereabouts was forbidden.

This is all great fun for the customer, but less so for Gallup or the BMRB before it. Ultimately, too, it wasn't that much fun for the record companies because *everyone* had those return-shop lists, and *everybody* seemed to be spending vast amounts just to cancel each other out. It was getting to the point where it might be hard to shift a record if it didn't have a free T-shirt. The clampdown came in November 1983, but a few months before it you could walk away with the following freebies: Rod Stewart 'Baby Jane' (WEA): free Adidas T-shirt; David Bowie 'Modern Love' (RCA): free poster; Kid Creole & the Coconuts 'There's Something Wrong In Paradise' (Island): free T-shirt; Level 42 'The Sun Goes Down (Living It Up)' (Polydor): free cassette; Robert Plant 'Big Log' (WEA): free book; Annabel Lamb 'Riders On The Storm' (A&M): free video; Big Country 'Chance' (WEA): free T-shirt; Haircut 100 'Prime Time' (Polydor): free T-shirt; Shakin' Stevens 'It's Late' (Epic): free beachball.*

Those are just the edited highlights. Even the majors could see it was getting out of hand: the BPI's new clean-up policy outlawed free T-shirts, books or videos, and anything else that had a saleable value, though posters and free records were permitted.

That code of conduct was important too in clamping down on other sales-force fiddles (including the offer of free albums in return for various favours concerning other albums), and was at last enforceable because of Gallup's vigorously efficient policy of returns-policing that was first introduced at the beginning of 1983 and continually refined. Granted that no chart will ever be totally hype-proof, that the tabloids need the headlines and that the industry desperately needs the showbiz, then the current Gallup system looks supremely hard to beat long term (that is, you can still fake it to

---

*Most of the accompanying singles were sizeable hits, but it's impossible to gauge to what extent success lay with the free gifts. As before, though, it's worth noting that the chart-return shops had them in abundance, and safe to say that those shops sold a lot of very cheap T-shirts . . .

number 147 but you certainly won't get near the top forty). And there's no doubt that it's a vast improvement on the way things operated even five years ago. Here's how it works early in 1986.

1 All sales figures from around 440 shops nationwide are entered on Dataport machines (a typewriter-sized computer box), 275 of which are then called up automatically by a central Gallup computer in the small hours of Thursday, Friday and Sunday mornings. The choice of the 275 is changed regularly, though not each week.

2 Each Dataport logs all sales made each day of the week at fifteen minute intervals, the resultant data providing Gallup with details of exactly where each record was sold, and at what time on which day. Any bulk-buying irregularities are automatically detected by the central computer checking against the norm.

3 The total sales figures for the selected 275 are then identified (the figures are keyed in at source by catalogue number(s) and are switched back to artists and songs at headquarters), and totals are added to leave a rough chart ready by Sunday night.

4 The figures are then weighted in an attempt to turn the sample into a representative whole by being mathematically balanced three ways according to the type of shop (for example, an indie or W. H. Smith's), the size of the shop, and geographically, in order to make up for any weekly changes in the panel of 275. Such things as chart-shop signing sessions are also put into weighted perspective. Gallup still doesn't get exact nationwide sales figures, but in a chart that represents the performance of one record against another that's never the idea anyway.

5 The resultant figures are checked over the phone on Monday morning against a back-up panel of 125 shops, selected from a total back-up of around 600. The performance of each new and climbing record is then matched against the check panel, and irregularities weeded out and weighted as before. The check panel is itself spot-checked. Fixed records will now be obvious, though Gallup cannot remove chart records or fine companies itself. BPI does that instead.

And that's it – the charts are made public on Tuesday morning. Or rather that's a very simplified version of the operation; the checks and security are in fact still more stringent, the fallibility of the system far less open to the loopholes manifest above.* You'd think that company managing director and sales reps would know better than to plot against it. Some chance.

They bribe. They get caught by Gallup and fined by the BPI. They fix. They get caught by Gallup and fined by the BPI. They buy their own records. The same thing happens. They juggle with catalogue numbers. The same. At times even the courts are brought in to deal with offenders.

In 1983 Arista was fined £3,000 when a salesman falsified entries against a Barry Manilow single. EMI was fined £10,000 for similar offences in March 1984. In April 1984, WEA was fined £6,000 for offering free copies of a Van Halen album to shops, including many on the Gallup panel. In September 1984, the distribution network IDS was fined £12,500 after a rep had made false Dataport entries. And in September 1985 Phonogram was ordered to pay £7,500, reputedly as the result of a rep offering a chart shop a record with the false catalogue number of another record that was genuinely selling well.

All were dismissed as isolated incidents by the companies involved, executives clearly taking great delight in blaming all on some ambitious sales greenhorn since sent packing. In other words, they put it down to showbiz.

Executives might also say: not to worry, the biggest legendary chart cowboys have already been rounded up. In February 1985 four men were served with High Court writs for illegal interference with the Gallup charts, accused of organizing an elaborate 'buying in' scheme, whereby they'd receive money from managers or small companies to buy their own records.

'The ringleader would run it like a sales force,' says Gallup chart manager Godfrey Rust. 'He'd have somebody in each area and he'd mail them a list of shops to go to. He'd deliver free copies of records to the shops, and then pay his guys to go out and buy them and then send the records back.' He would then ship them out again – in theory he could get a hit single just by the inspired juggling of about 200 records.

He must have made £200,000 or more out of it, [estimates Rust]. He would charge between £1,000 and £3,000 a week. I

---

*But the system doesn't come cheap. In 1985, Gallup's annual fee stood at over £300,000. Fifty per cent is met by the BPI, with the BBC and *Music Week* paying 11.5 per cent and 38.5 per cent respectively.

know one guy who paid him something like £8,500 to work the records for six weeks on the promise that it would be in the top forty in two weeks. After six weeks it had made number eighty-five and by that point it was really selling pretty well, and it was actually removed from the chart then.

Rust sees the ringleader as 'a con man basically', who's been doing a pile of outrageous things for years. 'We first thought he was a joke and eccentric – we knew he went around the shops buying his own records. He recorded himself, went into a shop, handed several copies of his record to the manager and said, "Can I buy them back now?" ' It was a nice idea.

The Sex Pistols
Cash from chaos

There's but one logical progression from record hyping: band hyping. Why waste money and energy and risk prosecution by trying to push one lousy single up the charts, when you can blow it all on pushing one lousy band up the charts – a band that promises relative longevity (a few years as opposed to a few weeks), as well as much more cash? And you can forget cheap publicity launches and record shop window displays and the odd picture disc single, because that's not real creative hype, that's just sprightly and opportune press and marketing. The big hype involves image creation – the art of something-from-nothing and the subsequent haul of big swag.

Not many bands or would-be Svengalis manage it, but two that have in the last decade are The Sex Pistols and Bucks Fizz. Needless to say, gorgeous hype is the only thing they *do* share.

Malcolm McLaren, the loquacious (then) 28-year-old fashion hound who steered the Pistols, can lay claim to changing a comatose industry singlehandedly. Exactly what the band stood for or sang about, or the way they behaved, was always less important than the fact that they couldn't be controlled. They might get banned, they might swear on live TV, they might cause a riot, they might wreck the room – no one knew. Before them, the whole industry knew *everything exactly*. There were few shocks. Most artists retired to a ranch and put out one album a year in a nasty cover.

The effect was a farcical major label quickstep the like of which has never been seen before or since. In McLaren's estimation, the corporate desire to 'tame' the Pistols was just as strong as the desire to make money from them. RAK wanted the band. So did Chrysalis. So did Polydor. In the end they went to EMI in October 1976 (signed in fact by A and R man Nick Mobbs shortly after bagging Lindisfarne's Ray Jackson . . .). The Pistols got a £40,000 advance on a two-year contract. Shocking behaviour and complaints from shareholders resulted in dismissal a few weeks later, and McLaren claimed he'd received a £50,000 pay-off. CBS and WEA then expressed interest . . . A&M finally got them for £150,000 . . . Off the label after one week . . . £75,000 pay-off . . . The punks sign with 'ex-hippie' Richard Branson's Virgin . . .

No one seemed to know too much about the exact money or why or who or where, but what counted was the attitude – the fact that McLaren talked gleefully, if hyperbolically, about the cash involved and the fact that a band could so upset a company by not knuckling under. Subsequently, of course, the backlash whipped hard and the industry of 1985 was as severe and as grimly in control as it was in 1975; as before, you danced to the chosen tune or you didn't dance at all.

The *attitude* was captured precisely by McLaren's concept of 'The Great Rock 'n' Roll Swindle' – the manifesto of embezzlement that was conceived with hindsight and boosted with pearly overkill. But remember that the Pistols' adventures in the industry were certainly directed as much by accident as design, and definitely by no fine-line manual of the sort that follows. This manifesto is simply a lesson in perfect hype – the most fun you can ever hope to have with EMI . . .

1 Walk into record companies and pretend that nobody knows you despite the fact that they asked you there in the first place.

2 Always announce your name in the most theatrical manner possible.

3 Show no interest in the music you are about to play them and even less interest in what they have to offer you in return, but display

a genuine desire to obstruct every other group's progress in order to advance your own group's career.

4 If little interest is shown, demonstrate that this group alone can create profit in their jaded industry and revive their flagging record sales. This is what every record company wants to hear.

5 Titillate them – play on their deviances and neuroses.

6 Understand their attraction for young, untamed boys.

7 Use this basic insecurity to play off one record company against another.

8 You are moving into the realm of politics, which with close advice from your lawyer, means even more money.

9 Forget the future and get as much money as possible on the dotted line.

10 Create a lot of different faces to provide intrigue.

11 Remember the man who sold the Eiffel Tower, twice.

12 Demand a formal signing to create credibility.

13 The next stage is to get the band off the record company as soon as possible, ensuring that you obtain as much money as possible in the process.

14 Intensify the group's misbehaviour in public.

15 Make the company think that *you* are an anarchist.

16 Remove any members of the group who show signs of developing musical ability. Replace them with gimmicks designed purely to upset people.

17 Shove drugs, incest, necrophilia and any other stories to the papers.

18 When your first record company eventually terminates your contract and pays you off, demand that they find an alternative to which you can sign for even more money.

19 Sign outside Buckingham Palace, and insult your queen.

20 Make the group threaten a TV disc jockey with his life in some famous late-night rock club.

21 Intimidate pillars of the pop establishment. They love being shat on, and great press coverage can be achieved by this.

22 Create a drunken rampage at the signing session.

23 Tell the group that sex is for the asking with all these record-company employees, and you can get off your second record company in as little as seven days.

24 You are now a contagious disease and are being given cheques simply for going in and out of doors.

Inevitably, perhaps, the Pistols ended up in court. In a band where the manager was as much the star as Johnny Rotten or Sid Vicious, a group split was always going to create problems over the rights to use names and claim future commissions. Rotten also called for a thorough audit of the Pistols' account. The final outcome was still undecided at the time of writing – some six years since the commencement of proceedings. Which means, no doubt, that the hype was fun, and the chaos was cool, and the industry was jolted, but that ultimately money came out king.

Bucks Fizz
Victory in Europe,
bitching in central London

In the realm of musical insults, the word Eurovision ranks high. In all but the blandest of music papers the word means commercial, unoriginal, sugary and unsavoury. Above all, it implies a cash-in – the ultimate example of finance over quality. What it ignores is that Eurovision, the only contest that virtually guarantees the victor instant success in the charts of over a dozen countries, is in itself an art-form, and one of the hardest to master. It is the biggest legal form of rags-to-riches musical hype in existence.

What's more, Europe just doesn't care if the act is entirely manufactured – the concern is not how many rotten pub gigs you've played, but how many 'baby ooh yeahs' you can cram into three minutes. And if you're the contestant's creator you don't want proficient hacks half as much as you want good-looking, fine-moving amateurs who'll do what you say.

The trouble is, acts have a reputation for being *so* ungrateful. The problem with band-hype is that sooner or later the machine will turn on its inventor and demand more say in its power source and better terms of employment, and it will maybe even demand to be switched off altogether. In Bucks Fizz's case this manifested itself in terms of sexual scandal, suicide attempts, court battles and rather nasty threats to personal livelihoods.

By the end of 1980, Eurovision had already been a dream of Nichola Martin's for some time. As a 26-year-old publisher, producer and singer with many unsuccessful groups, she had previously entered the British heats – 'Song For Europe' – a year earlier as a member of the trio Rags, convinced that victory was theirs on looks alone. It was mainly the BBC blackout that made them lose, she claimed later. But this year she redoubled her efforts and entered two songs. She sang on one, a little ditty from a band called Gem, and she sang on the other too, a song from Bucks Fizz. The double engagement was no problem because the first heats were judged from cassettes and only if you got any further did you need to worry about personnel and looks.

At the end of December 1980, the news came through that the Bucks Fizz song, 'Making Your Mind Up', had made it through and the next heat would be in a few weeks. Nichola Martin decided on a four-piece, a two boys, two girls affair, but chose to leave herself out – hopefully she would do a better job in the background. The band was recruited in two weeks: Mike Nolan was an old friend who had sung on the demo cassette and wanted to hang around; Cheryl Baker (real name: Rita Crudgington), an ex-member of two-time Eurovision finalists Coco and an occasional backing singer at the same studios that Martin used, was also in; Bobby Gee (real name: Bobby Gubby) was recruited through an advert in *The Stage*; and Jay Aston, an unemployed dancer working as a cashier in a Jersey amusement arcade, came through an agency. Nichola Martin signed them to Big Note Music Productions Ltd, the company she had recently formed with Andy Hill, the writer of the proposed Eurovision entry.

The group showed the contract to an Equity legal adviser, and agreed to sign after an hour's meeting at which no changes were made. The initial term was to be for six months only, but was extendable by four one-year options if they got a single in the top fifty or won Song For Europe. A request from Big Note for additional 'call masters' could perhaps further extend each option period.

Royalties were low at 5 per cent for the whole group, rising by 1 per cent with each option, and advances were similarly ungenerous: in the initial six-month period the group would split £8,000 only if they won Eurovision (the original clause in the contract specified this sum for winning Song For Europe, but was subsequently amended with the group's approval). If they didn't win, they'd receive nothing. Advances for subsequent option periods stood at £5,000 for the first, £10,000 for the second, £25,000 for the third and £35,000 for the fourth. All recording costs were also to be treated as advances against royalties. The group agreed too to surrender 50 per cent of their merchandising income to Big Note.

But, oh dear, who cared? In Jay Aston's words, 'We thought we were signing for a three-minute appearance in the contest . . .' Not so, says Nichola Martin, who claims she went through each clause in detail with the group and told them to seek independent legal advice. 'But that's the last thing you worry about,' suggests Cheryl Baker. Just not enough *time*:

> Right from . . . when we said, 'Yes, we will be a part of Bucks Fizz,' and signed the contracts, then that was it. The next day we had rehearsals, then dance routines, recording the song (because at that time it was still just a demo.) Then we won Song For Europe which straight away meant television in England and doing the promo films for Eurovision and rushing all over the place and making personal appearances. Then Eurovision – bang! We won that, and then you're doing the same as you did in England, and you're doing it all over Europe. You're doing personal appearances in Germany, France, Austria, everywhere. Really in that first six months your life isn't your own – you're whisked off and you eat, drink and sleep Bucks Fizz. Although we were thrown together like that, and had to do all that work just because we were successful, we didn't actually have time to know each other – not until we slowed down, sat back and said, 'Oh hello, I'm pleased to meet you . . .' It's a false situation and you're put in it and you have to face it.

By and large, they faced it well. Cheryl Baker clashed frequently with Bobby Gee and Nichola Martin, and petty jealousies over who sang lead vocals and designed outfits and routines were also common, but the professional combination continued to work post-Eurovision, and the pursuit of hits, the pursuit of money, the pursuit, presumably, of ultimate happiness, ensured at least the public image of harmony.

Nichola Martin, originally their manager for the first six weeks, gave up the position after the band saw the gaping conflict of interest, and was replaced by Jill Shirley of Razzamattazz Management, an old Martin acquaintance who was also responsible for the agency that recruited Jay Aston. Martin remained as a business and artistic consultant for two years and retained a considerable say in all live and recording work as well as all contract negotiations.

Dependence on the group's creator in fact decreased little in the first two years, not least because Andy Hill, the writer of almost all the band's lengthy run of hits, graduated from being Nichola Martin's business partner into her lover and eventual husband. RCA released the records, Razzamattazz handled day-to-day management, but it was Martin's and Hill's Big Note company that continued to pull most Bucks Fizz strings.

Fine, of course, when things continue to go well, when the songs keep on charting, when the band still feel indebted for that great early break, but infinitely troublesome when the factions widen, when the hits dry up, when an ego gets inflamed or when the contracts and royalty accounts get perused too closely. In Bucks Fizz's case, the early hype and image creation would only last as long as personal conflicts and egos remained in check. This was not, after all, a band formed on trust and personal admiration half as much as it was a band formed by the goals of money and success. So when Jay Aston slept with Andy Hill in mid 1983, and when Nichola Martin found out, well, there was bound to be trouble.

The brief affair resulted in Jay Aston's attempted suicide and culminated in her departure from the group. It resulted too in claims that Nichola Martin had subsequently totally ignored her and squeezed her out. Aston now believes that even after the expiration of her consultancy contract, Martin's influence remained so great that she succeeded in ruining her career for the eighteen months after her discovery of the affair. Moreover, Aston says that Martin's attempts to hold her to Big Note for a lengthy solo career after her departure from Bucks Fizz, could only result in a similarly disastrous creative straitjacket.

The way Jay Aston tells it, Martin

. . . accused me of foisting my attentions upon Andrew Hill to enhance my career prospects with a view to taking him away

from her. She told me that I was useless as an artist and without
her pushing my career, my career would prosper no more.
During this period I was informed by my mother (that she) . . .
implored Nichola Martin to show some sympathy but all she did
was abuse me.

Aston says that she apologized profusely to Martin and claimed that
it was Andy Hill who had pursued *her* rather than vice versa. She sent
Martin flowers via her wardrobe assistant, and attempted suicide after
hearing that Martin had crushed them and thrown them back. She
was found unconscious by her father and spent six days recuperating
in hospital.

Martin was informed by Aston's mother, Hilda Joan Aston, who
claims that 'she promised to write a note to Jay but the next day flatly
refused'. In the end it was Jay Aston who wrote first, regretting all in
a lengthy letter sent to Hill and Martin shortly after her release from
hospital. The spelling and the syntax here remain unaltered:

> Dear Nicola and Andy
> I feel I have to write to you both. Though I know the harm and hurt I
> have caused you both, is pretty well irrepairable, I have to write and
> try. I can not try to put the blame elsewhere. I am tottally guilty of
> acting in a selfish, foolish, unthinking way. That has only resulted in
> hurting two people most dear to me. I realise since we all met I have
> been in total awe of both of you. Nicola I have watched and copied
> your every move, trying to be like you, trying to be Nicola Martin. I
> have looked upon you both as my makers and creatures, and the givers
> of all this fame and fortune I am so unworthy of possessing, but I am
> able to admit this, to the world, if I thought it could help you both
> now, but I'm sure it could only cause more upset. I did what I did, out
> of total 100% love for Andy. Though it was totally selfish it was never
> to hurt you Nicola, I just finally felt the thought of loosing Andy more
> painful. I was totally convinced that Andy felt there was no hope for
> you both, but I realise now those things Andy said weren't meant, he
> was only ever totally in love with you Nicola. Why you panicked over
> getting married Andy I do not know. I have been secretly besoted like
> a child by you Andy, since we first met. I think as achievement and
> talent scores high in my book I was also bowled over by your talent
> and capabilities, yet you never seemed to throw it around. As my
> producer and creator, I was in total awe of you. I never planned to
> "get you". I always tried to tottally blank out my emotions and that is

why I have always found it quite a battle just to be in your company. That's why I have always been useless in the studio from day one. I used to hope you'd go out for a while so I could actually do something! I don't think I made advances to you first? But I realise, what you would say to me and talk to me as a friend when things weren't to good between you and Nicola I took as a possible message you wanted something between you and I. I thought that because I wanted to think that. I realise I've read things now, because of my feelings for you. I wanted to hear them. There seems to be very little grey in my personality. Things are black or white. A fault, I'm incapable, of rectifying. When I was talking to Nicola throughout this from day one of our sin committed I had a terrible conscience about it. I felt positively wicked and horish. I wanted to relieve my conscience the very next day but that was just my selfishness again. I absoloutly panicked with what had happened. I realised imediatly I could never be the wife and lover you could be to Andy. I came to see you because I was half easing my own conscience just by telling you what I felt, I could not tell you the truth, could never tell anyone, because it would be to painful for you. I think I realised then that I could never be Nicola . . . Some things I think are now getting a little twisted and misconstrued. I have never ever said that you were riping me off on this aerobics album.* I don't know where it came from. The only time it has been talked about was at the album cover shoot that was when the group were discussing the money they had been offered and that they felt ripped off. I never ever said that. I can only think someone misheard something I said. I would after all this admit it, if I had said it but I can't. I also never accused you Nicola of trying to damage my career, by telling the press office and Dee to cut me out . . . The other reason, that my parents have got so involved in this is because they have seen over these months how badly I have taken my guilt. When I took that overdose it was not for attention or sympathy. I planned it with total conviction to work. I reached a stage where I felt so worthless and shitty for my behaviour I could not live with myself any more. I left you a note Nicola just to say that I was so sorry. I daily regret that overdose being discovered. The reason I have not

---

*Aston was approached to record *Shape Up And Dance With Jay Aston* for another production company – a deal that would ultimately yield her a royalty of only 2 per cent. The album subsequently sold very poorly.

phoned or contacted you was because I felt there was nothing I could say. I couldn't talk for a few days, by then I felt you were probably getting over it. But I realise this now, isn't something you will, it may take weeks. But Nicola one thing I realise Andy does love you deeply and totally. He was always in love with you not me . . .

Again I am so so so sorry.

I don't expect you to ever forgive me.

I can't expect that, to believe me, I can hope. I love you both dearly.

                                                                                    The Slut.

In a sworn affidavit, Joan Hilda Aston recalled a phone conversation with Nichola Martin that took place shortly before the posting of her daughter's letter. She claimed that Martin told her that her daughter's career was now finished, and that she would personally ensure that it could never be resurrected.

Nichola Martin disputes it, but Jay Aston believes that that's exactly what happened. She feels she went from being the 'star' in the group to the leper, had her lead vocals snatched away from her, hardly featured in videos, was given a deliberately low profile in the press, and had no further say in photo sessions or costume designs.* Indeed, she looks back and sees conspirators at every turn:

> In the spring tour I had two songs in which I was dominant. In relation to one song I received an apology by the lighting engineer who said that he had received no direction at all how he should light it, and it, therefore, came over very poorly. In the second song, 'When We Were Young', I was portrayed at the very back of the stage in a poorly lit cage until the very end of that song. This song, in particular, had previously relied

---

*Her press was handled by the independent PR firm, Keith Altham Publicity. Six months before the Andy Hill flare-up, the firm had approved a Jay Aston story that eventually appeared in the *Daily Express*. The newspaper reported that Aston had completed a short-course triathlon event at Reading in six hours. 'This event nearly killed me,' she said after the event. 'It was tough in spite of all the training. The lake was ice-cold for a start.' The problem was, she didn't actually compete. The story had been written in advance by Keith Altham employee, Nick Massey.

considerably on an upstage dancing routine in which I was featured almost exclusively, as indeed I was in the promotional video. An audience had previously identified me with the song . . . the other three members of the group were in full light at the front . . .

On the advice of a friend, Aston sought the assistance of biz consultant Barry McKay, the man we've met previously in connection with Ray Jackson's successful attempt to sue EMI over its failure to honour its contract. A serious group coach crash had already delayed her desire to leave or at the very least pursue an independent solo career, and with McKay and a new solicitor she now reasoned that she could work not a week longer with Nichola Martin and the rest of the band. She sold her story to the *Sun* for £21,000 (money she says has gone to pay legal fees and hospital bills) and announced that she was quitting. The band immediately issued a statement saying they had already decided she should leave months ago . . .

Aston's departure was announced on 10 June 1985. One month later Big Note issued a writ seeking damages against both Aston and McKay, the former for breaking contract and the latter for inducement to break contract. Big Note also sought to impose restrictive injunctions on both defendants at least up to July 1986. The 'at least' is crucial here: though July 1986 was the expiry date of the original Bucks Fizz contract, a solo-option clause permitted Big Note to hold Jay Aston to a further maximum of five years of a solo career (in court the defendants argued that the term might be even longer). During this period she would receive no advances, and would have to pay for all recording costs out of her set royalty of 5 per cent.

The hearing followed swiftly. Aston repeated her claims above, arguing that her relationship with Big Note had now completely broken down and would therefore make any injunction intolerable, and that the terms of the existing contract were unduly onerous and unfair.

Nichola Martin, for Big Note, refuted each point in turn, and initially made a forceful case for Aston's retention. But on the sixth day Big Note dropped their claims and agreed to pay costs (estimated to stand jointly at over £40,000). Aston was now free from her Bucks Fizz contract and any possible claims on her solo career, but Big Note threatened that this was only round one, and that a full trial was yet to come.

Aston's solicitor, Richard Hart-Jackson, doubts whether there will ever be another trial. Certainly there was no sign of any further court proceedings as this book was being finished, only positive steps towards a new Jay Aston recording deal with another company.

Hart-Jackson further pointed out that the Attorney-General had been called in to investigate certain discrepancies between the original letter that Jay Aston had sent to Martin and Hill (used in court as evidence) and the reputed transcript of the letter that appeared in several national newspapers. There were fourteen differences in all, including the following: 'I don't think I made advances to you first' became 'I think I made advances to you first', and 'When I took that overdose it was not for attention or sympathy, I planned it with a total conviction to work' became 'When I took that overdose it was for attention or sympathy. I never planned it with a total conviction to work.'

There is no firm evidence as to how these differences arose, although Barry McKay claims that the changes were a deliberate attempt by Big Note to portray Aston in the worst possible light.

Bucks Fizz, Nichola Martin and manager Jill Shirley held auditions for the new Fizzer within days of Jay Aston's departure.

Over 1,000 hopefuls (all under 5 feet 4 inches lest they dwarf Mike Nolan or Bobby Gee) showed up at the Prince of Wales Theatre, most to be rejected on looks alone. The shortlist was whittled down to forty on the first day and to a dozen the next. They sang and were videoed. They were interviewed for about an hour. 'The whole thing took about four or five days,' says Cheryl Baker, 'which really isn't enough time for such an important decision . . .'

The lucky girl was the 21-year-old Shelley Preston, a pimply, waif-like blonde with no singing experience outside school choirs and amateur operatics. Six weeks after she joined she was crunching cough sweets to rescue her voice from the rigours of furious rehearsal. She was clearly thrilled to be on board. 'As soon as I was told (early July 1985) I was whisked off for a photo session, and then we had to do the track for 'Wogan', and then I had a Sharp photo session . . . then we had rehearsals for 'Wogan', and then the second week I started the routines, then I did the vocals, then we went into the studio . . . it's just been one thing after another, and learning all the time. And I love it all – it's such fun.'

What are the terms of your contract?

'Oh, no, I don't want to talk about it . . . I don't know how anything goes on really, but as each thing comes up it's explained to me. If ever there's something I'm not sure about or worried about, I can just go to any of them . . .'

6

Thank you, Sheffield,
and good night

What really happened when Barry Manilow
and Duran Duran played in the open air

As kids, most current rock promoters watched their parents'
letterbox with a mixture of fear and dreamlike joy. Even a podgy,
bum-fluffed Harvey Goldsmith would waste time gazing at the metal
flap. Were the Cliff tickets coming? Was he going to see Buddy Holly
after all? If he sent off at the end of March, he'd probably know the
outcome by the middle of April. And if Harvey was unlucky, the
whole damn dream would begin again – either an endless queue at the
box office or another couple of weeks of nailbiting postal lottery.

Twenty-five years on, the kids are still watching the letterbox, only
this time Harvey Goldsmith and others like him are running the show.
And things have got a little out of hand. Oh, the show's just about the
same – still selling rebellion to the kids – but it's the promotion that's
gone a little crazy: every year there are more artists seeking gigs than
ever before; every year there are probably more ticket applications
than ever before; every year the value of gross box-office receipts hits
new highs; every year the venues get more bizarre; and every year the
myths surrounding the work of the rock promoter grow larger and
more distorted.

'The belief that we all carry home huge plastic bags of money after
every gig is ludicrous,' say the poor, less-established ones. 'The
thought that we're all corrupt ego-maniacs is absurd,' say the wealthy,
flashy ones. 'You've really got to be nuts to do it,' says Harvey
Goldsmith. 'All this talk of cheating and corruption is ridiculous –
you'd never stay in business.'

And yet the potential for constant swindling and embezzlement is enormous. Take that kid waiting at home for his tickets. Little Johnny sent off six months ago to see his great white hopes, and with two weeks to go he's still heard nothing. And why? Because his cheque has been banked at high interest along with 30,000 others. With ten days to the gig the promoter (not Harvey Goldsmith, of course) will write him out a new cheque, return it in the s.a.e. provided and attach a little slip saying, 'No dice – sold out.' He'll do that 25,000 times and walk into that particular gig having already made a cool £10,000. You need a smooth, well-oiled machine to do it efficiently, and most of the big promoters have just that.

On a strict, above-board level, rock promotion is no longer the gold mine it used to be. But as the increasingly shrewd negotiations of artists and their agents ensure diminished profit margins and fewer regular legal killings, so the attraction of underhand dealings increases.

Open-air shows provide the biggest potential for both massive profits and crippling bankruptcy, and the 'big play' has become the central focus of many. Goldsmith cites Dylan at Blackbushe as his largest single success (excepting Live Aid), while younger promoter Paul Loasby singles out 1984's Barry Manilow gig at Blenheim Palace as his greatest disaster. The struggling Wilf Walker, the best-established black promoter in the country, organized his first big play in July, an African National Congress Benefit gig at Crystal Palace Bowl, with Jimmy Cliff and Aswad among others. The gig could have netted profits of £48,000; in fact, it lost £23,000, most of it paid for by the Greater London Council. Walker could have retired for a year on his slice of the potential takings; instead he almost lost his flat.

Even on a much smaller gig you can lose your shirt. In London on any one night there are as many pub, club or large-hall promoters losing money as there are those making it, and the potential for profits and the risk of loss are both consistently greater for the promoter than the artist.

Strangely, for such an important area of live entertainment, remarkably little is known about the promoters' twilight world. There is still no governing body to serve as a watchdog, and with the exception of council safety regulations, codes of practice are arbitrary and laid down in secrecy.

Most promoters are willing to talk about their work in general terms, but few will discuss specifics. Only one would open his files and discuss the breakdown of a loss-making gig. And the majority still remain slightly uncertain about their own motives. Harvey Goldsmith says he enjoys the challenge of organization and risk-taking: 'It's like betting on the 3.30 every day – and I just back a lot of winners.' Even the unsuccessful ones say that they love the live arena, and most admit that promoting is just about all they know how to do. But a love of organization and a love of music are consistently ranked lower in priority than the love of making money. A 'good' promoter is invariably defined as one who makes as much money as possible.

Every day, just after lunch, hundreds of people lug amps and instruments into small pubs and clubs the size of London's Dingwalls and the Rock Garden, and know they're being robbed. There comes a point in rock promotion when meanness and sharp business practice give way to cattle prodding and immorality, and eager and struggling unknown bands have to put up with the last two with alarming regularity. Invariably paid only a fraction of the stipulated minimum Musicians' Union (MU) rate of £17.25 per performer, often not allowed to soundcheck, and frequently employed without a written contract, most artists remain either too desperate or too intimidated to complain or refuse work. Never before have so many bands chased so many prestigious gigs, and never before have venue managements been able accordingly to exploit so freely. Nor has the role of an agent ever been so important.

As the central cog in the management of an artist's live career, agents serve as a workable alternative to an artist negotiating direct with promoters or venues, taking a 10 to 15 per cent cut of their gross earnings. Their vicelike grip on the live scene means that without one a new band is fairly powerless.

Dingwalls in north London remains one of the largest and most hallowed daily venues where it is still possible to get a support gig without an agent, but a gig there tonight may well leave an unrepresented band deep in the red. In August 1984, for example, an unsigned but highly promising rock band, Then Jerico, turned in a stirring forty-five-minute support slot at the venue and got paid £40. Out of that they had to pay £10 for the use of the house public-address system, and 10 per cent commission plus VAT went automatically to the venue's own booking agency. The band had to shell out £15 for a van and roadie, and on that particular night the guitarist needed an amp and the keyboard player needed a keyboards stand. They added it up and they'd lost out. The gig had cost *them* around £30.

The fact that the band's manager originally wanted to remain anonymous (along with the band) for fear of not getting future gigs is one of the reasons the situation has lasted so long. He feels that not only was the situation typical, but that they actually 'got off rather lightly that night. Desperation counts for so much that it's almost worthwhile paying the venue so that you can play there.'

The MU says it is helpless just as long as bands remain desperate and accept anything that's offered. A stream of complaints in the late seventies prompted the union to demand that the management of the Marquee, a particularly bad offender, paid each musician a minimum of £9 per performance. The venue agreed only after the threat of a widespread MU strike shortly before the Marquee-organized Reading Festival, but swiftly demanded that the minimum support payment be made by the headliners. The headliners in turn invariably charged the support band for the use of their PA rig, and the situation is now very much back as it was. 'Because the whole rock world is goal oriented,' says ex-MU rock worker Mike Evans, 'it's only worth being in the First Division. Third Division bands aren't worth a bean.'

London's 'medium play' arenas – the Lyceum, Hammersmith Palais and Odeon, Electric Ballroom, Brixton Academy, Wembley Arena, Earls Court and less regular oddball venues like West End theatres – have provided most established promoters with their bread and butter for years. In theory anyone could do their work, but to do it well you need massive experience, great judgement, impressive financial resources and luck. What you don't need is any appreciation of the music you're trying to flog; you must know its market, but you get no points at all for knowing what a band's songs are about. And that's one of the problems: the reason there aren't more successful promoters is because a huge amount enter the world with a deep love of the music and are forced to learn the hard way about the rest of it.

A promoter's task of organizing a one-off gig in a 4,000-capacity hall can be broken down into a number of steps, each blurring heavily at the edges. Each carries headaches and heart attacks of its own.

1 *Clinching the deal*   Unless horrendously popular or desperately obscure, most artists will be offered to a promoter by an agent. The band, say Culture Club, will decide in liaison with its management and record company exactly when and where they intend to play and the agent will in turn present their wishes to a number of promoters in the hope of securing the largest fee (and hence the largest cut for themselves). Each promoter will then specify the maximum fee he's willing to pay in order to cover all costs and still emerge with a sizeable profit based on anticipated receipts from a full house. His offer is often a matter of bluff; with the exception of the venue hire (which will be checked early on for availability), there are no such things as standard costs. But too low an offer and he'll lose the band, too high an offer and he'll probably lose money. Promoters may often act jointly to lower a band's fee; shared profits may well be greater than those resulting from the fee made unnecessarily large by attempts at outbidding.

Increasingly of late, costs have been subsidized or paid outright by a sponsorship contract, engineered almost certainly by a multinational with eyes on the youth market. So for £50,000, Levi's got the advertising hoardings around the David Bowie stage when he played England in 1983 (as they had done also with Roxy Music and Ultravox), and they got their name on the posters and the programmes, but Bowie himself didn't even have to wear the things. The mid eighties have seen the UK pair-ups of The Police and Guinness, Japan and Maxell Tapes, Duran Duran with Sony Tapes, and Bucks Fizz with Sharp. Whether Sting actually even likes the thick black stuff is an irrelevance; he is seen to like it, just as its Dublin manufacturers are seen to like songs like 'Every Breath You Take'. The reality is that the brewery shifts a few more bottles and The Police break even or turn what may have been a large loss into a small profit.

But compared to the US, where Pepsi spent $60 million on linking their fizz with The Jacksons ($8 million was pumped on to the scene of their major gigs in 1984 and the rest on TV and other advertising), UK sponsorship remains relatively small fry and seldom worth administering for anything less than a nationwide tour or a trail of arena gigs. For our Culture Club one-off, the band, agent and promoter will have to wrestle with costs by themselves, conceivably with some contribution from the group's record company.

2 *Drawing up the contract; dealing with the prima donnas* Say that Culture Club have agreed to play the Brixton Academy for a fee of £4,500 with their selected support band, The Unknowns, playing for nothing. The Unknowns have in fact 'bought on' to the gig, a common practice, and have paid Culture Club £1,000 (laid out by their record company) for the exposure. They know they'll make a loss, but hope it will be recouped by record sales and by securing future gigs. For a tour, a headliner playing thirty dates may conservatively expect a support band to buy on with a payment of £8,000. Tales of record companies outbidding each other to place their new darlings on a prestigious nationwide outing are common.

A contract will be drawn up by the agent specifying fee, date, time, place and length of appearance, soundcheck times, venue capacity, maximum ticket prices and possibly assurances that the band will not appear within a twenty-five- or thirty-five mile radius of the Academy in the same week or month. In this case, Culture Club will receive a set fee payable directly after the show. But in many cases the contract may also stipulate that an artist receive a set amount (say, 25 per cent) of all gross box-office takings, and also that part payment (often one-half) should be made in advance. Each contract invariably carries a rider detailing such things as power supply, placement of mixing desk, size of stage and – often the subject of much ridicule – dressing-room demands. These normally run to a few lagers, a couple of bottles of wine and a light meal, but it is the truly outrageous riders that add that golden sense of magical mythmaking for most promoters, and maybe they will try to carry out even the most childish ones for the pure hell of it.

Howard Jones's demands, for example, are already the subject of hilarity. On a college tour in 1983 he insisted on the daily provision of eight pounds of brown rice, six large aubergines, three pounds of courgettes, three green peppers, three pounds of onions, one head of garlic, three French loaves, three pounds of fresh tomatoes, one tube of tomato paste, one whole pineapple, twelve mixed yoghurts, twelve bananas . . . and the list goes on for ever. He also insisted that the stewards must not have guns or dogs; that the dressing room possess a 'sweet-smelling ambience'; and that he must have physical contact with the audience.

The Smiths, whose lead singer Morrissey was afflicted at one time with a nasty habit of covering his audiences with flowers, had a request for £50-worth written into the band's contract. It specified that gladioli must be included, and that there should be 'no roses or other flowers with thorns, please'.

For a British appearance in 1984, Van Halen got eight litre bottles of Jack Daniels, eight litre bottles of brandy, eight litre bottles of vodka, sixteen cases of domestic beer and a worldwide selection of cheeses. At previous gigs they reportedly also requested 'huge bowls of M&Ms [US candies similar to Smarties] with all the brown ones removed'. Harvey Goldsmith says: 'The days of having special rooms for snakes with Alice Cooper have gone because the acts have grown up a lot . . .' Quite.

And for more stories, your choice is as wide as Harvey Goldsmith. A while back David Bowie confidant Iggy Pop had the following written into his contract: 'It is absolutely essential at the conclusion of the show that there is a nurse in attendance with two cylinders of oxygen with masks . . .' And Pere Ubu's lead singer David Thomas set new limits for meticulous sandwich-making at a gig at the University of London's Union: 'NOTE,' the rider ordered, 'a sandwich is defined as three pieces each of meat and/or cheese, one-inch thickness of lettuce, a half-inch thickness of onion, mayonnaise, two slices of three-quarters of an inch of tomato, all between two thick slices of wholewheat bread. NO BUTTER. AND I WILL REPEAT: NO BUTTER OR MARGARINE PERIOD.' It also specified that no support band may have a political, religious or 'vulgar' message, and even the stage crew got the same rigorous inspection. It was stressed that 'no outrageous fashions are permitted' and was preceded with the tag: 'I can't tell you how much I will be disappointed if this rider is ignored; nor can I tell you how pleased I'll be when I find that you've been attentive to my needs.'

That last comment is reminiscent of the supposed classic last line on an American rider of a hugely popular drug-ridden touring band: 'No snow,' it said, 'no show.'

Even if riders do extend to the provision of drugs, it's unlikely that the promoter will be the one left footing the bill; a rider estimate will simply be deducted from the agreed performance fee when the promoter's original costings are drawn up.

3 *Venue, equipment and workforce*   At the time of the gig, early in
1985, the Brixton Academy cost £2,500 and 5 per cent of the gross
box-office receipts to hire for one night, and the promoter may have
to secure it with a deposit. This compared with the Lyceum charge of
£850 or 18 per cent of your gross takings (whichever is the greater).
And the Hammersmith Palais charge of £1,100 plus VAT. The venue
contract would specify the fee, age restrictions, and the supply of such
things as bar and security facilities. Assuming that Culture Club
decide not to supply their own PA and lighting and effects rigs, these
would be hired to the band's specification, and taking into account
the cost of technicians, humpers, van hire and piano tuning, the
promoter ends up paying a neat £1,500. Security is another problem.
While Mecca Halls such as the Hammersmith Palais supply their own
bouncers as part of the deal, the Academy requires that you find your
own. Forty heavies and two dogs are about right – and at £40 a head
that's another £1,600.

4 *Publicity*   Even for Culture Club a promoter requires a fair bit of
advertising. Press ads and street posters are likely to cost an easy
£1,000 – more if the tickets are going slowly. Printing the tickets will
be another £100. In most cases the venue's box office and the
established ticket agencies will handle all sales, releasing takings only
after the show's been played. If the Culture Club date is set
sufficiently far in advance and vocalist Boy George looks like
remaining popular for at least a few months more, the promoter could
decide to set up his own postal box office – essentially to assist with
cash flow, and conceivably to operate the cheque-banking fiddle
above.

This might also limit the likelihood of Culture Club fans being
fleeced by the touts. Because that's another major headache . . . A
professional heavy queues up at the box office for the tickets that are
bound to sell out. There's a four-per-person maximum, so he queues
up again. And he ropes in ten mates to queue up for him. That's
almost fifty tickets to play with and by setting up a phoneline or just
flogging them outside the venue on the night, those seats would
certainly go for double, if not quadruple the face value. Police action
doesn't seem to have much effect.

Setting up a postal box office wouldn't eliminate the problem, it
would just make it more complex; you'd need a load of different bank

accounts, a pile of separate addresses, and, if Culture Club were in real boomtime, a bit of luck as well, because there would probably be more applications than tickets. There are, however, certain name touts to whom even this is no problem – their machines are oiled and programmed sufficiently well to ensure that the tickets will always end up in their fists somehow.

Yet even the sharpest London touts are schoolboys trading bubblegum cards compared to the biggest US ticket 'scalper' Bill Meister, a squinting Cincinnati kid in his mid-twenties, who made millions in two years, before being hauled in by the Ohio Securities Division investigating some $9 million in missing funds. His empire collapsed (possibly only temporarily) early in 1985 when it was disclosed that he had illegally sold unregistered securities in a scheme to double any investor's outlay in a massive ticket buying and selling wheeze. It was the securities that were the problem, not his ticket touting itself – that in fact had been legal in Cincinnati since 1982. And since then he'd pulled off such things as buying up a few Prince tickets –over 12,800 in all – by hiring college kids and paying them up to $100 if they got him good seats. He sold them at about double face value in his video store and made a personal net profit of around $120,000.

Mobster rule tends to dominate another area of pre-gig headaches too, that of street advertising, but this is one where the regular promoter invariably comes off better than the novice. In fact it looks like Bill Stickers isn't so much prosecuted these days as up for scrutiny under the Monopolies Commission. Everyone's favourite put-upon hoardings advertiser isn't in fact the gutsy local hero with a bucket of flour and water, but a few highly organized muscle crews headed by big boys Terry 'The Pill' Slater, Dave Walker and Dave Hutton. Between them they seem to hold the franchise to just about all the popular free ad space in town. So put a poster up for your local jazz festival and it might mysteriously disappear overnight, either covered up or ripped down. Thames Television recently tested the theory by placing 400 bogus posters on prime London spots, and within hours of them going up most did indeed vanish, some within full view of the cameras, and a few coupled with threatening confrontations.

5 *Insuring against disaster while dreaming about victory* A wise promoter will insure himself against the worst – late cancellations due to accident, flooding, a group splitting up – but no promoter can insure himself against his own incompetence, and it is clear that the risks are high. Adding show-day extras such as hospitality and Valium (£300) to the cost pile he's got already, Culture Club in Brixton will cost the promoter £12,000. With tickets priced at £4, he'd have to sell 3000 just to break even. Pack it out and he makes £4,000. Half fill it and he loses £4,000. A promoter can maximize profits by (a) shrewdness, (b) hardness and (c) corruption. Most go for all three.

'I think I've probably made more errors than most,' says Paul Loasby in a cramped office near London's Angel. He's not wrong. Small, boyish and engaging, Loasby's been in promotion since his university days. Still in his early thirties, the man has had disasters like Andrew Lloyd Webber has successes – and somehow he just manages to keep on top of them all. Not many people know that you *can* fail with Duran Duran, Queen and Barry Manilow, but Loasby's managed it somehow, and in style.

He conceived 1984's Barry Manilow gig at Blenheim Palace as 'a classic romantic vision of going away to Woodstock for a dirty weekend', and three years ago he had dreamed of promoting The Rolling Stones and Genesis there. By the time the necessary arrangements had been made with the Duke of Marlborough, only good ol' Barry presented himself as the surefire money spinner Loasby yearned for. He roped in four co-promoters and billed the thing as a mum's dream – a gorgeous, big-nosed crooner in the gorgeous shadow of a gorgeous stately home.

As it turned out, the stately home was acres away – all he could get was a *field* in Blenheim. More disastrously, he went on sale far too late at a time when thousands of Manilow fans had already booked or departed for their holidays. 'It was a long, hard slog and it certainly wasn't worth it,' he now admits. 'It was a walking disaster area. We didn't sell. It stiffed. A classic mistake. I thought it would be a licence to print, and thank God I wasn't in it on my own.'

A nationwide string of concerts by Japan around five years ago proved equally calamitous for other reasons. The pretty synthesizer band were at the height of their success, tickets had gone on sale almost six months before the tour was due to begin, and the whole thing had sold out within hours. The top price seats cost £7, almost

£900,000 worth of tickets had been sold, and the whole thing should have been a promoter's dream. Loasby, the band, the band's management, the band's approved merchandisers, everyone concerned, should have made an absolute killing.

The problem was that despite experiencing serious cash-flow turmoil, Loasby had agreed to make a massive advance payment of £100,000 to Japan almost six months before they even played a note. He then found himself unable to come up with the cash (he owed around £40,000 with four months to go), the box offices throughout the country refused to release their takings until the shows had been played, and if the band's management had decided to pull the band out as threatened, Loasby's reputation would have been ruined.

He avoided disaster, but only just. Promoter Barry Marshall bailed him out by putting up the rest of the advance, assisting with the tour logistics and emerging with roughly half the profits. Loasby keeps at it, insisting that this is the only life he enjoys. 'It's still the rock 'n' roll life and it's still a great challenge of organization. It's certainly not a glamorous pastime.'

Indeed it isn't. Like all promoters, most of Loasby's time is spent pulling his hair out over the phone. He comes back from lunch and he's got fifteen messages waiting for him, all of which concern his Echo and The Bunnymen tour. Have the right number of seats been removed to accommodate the mixing desk at the Manchester Apollo? How many lagers do the humpers get after setting up the amps in Sheffield? Do the bouncers at the Academy wear monkey suits or T-shirts? Will the dressing rooms have three separate sink units as requested? How many free tickets should the Liverpool shop owners get for pinning up the tour posters?

'It's a thankless task. You're likely to be going out there to make £500 or £600 a night risking anything up to £20,000 to do it, which is nuts.' Yet Loasby remains one of the few who claims to understand the heavy metal market. And the knowledge has recently done a lot to keep him afloat. On the day we met he was off to Walsall to pick up his 'very, very considerable' earnings from a recent Castle Donington Monsters Of Rock festival. 'I'd tell you how much I made if only I knew. But it's a lot . . . thank God.'

But Loasby would be the first to admit he's not yet made it to the first league. One who has, one in fact who stands as the first league's Manchester United, is Loasby's former boss, Harvey Goldsmith. The

contrast couldn't be greater: Goldsmith relaxes in a sparkling office at
the Bond Street end of Oxford Street and it's a million miles from
Loasby's Islington. He'd make a great, if slightly elderly, rugby prop
forward. Bearded, heavy, slightly gruff and in his early forties, he's
surrounded by mementoes of achievement. Plaques, posters, gifts and
tour junk line the walls and shelves as testament to the fact that he's
handled them all: Dylan, The Rolling Stones, Pink Floyd, Elton John,
Led Zeppelin, Stevie Wonder, Bowie – you name it.

Goldsmith also began promoting at university, and now, twenty
years on, he's the best known, flashiest promoter in Britain. He's
undoubtedly one of the wealthiest – at the end of 1984 he announced
plans to go public and launch himself into TV and film to further
maximize his profits.

Most who have had dealings with the man speak highly of him,
possibly out of fear. Modern Publicity director Alan Edwards recalls a
meeting with him about The Who: 'He was banging his fist and the
coffee was flying off the table, saying "I want the fucking front cover
of this paper!" or something like that. And I promise you I was
absolutely terrified. I'd never been so frightened of anyone almost in
my life . . . Like this bloody monster in front of me.'

By contrast, management executive and old Goldsmith acquaintance Sandy Campbell reckons that, 'He's a real softie at heart who has
an incredibly tough job looking after all those prima donna artists.'

The bands themselves all talk of fair treatment and superbly
organized shows, putting his hard nut image down to accepted
professional conduct. 'But the man hasn't got a clue what's going on
musically,' says Loasby who relates how Pete Wilson, Goldsmith's
right-hand man, had been negotiating a deal to present Wham! at
Wembley Arena over the prestigious Christmas period. Goldsmith
returned from a trip abroad to be confronted with the idea. 'Who *are*
they?' he asked. 'They haven't had any hits, have they? Give them two
nights at Dingwalls!'

But Goldsmith booked Wham! in for four nights at Wembley as
advised and the dates were sold out many times over. He didn't foul
up like Loasby did with Japan. It's most likely that he made a fortune
from it. He had fourteen people working for him to make sure of that.

Bono of U2 said recently that Frank Barsalona, one of the kings of
American promotion, 'is so rich that he's honest', and the same may
well be true of Goldsmith. He claims he takes neither punters nor

artists for a ride, and disowns any of the regular promoters' fiddles. He denies practising what has become known as 'rubber walls' – breaking fire regulations to jam more people into a venue, invariably behind the backs of the band and venue managers.

Goldsmith does not dispute, however, that at the large and popular unseated venues such as the Lyceum, the Hammersmith Palais, Heaven, and the now defunct Venue in Victoria, there exists a vast propensity for promoter dishonesty. The Lyceum, for example, officially holds 2,100. But pack it out to pogo-room only and you can comfortably add an extra 1000 – most promoters would argue that there would be no atmosphere unless you did. And even if the promoter colludes with a band and admits that he's let in an extra 400 people to see them (and gives them the receipts) it's highly likely that he's in fact let in 800 and pocketed the extra cash himself.

'I'd be a fool to say that rubber walls aren't part and parcel of the trade,' says Paul Loasby. 'But some of the halls would be half empty if the fire regulations were adhered to absolutely.'

'I'm very nervous about rubber walls,' says Harvey Goldsmith. Had he ever thought of doing it? 'No, not really. Sometimes these things happen. I'm nervous about safety and always have been. One day there's going to be a terrible disaster.'

And what about banking cheques well after a venue has sold out? 'We don't do that,' says Goldsmith. 'We only bank the cheques of the people who get tickets. Sure, you can make cash out of it if you want to go through that aggravation.' Ten minutes pass as Goldsmith talks of other things. Then he says: 'Sometimes we bank a little bit more because we may get a lot of bounced cheques. Then at least the people in the wings get the opportunity of getting tickets.'

On the positive side, Goldsmith talks of his repeated attempts to form a promoters' association: 'Three times I tried to get all the promoters together, but nobody wanted to know – they all thought I was doing it for myself. We had a big lunch where I said that if promoters break the rules, they should be dealt with internally. The other promoters always suffer because of the one guy who screws up . . .'

Wilf Walker is the same age as Goldsmith and has been putting on concerts since 1978. He emerged from jail after a short drug sentence in the early seventies armed with a strong desire to see black artists handled by black promoters (he was born in Trinidad).

Walker says he's encountered racism all the way down the line. Agents, venue managements and even black artists doubt his ability to organize on account of his colour and his tiny size of operation. Accordingly he's often had to bypass agents and deal with the likes of Gil Scott-Heron and Jimmy Cliff direct, offering higher fees than they could get elsewhere in an effort to establish a reputation.

And this he's certainly done. In six years he moved from small Rock Against Racism gigs with Aswad and Misty in Ladbroke Grove through the annual organization of the Notting Hill Carnival to sell-outs at the Hammersmith Palais and the Lyceum. But the heavily overladen desk in the 'office' corner of his Notting Hill flat is testament to the fact that he's only barely managed to keep his head above water. Six years in and he had still never handled what he saw as the really big play – the killing fields of a big-bill open-air gig.

July 1984 saw Walker gearing up frantically for one at last – a massive eight-act benefit bash for the African National Congress (ANC) at the 25,000-capacity Crystal Palace Concert Bowl.

It was a disaster. It drew only 6,000 and Walker lost thousands. The Greater London Council had agreed to back the event and ended up losing tens of thousands. Only the artists came out of it well. The crowd believed the bands were playing the ANC benefit for expenses only; in fact, Jimmy Cliff and Gil Scott-Heron both demanded fees on top of expenses. The music itself was occasionally inspired, but behind it lay an ugly heap of greed, exploitation, disastrous delays and hypocrisy.

Walker had first tried to organize a gig at the Crystal Palace Bowl the year before, but was forced to pull out with only three weeks to go: the bureaucratic delays in getting the site, insurance and other contracts meant that he had nothing like sufficient time to sell the 25,000 tickets. This time round he was determined things wouldn't happen the same way again. Unfortunately, things got even worse.

Walker approached the GLC in early June for permission to use their site for the benefit on his birthday, 28 July. He received their official blessing only at the beginning of July – again, three weeks before the gig. Walker had also approached the GLC for a guarantee against loss of £20,000, based on a maximum total expenditure of £42,000. Again, he received nothing in writing for weeks. He still hadn't heard with two weeks to go, and by then it was already far too late to pull out.

'I was having heart attacks, but I had to go through with it. I thought I was going to be the guy who never gets into festivals for real unless I take this chance now.' Even with two weeks to go, Walker stood to lose a small fortune. He'd already paid London's *Standard* £750 for an advert, and press advertising overall had cost him £2,500. He'd spent £1,500 on printing and putting up his posters. He'd already given his security men £3,000. None of that was recoupable. Most unacceptable of all, he felt, would be the loss of the advance he had already given Gil Scott-Heron.

On 20 June Walker signed a deal with Scott-Heron (an American artist highly respected for his fight against apartheid), by which he would receive an advance of £1,500 as well as an additional £3,500 to be paid after his performance. 'I wanted him to sing "Johannesburg" [a damning anti-oppression song],' says Walker. 'But he demanded £5,000 *plus* air fares and accommodation, which actually puts another £2,000 on the bill. So Gil Scott-Heron is actually supposed to earn £7,000 for a *benefit*. For Nelson Mandela!'

Desperate for name attractions, Wilf Walker agreed to Scott-Heron's terms. As it turned out, he wasn't the only artist on his list who demanded large fees. The bill was topped by Jimmy Cliff, hit-maker of 'Many Rivers To Cross', 'You Can Get It If You Really Want It' and 'The Harder They Come', the title track of the film in which he starred. Cliff's deal had been clinched on 7 July, three weeks before the gig, and only after assurances from his agent that he would publicly denounce the South African régime, despite having previously played there himself. He demanded a £5,000 fee (to be paid in full on the day of the gig) plus payment for accommodation, food and internal transport for his entire entourage. For a regular appearance it would have been a knock-down price; for a benefit Walker considered it quite outrageous.

Aswad got £4,000, Hugh Masekela £2,000, Gaspar Lawal £800 and African Woman £500. (The majority, if not all, of these payments were to cover expenses, which in some cases seemed quite extravagant, and in others were just a result of poor planning. Despite his £2,000, for example, Hugh Masekela still lost money. He was in the middle of a European tour at the time of the concert, and had to fly in with his twelve-piece band and all their equipment especially for the date.)

Aswad presented a further problem. Despite the draw of Jimmy Cliff, London's most popular reggae band were likely to attract the largest crowd and were duly guaranteed the last slot of the night. But they had also agreed to play the Capital Radio-sponsored Reggae Sunsplash at Crystal Palace Football Club three weeks earlier, and their contract dictated that Walker couldn't advertise any future appearances until the Sunsplash was over. Hence he was forced to hold out on the news of his biggest potential draw until there were under three weeks to go – and he knew well that that was far too late.

The GLC's guarantee to cover a maximum loss of £20,000 finally came through with ten days to go. They were fully aware that the artists were being paid, and it was only on seeing a full breakdown of Walker's costings that they agreed to cover him for such a large amount. But in return Walker had to agree to a massive moral compromise – that the ANC's receipts from the gig should only be 50 per cent of the profits (not 100 per cent as planned), and that the GLC received the other 50 per cent. Walker had either to agree or there would be no gig and he would have lost more than £10,000. He duly informed the ANC of the compromise.

But profits? Even with ten days to go, Walker held out little hope. He had already forked out what he considered to be quite excessive costs, and claimed he was greatly overcharged by his production company. 'The catering cost me £2,000 and I had three cups of tea in a plastic cup! But I was hooked. I had to go with *any* costs or it wouldn't have happened.'

Walker's total expenditure broke down as follows:

Promotion expenses	£ 4,921.00
Promotion costs	£ 6,973.00
Site charges	£ 4,351.00
Administration	£ 9,273.00
Travel	£ 3,573.00
Equipment	£ 6,160.00
Artists' fees	£15,360.00

His total costs (allowing for miscellaneous additions) worked out at £51,113.00.

He pegged the ticket prices deliberately low: £4 advance and £5 at the gate, an obviously desperate move to fill the arena with some sort of atmosphere. It was a glorious day and around 6,000 people turned up, a few of them with forged tickets. Receipts totalled £27,502.00. He had lost just over £23,500.

The concert itself was a mixed affair. It was dogged by PA problems and Gil Scott-Heron never played. He had missed his scheduled flight and by the time the next plane got him to the site, hours after he was supposed to have soundchecked, Walker said there was no place in the running order to put him on. He kept his advance and never did get to play 'Johannesburg'.*

The next day Wilf Walker faced a bank overdraft of £7,000 (his bank manager suggested he take out a second mortgage on his flat) and had debts of £17,000 outstanding elsewhere. The GLC's guarantee only obliged it to cover the losses up to an expenditure of £42,000 and hence was bound only to compensate Walker for £14,500 of his losses. After meeting him again, they upped their cover to £20,000, leaving Walker to pay the outstanding £3,500 himself.

The ANC took the news of the losses philosophically. (Walker sank further into debt when he gave them £200 as a token of his own support.) The GLC told Walker they were impressed with the way he had organized the event in the face of all the obstacles, and later agreed that he should organize another.

Walker himself puts the affair down to inexperience and adopts a cool 'win a few, lose a few' attitude. 'I think that going from Acklam Hall to the Crystal Palace Bowl is a very large step,' he suggests. 'And it could have been a lot worse. I could have lost my flat, and my wife and my kid could've been out on the street. Yes, it could have been worse. It could have rained.'

When it was announced that the beautiful and bronzed teen idols Duran Duran would take part in another charity concert at a Midlands football ground, the cynics wanted to know what was in it for them. When it was revealed that the charity would be MENCAP,

---

*Gil Scott-Heron's advance was £1,500 plus six return air fares.

the Royal Society for Mentally Handicapped Children and Adults, the cynics pounced: 'It's like they say – charity begins at home.'

The massively successful five-piece were, in fact, doing the concert purely out of the goodness of their own hearts. There was one ulterior motive, but an honourable one, in so far as lead singer Simon Le Bon's mother helped out in a special school for the mentally disabled. And once that was made clear, everything should have been fine.

Inevitably, maybe, the concert was a major disaster. They played well enough – their top five singles, their chart-topping albums – but MENCAP made rather less than the £75,000 they had been led to believe they could anticipate. Instead they got little but a pile of hefty legal wranglings. Because from the concert itself, attended by many thousands, they received hardly a penny.

Rob Hallett, a representative of Derek Block Concert Promotions, first approached MENCAP with the idea for the gig in February 1983. An ideal opportunity for mutual benefit, he suggested. MENCAP would get the profits and the Durannies would ease their collective conscience by donating to a fine cause. The Derek Block organization would cover their normal administrative and other costs but nothing more – they would not take a profit slice.

Which seemed great. But to an organization like MENCAP, which almost daily receives several requests to lend its name and support to other fund-raising events, their usual early 'What's-in-it-for-the-fund-raisers?' scepticism threw up a significant side interest that hadn't been raised from the outset. Alan Leighton, MENCAP's group director of marketing and communications, now suggests that the venue – Aston Villa football ground in the band's native Birmingham – had already been booked. But with the date set for July and preliminary arrange-ments already pencilled in, the local authority had refused to grant a licence for its use and all the plans looked suddenly bound binwards. Enter the charity idea: if MENCAP put their weight behind the Derek Block organization's application, then maybe the authority would have a sympathetic change of mind. At the time, Alan Leighton thought that, 'if that was the reason for wanting our involvement, then that was reasonable enough,' and accordingly drafted a letter suggesting that if permission to use the ground was not forthcoming, MENCAP would stand to lose a considerable sum of money. It worked too; the local authority, faced with a mild measure of emotional blackmail, presum-ably looked to its conscience and said yes.

Leighton is a large, middle-aged, ex radio agony uncle with a tough northern accent, a bulbous face with thin, greying hair and a horseshoe moustache. In his streetwear of heavy brown full-length leather coat and fedora he is surely one of the dandiest representatives of his profession. His equally colourful boss, MENCAP secretary-general Brian Rix, used to drop his trousers most nights on stage. Both are highly respected expert charity workers who will tell you even now that their knowledge of concert promotion is slight. Accordingly, they decided to leave the Duran gig to the experience of the Derek Block organization, and concentrate instead on how they'd best use the proceeds.

They chose a scheme they'd already begun formulating some months earlier – the establishment of an Open University course designed for those who worked with the mentally handicapped. Brian Rix even discussed the possibility of Duran's Simon Le Bon presenting a part of the series. The cost of the OU course had been estimated at £150,000. Rob Hallett suggested that a cool half of this could be met by the concert profit, and even though he had no direct personal contact with MENCAP about the organization of the show after the first month, the anticipated £75,000 was held up as a target figure right up to the gig itself.

There were the inevitable organizational hiccups. The crowd capacity, originally anticipated at 48,000, was reduced to 28,000 for safety reasons and the ticket prices were hiked accordingly from the original £5 to £8.50. If Villa sold out, the gig would still take in a gross income of £238,000. It was acknowledged that the cost to a young fan was high, but it was also thought that for Duran Duran most kids would sell their mothers to get in. And there was more good news: Aston Villa club chairman Doug Ellis charged the Derek Block organization only £15,000 in place of the normal £25,000, believing he was making an indirect donation to MENCAP's profits.

Like everything else on that day, it was consumed within a vast spiral of costs that failed to be exceeded by income. Only around 18,000 people came through the gate – and that was barely break-even point. According to Alan Leighton, he was taken aside on the night to be told, 'Sorry mate, it doesn't look as good as we had anticipated.'

Something indeed had gone wrong with the Derek Block company sums. Either the band and its far less popular support acts weren't enough of a draw, or even their fans didn't fancy a crush on a football field, or people expected rain (in fact it was fine), or the ticket prices were too steep. Or perhaps the costs were just too high.

Around £170,000 had been taken in ticket sales and merchandising. It seemed that to swallow all that in expenses, Derek Block would have had to fly the artists and entourages in from all parts of the world, and that of course is exactly what happened. Forty-six people jumped on jet planes for the concert. For the bands and their technicians it was a pleasant enough trip for free.

Duran flew in from a studio in the Caribbean some days earlier to take part in a London concert in aid of the Prince of Wales' Trust (which, incidentally, made a profit of around £30,000). The band's management company, Tritec Music Ltd, claimed that although the Duran contingent consisted of twenty-six people, not all the expense of their flight and accommodation was borne by the Derek Block organization; rather, the Prince's Trust concert, which the group also played without payment and which was sponsored by the BPI, was also asked to contribute to the costs.*

Apart from Duran Duran, the other flight tickets went to the Robert Palmer crew (eleven people at a total cost of £12,404 including air freight) and to the nine-piece Prince Charles and the City Beat Band line-up (total cost £4,563). Given that neither act was a major draw, it was surprising that so much had been spent on bringing in overseas bands. From the outset it looked as though neither would have any significant effect on the total attendance but both would add a lot to total costs.

A deeper mystery centres on the merchandising receipts from the show. Although a letter from Derek Block's promotion company to Doug Ellis written two days before the concert says that all merchandising profits were intended to go to MENCAP, a report in the *Standard* later suggested that Block himself had issued statements which suggested that this was not the case. The sale of T-shirts, scarves, programmes and the rest grossed around £40,000 and produced net profits of around £20,000. But even with this additional boost, total income was still vastly overrun by total costs. Which was all a massive disaster in itself, argued MENCAP, if all the figures were

---

*I am indebted to a report in the *Standard* by Peter Hounam and Andrew Hogg for some of this information.

true. 'Let us do an independent audit,' they said. Sure, said the promoters.

'But the accounts were never forthcoming,' says Alan Leighton. What MENCAP did get was an *in gratia* payment of £5,000 from Duran Duran personally. 'We were advised by our lawyers not to cash it – that would have implied acceptance of the amount. £5,000 is very different to £75,000 . . .'

In fact, the £5,000-cheque was mounted alongside a Duran Duran photo and pinned up on Leighton's wall in a glass case. And for well over a year it looked down and witnessed a tedious, knuckly legal battle over the non-materialization of accounts. Settlement, in fact, took twenty months from the date of the concert, and ended with MENCAP agreeing with the final sums and accepting a donation from Duran Duran that exceeded considerably their initial contribution.

But that original cheque is still up there on the wall, and it's highly unlikely ever to end up in one of those Sotheby's auctions of rock memorabilia. 'It's up there as a reminder,' says Leighton with a sigh. 'It's not just up there to decorate the office.'

There are, however, no pictures of old-time songsmith Brenda Arnau. In January 1985, she held her comeback concert at the Albert Hall and she too promised to donate the profits to MENCAP. Her husband had booked the hall for £3,500 and pegged ticket prices between £5.50 and £10.00. The costs were low – no world-girdling flights, no massive crew – and the hall's capacity of 5,500 would guarantee a good net income if full. But only around 100 people showed up. MENCAP didn't make much money from that one either.

7
Wham!

Young guns fall for it (again)

Early in October 1983, Mark Dean received a letter that told the story of Wham! in a way he'd never read it before. As the managing director of Innervision Records and the man who had signed the unknown duo to his label about a year and a half earlier, the 23-year-old industry whizz had already seen perhaps fifty accounts of the group's fabulous career to date, most concerned with their thoughts on politics, fashion and their own music.

But this revised account, from Wham!'s solicitors, Russells, concentrated instead on the reasons why Wham! could now consider themselves free to break their Innervision contract and record with any other company of their choice; on why, also, the duo could even claim the rights to all the master recordings they had already delivered. In short, the twenty-four page letter was a blistering attack on Mark Dean's competence, alleging, among other things, that his contract with Wham! contained numerous unfair terms and was made in circumstances where there was strict inequality of bargaining power.

The implication was not only that Dean's ten-year claim on one of the most popular bands in Europe was at an end, but that he'd been immensely fortunate even to have had them and their success for eighteen months.

The way Russells told it, Wham! – aged just 18 and 19 – had stumbled deep into each classic pitfall and then some. They were on live television and couldn't afford to get home; they turned up at nightclubs and had to pass on buying their round; they topped both

singles and albums charts, sold millions of records worldwide, and
were still only on around £40 a week. For a 23-year-old, it appeared
that Mark Dean had done an awful lot of wrong.

As old friends, Mark Dean and Wham! guitarist Andrew Ridgeley
swilled beer at their Three Crowns local in Bushey, Hertfordshire.
Music invariably dominated the conversation, Dean spinning tales of
his A and R work with Phonogram and his involvement with hit acts
ABC and Soft Cell, Ridgeley talking of his hopes for the new band. By
February 1982, when some rough-edged Wham! demo tapes had been
widely rejected by various major recording and publishing companies,
Dean agreed to listen to his mate's recordings almost out of courtesy.
And of course he thought them a marvel. One of the songs in
particular, 'Wham! Rap', seemed a certain hit.

Fortunately for Wham!, he said, he was in the process of
negotiating a deal with CBS whereby he'd run his own licensed label –
Innervision – in the hope of discovering new worldbeaters. Wham!,
he enthused, might make his ideal first signing. The more demo tapes
he heard, the more Dean enthused. The duo, comprising of Ridgeley
and singer–songwriter George Michael, began to discuss possible
producers and certain success. The contracts, said Dean, were on
their way.

The draft agreement, drawn up by Innervision's solicitor Paul
Rodwell, and dated 5 March 1982, was a standard but lengthy blank
CBS contract that had been completed by Dean with regard to the
specifics of royalty payments and advances, and in the absence of a
Wham! manager was sent to Andrew Ridgeley direct. A covering note
detailed that Rodwell himself would be away for the next ten days
and that Ridgeley should 'liaise' with Dean over the actual signing of
the deals. Rodwell closed with the regular and very proper, 'I must of
course mention that you should of course seek independent legal
advice with regard to the contract before completing same.'

George Michael took the contract to Robert Allan, a specialist
music-industry solicitor recommended by a customer in his father's
Greek restaurant. He was advised that it was a poor deal that needed a
fair amount of financial and creative counter-attack. Accordingly,
Allan wrote to Paul Rodwell suggesting a meeting for the purpose of

'discussing your client's proposals and putting forward some proposals of my own'.

But according to Russells, the days that followed saw Dean telling Wham! categorically that Innervision refused to negotiate the commercial terms of the agreement, save that it would pay the two of them an advance of £500 each and confirm that their royalty rate would not be reduced by any payments to their producer. Additionally, Dean's pressure on George Michael to conclude the deal swiftly lest it might not be concluded at all, resulted in Michael telephoning his solicitor to instruct him only to negotiate 'on legal points'. The overall fairness of the contract should not now be of concern to him, he said.

Robert Allan wrote to Paul Rodwell with numerous amendments to the original draft contract, despite his now limited brief. That was on 20 March. He didn't hear from Rodwell again until a letter dated 26 March reached him on the 29th. And by then the signatures on the Wham!/Innervision deal were already five days old.

The train of events had made a mockery of the whole idea of independent legal advice, claimed Russells. And if what they claimed was true, then they certainly had a strong point.

On 24 March Wham! were rehearsing in a poorly equipped studio in Holloway, north London. Two hours in, Dean arrived with the final contracts and an ultimatum. The band either signed then and there, or would have to wait a further five or six months; CBS, his paymasters, needed the signed contract, he said, or else they wouldn't put Wham! on their upcoming release schedule. Dean also revealed his interest in various other bands he might sign in place of Wham! if they decided to delay their contract any longer. But if they did sign, then he would also transfer them to a better-equipped rehearsal studio. He stressed that he couldn't afford to risk the outlay of any more cash until they had committed themselves.

Thus coaxed, the three of them adjourned to a nearby café to sweat out the details further. George Michael flicked through the contract on the café table, acknowledged the handwritten changes, and signed the deal along with Andrew Ridgeley. The next day they did indeed find themselves in improved rehearsal rooms.

Within a week Robert Allan had discovered that a large chunk of his proposed amendments had not been instituted, and worse, that Innervision's solicitor Paul Rodwell had added some changes of his own in the belief that these would be seen by Allan before signing. Dean's haste meant that Wham! agreed to a deal that any solicitor with any knowledge of the industry would have laughed off his desk in an instant.

Those at least were some of Russells' allegations. In court in November 1983, some nineteen months after Wham! had signed, the same allegations also formed the bulk of Andrew Ridgeley's and George Michael's affidavits against Innervision. For his part, Mark Dean did not specifically deny the exact details, but issued a general challenge as to their overall validity. He was in court pressing for an injunction to prevent Wham! signing elsewhere. It looked like the start of another immensely gruelling case.

The whole affair took around six months. Dean and Innervision lost Wham! in an out-of-court settlement, even though he had won that first temporary injunction. The band expressed delight at their victory, and though beaten, Dean showed great relief that the whole affair was at least over. He told his closest friends he never wanted to go through anything like it again. They in turn perhaps weighed up the fabulous story and assured him that the chances of that actually happening were fair at a thousand to one.

Of average height but heavy build, and most frequently dressed in checked shirt and heavily buckled jeans, Mark Dean passes as the most archetypically impressive mid twenties industry hard man you could hope to find. And, partly by luck and design, the super-firm handshake, tough zero glare, slightly wild black curly hair and harsh, bleak features, all provide a certain visible aggressiveness that can't but enhance what many will always perceive as the necessary biz image. He talks with hard conviction and mature realism and he rolls with a steaming enthusiasm through all of it. At the start of 1984, with the Wham! affair still in litigation, he spoke with a certain sparkle about how he'd emerge victorious. When it was already cold and lost, the following June, he spoke with equal conviction about the likelihood of his other signings emulating Wham!'s success. 'You just watch,' he said.

He made no bones about his overall attack:

> To be totally ruthless about it, our job at the end of the day is to see the trends coming on the street, steal them off the kids, and then sell 'em back to them ... But nothing's new. *Nothing*.

Nothing is original either, the only thing that can be new is the attitude until the band breaks, and then the attitude goes back to exactly what it was before over twenty-five years – and that's to make as much money as possible.

According to Wham!'s George Michael, Dean 'came into this business with the attitude that if you don't step on people, they'll step on you'. If only he had known that before, he sighs.

At the time, of course, Dean's fighting spirit was dandy. Besides, they were all old friends. Everyone else had turned them down, so why not go with Dean? He had, after all, just established the necessary machinery to carry them in on his own. Innervision Ltd was formed with a paid-up capital of £100 several weeks before those tentative pub discussions with Wham!, and could boast two main selling points. First, the combined efforts of its two directors were held up as that old unbeatable combination of youth and experience. Mark Dean had worked in publishing and A and R, and the duo knew he had a sterling reputation as a forceful developer of talent; and solicitor Paul Rodwell, the second director, would surely provide all the necessary legal fine-tuning to ensure smooth running. And second, a deal was being negotiated with CBS whereby the parent company would fund Innervision and manufacture and distribute all its product, and pay the company a royalty for each record that Dean's signings sold. So not only would Wham! get personal, friendly attention from someone they trusted, but they'd also see their records in every shop in the country, and probably every country in the world.

And if the glimmer of fame up ahead with Innervision wasn't enough, George Michael, the true powerhouse of the duo, found that he was being pushed by his parents from behind too. As a Greek Cypriot who knew little of the rock industry, his father gave him six months to become a pop star. If he failed, he'd be pulled into the family restaurant business and maybe revert back to his real anglicized surname of Panos. With that sort of incentive, suggests his current manager, he would have signed *any* deal: 'So when there were a lot of difficulties with that contract, and the contract didn't seem to be right, he just wanted to override it, sign it, and get on with it.'

As to that tale of coercion, those allegations of unfair contracts, all that under-utilized legal advice, well, that would all have counted for nothing had the pessimism of George Michael's parents proved well founded, and if they had shown their son's musical ambitions to be so much idle dreaming. Trouble was, they were wrong; George Michael really had something.

Wham!'s first hit, 'Young Guns (Go For It)', charted high in November 1982, eight months after they signed. And of course the more records they sold, and the more they appeared on 'Top Of The Pops' celebrating subsequent hits, the more the old syndrome took over: the 20-year-olds began looking around for the rewards they believed to be theirs, and there were none. There was a luxury of sorts, but it all added to their overdraft. The first Christmas they went home to their parents and money was as tight as ever. The same the following Easter, and next summer too.

In the company of their present manager, Wham! could look back on their Innervision deal of that summer and find a trail of clauses that they still didn't fully understand – though they knew that most of them had been a great mistake. It was almost enough just to look at their advances and royalty payments. At a time when the majors were paying crazy money for potential chart talent – shortly over a year later singer Alison Moyet was rumoured to have received a £250,000-per-album advance from CBS – Wham! each received only £500. Royalties worked out at just 8 per cent for UK albums and singles and only 6 per cent and 4 per cent respectively for albums and singles sold in the US or the rest of the world. Even an unknown signing could have expected at least 10 per cent or 11 per cent, a chart-topping one 15 per cent to 18 per cent.

Dean's defence, and the one he impressed on Wham! in frequent negotiations over their lack of income, was forceful and three-pronged. First, he suggested that Innervision was out to make profits like all other record companies, and he did not see Innervision as a latterday Apple; he had offered them a deal and they had jumped at it. Secondly, his company broke Wham!, and he argued that without Innervision they wouldn't have achieved massive success when and how they did. Further, he claimed that CBS began taking an interest in his two mates only after he'd hired an independent strikeforce and plugger to make 'Young Guns' a hit. 'We began showing up their system. The thing that they had created [Innervision] had turned into a monster.' And thirdly, he stressed that his hands were tied; he couldn't offer Wham! more than he was earning himself.

He now admitted that he too had made a grave mistake: his

licensing deal with CBS, only finalized the day before he signed Wham!, fell horribly short of the ideal. With less impatience and ambition, and with a cooler head, he too might perhaps have worked over the details a little longer and wouldn't have agreed to all the clauses. As it was, he now almost justified Innervision's meanness towards its first signing as a necessary result of the deal he had himself signed with his parent company.

In summary, Innervision's deal with CBS specified:

1 CBS would manufacture and distribute records of the artists Innervision signed and recorded, and in return pay the company royalties. The licensing deal could last up to five years, and in the first three years the basic album royalty stood at 15 per cent in the UK and 13 per cent in the US. The royalty rate for seven-inch singles was 11 per cent for UK sales, 8 per cent for US sales. Out of this Innervision were expected to pay all artist royalties, as well as those of any one else working on the record such as producers or mixers.

2 CBS paid Innervision a first-year advance of £150,000 to be used for making master recordings and advances to artists. This was fully recoupable against the royalties accruing from successful Innervision releases. Innervision also received a maximum facility budget of £75,000 in its first year, essentially a loan to assist with working capital and capital expenditure requirements.

3 Twelve-inch singles, once used almost exclusively for promotional purposes but now selling regularly in tens of thousands (especially for dance records in which Innervision specialized) would only be subject to royalty payments once sales had exceeded 30,000.

4 Innervision would only receive *half* the royalties on a particular record promoted by a 'substantial' TV advertising campaign, not only in the four months following the campaign, but also for records sold in the two months *prior* to it.

Though apparently not to dissimilar from an equivalent licensing deal struck between ZTT (the label that spawned Frankie Goes To Hollywood) and Island Records a year later (a deal, incidentally, also negotiated on ZTT's part by solicitor Paul Rodwell), the clawback points 3 and 4 ensured that Innervision might receive dramatically less than Mark Dean might have hoped for. The ZTT/Island contract which provided ZTT with UK single and album royalties of 12 per cent and 16 per cent and advances of £120,000 on signature and an additional £40,000 after nine months, did not contain comparable CBS clawbacks, and was also considerably more generous in its terms: the Island advances were only recoupable against 40 per cent of ZTT royalties, not 100 per cent as CBS recouped from Innervision (hence the recoupment period would be a lot slower in Island's case, giving ZTT far more room to breathe).

Dean's deal with CBS thus prompted the following summarized Innervision contract with Wham!.

1 George Michael and Andrew Ridgeley each received advances of £500 recoupable against their first royalty payments.

2 Wham! were signed to Innervision for an initial contract period of one year and four further years at the company's option. During each of these periods Innervision were entitled to one album and could ask for another if they wished, making a possible ten in all. If the duo broke up, each member could be bound to Innervision for a further ten albums, even if the split occurred towards the end of the band's ten-album period. If this happened, each member would only receive three-quarters of the agreed royalty.

3 Royalty rates were 8 per cent for UK albums and singles in the initial, first and second option period, and 6 per cent and 4 per cent respectively for albums and singles sold in the rest of the world (including the US). These rates were exclusive of any royalty payable to the producer. Further, royalties would only be paid on 90 per cent of net sales.

4 Wham! received no royalty payment on sales of twelve-inch singles, *even if* sales exceeded 30,000 copies.

5 TV advertising halved royalty payments from *three* months preceding the campaign, and up to the end of the second accounting period following the final advert.

6 As with Innervision's deal with CBS, royalties would be halved if any record was issued in a coloured vinyl other than black, or if a double album was issued at fractionally less than double price.

An additional clause specified the payment of per-album advances ranging from £2,000 to be paid on the delivery of Wham!'s first album, through £12,500 paid for their fifth album, to £35,000 paid for their tenth. It was further evidence of Innervision's frugality; any band successful enough to produce ten albums for the same label can expect an advance against album sales well into hundreds of thousands. Deals of advances worth £1 million are also not uncommon.

It wasn't hard to understand why the bigger the hits, the greater Wham!'s despair, and the more sour grew the band's relationship with Dean. Dean had even taken on the role of quasi-manager for the first year, and Wham! agreed he was initially very good for them. With time, however, they assured themselves that anyone would have made a success of them eventually. In the words of the late Rolling Stones manager Andrew Loog Oldham, 'They were there already, they only wanted exploiting,' – and they began to look elsewhere for a new manager who could free them from the Innervision ties.

They turned first to their solicitor Robert Allan, but three months later in July 1983 found themselves not only in the hands of a new legal force – Russells – but also in those of a new manager whose fearful reputation for hard-nut biz arrogance was sufficient to make Allen Klein look distinctly sheepish.

Simon Napier-Bell, one of the fabled names of sixties rock and, more recently, Japan's manager for several years since his comeback from retirement, saw in Wham! a rare and enviable level of energy and professionalism, and in George Michael an uncanny ability to sit down and write hits. He had first seen them on 'Top of the Pops', and he was especially taken by their unmistakable buddy-buddy image – the Butch and Sundance or Blues Brothers feel that might make them as attractive to young male fans as they were to girls.

Speaking in his opulent but exceedingly grubby deep-piled Marble Arch house, looking not unlike a well-fed, well-tanned hamster (the result of a recent trip with Wham! to Miami), he exhibits a great and seemingly insatiable appetite for the gutsier workings of the UK rock industry, and he's clearly thrilled to be a force in it once more.

He's almost twice Mark Dean's age, and Wham! have little doubt that he's the sort of big hitter who can now see them out of any tight industry corners they may still encounter. His past tactics had been both brutal and painfully direct. In the mid sixties, for example, his group The Yardbirds asked him for houses. 'It was a bit of a nuisance because I had a busy schedule of eating and drinking to maintain,' he wrote in *You Don't Have To Say You Love Me*, his memoir of the sixties rock world. 'However, I found time to pop down to EMI Records and tell them I'd decided their contract was no longer valid, and The Yardbirds were off to look for a nicer one elsewhere . . . I told them that £25,000 would be enough to change my mind.'

Indeed, George Michael even seems rather proud that his past dealings have won him many enemies. 'He has a huge reputation as a real asshole,' he says with a smirk. 'And there's no doubt that Simon will make a lot of money out of us. But what he really wants out of it is to be responsible for managing a group that is one of the biggest in the world.'

Though it's likely that he's on at least 20 per cent, Napier-Bell probably still hasn't signed a formal management contract with Wham! – at least he hadn't at the close of their first year together. 'There's never really any point,' he shrugs. 'Once you've agreed something verbally, you either keep to it or your relationship's worthless. You need full two-way co-operation to keep both parties happy. If things break down, it's the easiest thing in the world to pull out and make sure the other side can't work.' Certainly this was true in the latter stages of the Innervision–Wham! relationship.

Mark Dean suggests that Napier-Bell did more than just help Wham! out of their contract; he claims he also made their departure inevitable. 'Despite what Wham! might tell you, it was definitely Simon who built a wedge between the group and the record company.'

Wham!'s ultimate pull-out, of course, was set in motion by Russells in the blunt terms of that letter above. Innervision's response, the attainment of a temporary court injunction, was followed by another writ, soon dropped, that saw Dean on the counter-offensive. For a short while he attempted to sue Napier-Bell and Tony Russell for conspiracy and inducement to break contract.

The entire matter was settled out of court in March 1984. Innervision lost Wham! but gained independence from CBS and a considerable pay-off loan. The break had cost the small company dearly: the amount they owed CBS was initially estimated to be around £450,000, to be paid back by a 1 per cent royalty on the future sales of all Innervision releases. Wham! signed to the major CBS subsidiary Epic for a far higher royalty rate than that agreed in their first contract (rumoured to be as high as 20 per cent) and are clearly now well into the millionaire bracket.

The end of the affair found George Michael and Andrew Ridgeley seated in their publicist's basement room in confident, even arrogant, mood. Michael even regards the enforced legal break as something of a blessing: 'It's been more of a help than we could imagine, certainly for me in writing. But I think you've just been bored, haven't you, Andrew?'

'Bored? Yeah, sometimes. But I went and got a skiing holiday – that was quite fun. But it's good to know that we're going to be number one soon . . .'

As with their manager, a recent trip to Miami has helped their suntans no end, and they take delight in preening themselves during questions and smoothing in skin moisturizer when answering. George Michael does most of the talking, just as he does most of the creative work in Wham!. He tells of how he talked his way out of the first day's shoot for the video of his 'Careless Whisper' solo single because his hair wasn't exactly right.

As for his old friend Mark Dean, he expresses little sympathy.

He was unlucky. He didn't really know what was going on at the time because he only had a few rough demos. Maybe if he had the demos we gave him three days later . . . [he admits that his main error was his desire to sign *any* deal] but it doesn't mean you have to pay for it by giving your ability for someone else to rake in the money for the rest of your life.

Things even went OK initially because we were both working towards the same goal. But we knew that one day there would be a lot of aggro, and he must have known that as well. He really counted on CBS coming to help him, which they didn't. He made the mistake of making that lousy deal thinking he could renegotiate it when things got better, but found that he couldn't because CBS weren't giving him the room. If he was not a greedy man, he could have been a very rich man by now. Probably still will be, but the point is he could have been a lot richer . . .

The irony, perhaps, and a certain testament to the hitting strength of the biz big boys, is that Dean lost out as much, if not more, than Wham!. Dean admits defeat at least in part, but suggests that his current roster of Innervision acts can only benefit from his experience. 'You can't afford to get bitter and twisted after something like this,' he offers with a sigh. 'The industry goes on quite happily without you. If you get bitter in the music world, it's time to quit.'

Dean's resolve was further tested after the Wham! affair by the bust-up and departure of two other, less popular, Innervision signings. Most hopes were pinned on his fiercely ambitious young teenies Girl-talk, those Ronettes sound-alikes who still attend school. So far, two singles have brought little success, but the girls believe they'll crack it eventually. They still think they'll be as big as Wham!, but it was an early setback to learn that they wouldn't see the two golden boys in the corridors at Innervision. Maybe they got over it towards the end of 1984 when Mark Dean could have told them that they would now see them in the corridors of his brand-new lawyers. Dean had just switched to Russells.

And Wham! themselves can lay claim to being the most successful worldwide pop act of the mid eighties.* The metal discs, the number ones, the magazine and tabloid covers and the songwriting awards have become almost weekly events since the break from Innervision. A feverish America has welcomed the duo as the 19th British invasion, and George and Andrew even enjoyed a historical exploratory tour of China.

And if the Chinese kids couldn't understand the words, and weren't allowed to dance, and if they didn't even care, then why should anyone else worry? You could almost see the platinum discs flicking over in the glaze of Simon Napier-Bell's eyes. There would be problems at customs, but China, surely, was an untapped market of some size.

---

*In February 1986, George Michael announced that Wham! would soon be splitting up.

8
Beaten by the beast

The starry rise and crashing fall
of Hazel O'Connor

Hazel O'Connor was not the victim of any major fraud. Neither was her downfall as spectacular as some. She was quite simply ground down, and her story is typical of many.*

> I haven't got any money still. I'm not going to have any money for years, if ever. There were times when I thought if I wasn't naturally strong I might have done myself in . . . At one point I had writs arriving every week. Such bastards! How dare they treat me like this.
>
> Hazel O'Connor 1985

All rock stars have at least one big break, and the way it happened to Hazel O'Connor was like this. In January 1979 she was filling in for a couple of weeks on the switchboard at Albion Records, a small, newly established independent company in London's Oxford Street. It wasn't exactly the sort of work she had had in mind when she signed a one- single deal with them a few months earlier, but then things hadn't worked out quite as she hoped they might.

Her dream was to release a single and go top twenty. The reality was that it happened like that to maybe one in every thousand, maybe ten thousand. O'Connor was just another statistic; she had recorded a single for Albion that was judged as being so bad that neither she nor

---

*Events described in this chapter are drawn from official documents and interviews with almost all the protagonists. Where there has been a conflict of information, I have chosen to rely in the main on Hazel O'Connor's version of events.

her record company thought it worth releasing. She was told to go away and write hits, but poverty necessitated she do odd jobs on the side, and hence the relief switchboard work. But it wasn't all bad: on the first day a call came through asking to talk to one of the Albion directors. They weren't in. Could she help? 'Actually, no. I need one of the directors. I need to talk to someone about Hazel O'Connor.'

O'Connor said that that was her.

'No, no, no. This one's a singer.'

It went on like that for a while. The caller was from Esta Charkham's casting agency. They were looking for actors for a big new movie. Someone had given them O'Connor's name. Was she free for a chat? Could she, in fact, come for lunch with film director Brian Gibson?

Gibson's TV success with 'Joey', 'Billion Dollar Bubble', and 'Blue Remembered Hills' had landed him with a £1½ million budget to write and direct what was hoped would be the first wide-appeal big-screen new-wave musical. 'Rock Follies', the successful TV series which traced the rise and manipulation of a women's singing trio, provided at least some of the inspiration, although the lead in the movie would almost certainly be male. More than anything, Gibson seemed to want a rise-and-fall story: rock singer struggles, makes good, gets ripped-off, freaks out, shoots up, screws up and falls into obscurity. A horribly common tale incorporating an inside look at the biz. Sounded corny as hell, in fact.

It would take a similar approach to that of *Stardust*, the hit Michael Apted film starring David Essex, and maybe steal a few clues from David Bowie's Ziggy Stardust concept on the way. Avant-garde it wasn't, but then that wasn't the idea. It would be an accessible rebellion movie which was bound to make a big star of its rebel.

If the rebel ever showed up. Gibson had been searching for a relatively unknown male lead for months. The film's producers, Davina Belling and Clive Parsons, still coasting after their critical success with the banned Borstal movie *Scum*, had also been looking. There were enough punk singers, new-wave posers and rhythm 'n' blues belters around, but few had had any acting experience or appeared articulate, self-assured and willing to take direction. And they were looking for supports as well – which is where O'Connor came in.

Although she had as yet seen little success, O'Connor was at least a face in a Covent Garden clique that moved from club to pub to party most nights in search of booze and the right music, which invariably meant their own. It was true that The Sex Pistols had blown punk wide in 1976, but throughout most of 1978 the prime movers of the punkish, wiggly crowd were still concentrated and distinct enough to hang around in a fairly large gang. One pivot was a building in James Street, a quasi-squat, total rent £7 a week. The Clash played at the party to open the place and The Sex Pistols came and threw bottles at them. The Stranglers had their own birthday party upstairs. Chrissie Hynde, later to form The Pretenders, used to hang around bumming cigarettes on the stairs. It was an allegiance built occasionally on moral and physical support but often on little less than jealousy, but you still had to keep in to get ahead.

Hazel O'Connor was a relatively latecomer to the scene. She was 23, older than most of the hangers-on, but she had a fistful of world-weary stories and her outwardly tough, fighting stance seemed to impress most of those around her. She had an angry ambition, some noticed. She looked the part – tastefully vulgar – in short skirt, black tights, harshly cropped blonde hair and double-width eyeshadow and lipstick on a drawn pale face that was often described as striking but rarely as pretty.

Another member of the crowd, Stephen Lavers, an ex-music writer currently working for A&M Records, had heard of the film in search of actors, and suggested that O'Connor's name be put down on the list. And now, at lunch with Brian Gibson and her Albion label director Dai Davies, the list had shortened and O'Connor did her best to impress. Gibson, clearly fascinated by the industry in general, pressed Davies for usable titbits. Albion were at that time in litigation with The Stranglers, and Gibson wanted to know why. What was it all about? What was the likely outcome? Were legal proceedings as common in the industry as he had heard? Davies answered cautiously as best he could. O'Connor sensed maybe she was there as a front – maybe Gibson just wanted some industry meat from her employer. Still, she let rip gleefully with her career story thus far. Davies had heard some of it before, Gibson had heard nothing, and both appeared to be thrilled with it.

And quite alarming it was too – not a singing lesson or the-day-I-auditioned-my-bass-player yarn in sight. She was born in Coventry in 1955 to an Irish factory-working father, a hotel receptionist mother and a 2-year-old brother. Her parents separated when still young, leaving their daughter feeling scarred as something of an outcast and

romantic loner (this is the way she told it, anyway). That was followed
by a frugal youth at her grandparents, underage sexual experience, five
O levels at school, and six months at art college.

Then it started getting ugly: a terrifying rape, aged sixteen in
Marrakesh, au pairing in Morocco, hippying in Amsterdam, dropping
acid in Paris, living in a nudist squat in Swiss Cottage, London, the
briefest of teen marriages to a Polish cellist, erotic dancing with a
French company in Tokyo, seedy cabaret in Beirut aged 19, hot nights
with an Arab prince, soft-core porn film roles and nude modelling back
in London, the first singing job in a harmony trio called Lady Luck, the
first she read of The Sex Pistols in *Melody Maker* . . .

She was called up to read for a part at the offices of the film's backers,
United Artists, the following day. Singer–actress Toyah Wilcox, who
had already appeared in Derek Jarman's punk film *Jubilee* and had
recently begun a successful chart career, sat next to her in the waiting
room. The film now had a working title, *Breaking Glass*, and O'Connor
read three parts, thinking the script immensely weak. But she also
thought she had impressed Brian Gibson sufficiently to land a walk-on,
and the money looked good – in fact *anything* looked better than the
prospect of continued work on the switchboard of her own record
company. It would probably be a while before she heard, but it was a
dream well worth nurturing.

Albion Records certainly wasn't in what you might call the big league.
In fact, compared with the US-owned multinationals CBS, WEA and
RCA, Albion wasn't even on the map. Or it was there, but on the
outskirts of town, along with maybe 100 other small independents that
had sprung up in the wake of punk. It had a vague, fighting spirit to its
name, but even that was more image than action. Apart from that, it
had little to recommend it.

The company was barely a year old when O'Connor had first
approached it. It had so far had little success, only the most threadbare
full-time staff, and within only a few months had already succeeded in
shattering her dream of success with her first recorded single.

When she first met Albion managing directors Dai Davies and Derek
Savage in early 1978, what she wanted was live work and a management
deal. Recording deals at that point seemed such a distant hope that she

convinced herself that as yet she didn't need one. She did need money, and believed she could earn enough just by playing live with her newly auditioned band. Somewhere in her lay a will to rebel a bit too, to shout down authority with a four-four drum beat, but the desire was never awfully strong. She wanted above all to perform. She would probably have juggled chickens if it paid. And she knew that Albion were in an ideal position to provide her with live venues.

As a live agency, Albion was one of the few accessible and hip music-business operations on the rebel scene's lips, and just about the only agency putting on the sort of music they wanted to hear or perform. When Hazel O'Connor first telephoned she was told that an appointment would take two weeks.

She spent them writing songs, designing posters and preparing a demonstration tape. She could then go in and tell them she sang, wrote songs, played guitar a bit, was photogenic and had designed a poster campaign which featured slapping pictures of herself all round town inscribed with the legend 'Where is Montana Wildhack?', one of the characters in Kurt Vonnegut's *Slaughterhouse Five*. She walked in and did just that – a massive ego puff. Dai Davies and Derek Savage, seated at the same huge desk opposite her, collapsed in hysterics. O'Connor felt she had impressed them. Davies and Savage calmed down to a snigger. She definitely had something, they felt, and they would try and help her if they could.

Formed as a record company in mid 1977, Albion had begun primarily as an agency and publishing operation two years earlier. Davies and Savage had first worked together in 1973, when Davies was managing pub-rock bands Brinsley Schwarz and Ducks Deluxe, and Savage ran a small booking agency specializing in earthy bands and small venues. They seemed an odd pair: the Welshman Davies, podgy, cherubic-faced, bounding with energy and on-the-road tales of rock misadventure; and Savage, the more sober, bearded and increasingly reserved character who had spent the last two years only organizing but not participating in road tours for other bands. But their relationship was bonded strangely by the mid seventies' oil crisis – the soaring price of petrol hitting the extent of an artist's travel, causing both of them to suffer from the drop in work. It was clear that booking a string of London pubs would cut down the need for travel almost completely (London was, after all, where you got maximum exposure), and if a new agency could provide a band with the guarantee of work for a week in different venues around town, then any band would find it worthwhile even to travel from Scotland. Davies had previously applied to the Nashville country-and-western pub in Kensington to run the place for the exposure of his own and similarly hard r 'n' b groups, and he formed Albion with Savage shortly after he got the go-ahead in 1975.

It started small and by the end of its first year had grown little. The Nashville was a fun venture, but it didn't make them much money. Graham Parker started out there, as did Elvis Costello, but with admission free from Mondays to Wednesdays and Thursday to Saturday prices generally at only 75 pence, it was hard to make a killing even on popular acts. Bands got paid £40 a night on the free days and 75 per cent of the door takings on charge nights. A couple of Albion's larger promotional enterprises around that time involving the flying in of Jamaican reggae act Toots and the Maytals and the American Ramones, ended in disaster, and it became clear that they badly needed something to change their fortunes. Then along came punk, and things began to look up.

It was still a long haul: although O'Connor was now dealing with them at their reasonably comfortable Oxford Street set-up, Albion had operated for the first two years in decidedly less salubrious premises – a cramped flat-cum-office above a hairdressing salon in Putney, south-west London. If you'd first been there on a Monday, you'd never return on Monday again – such was the pungency of the perming process below. But Davies's and Savage's rent was only £6 a week and as yet they couldn't afford to move elsewhere. Their grip on the London pub scene increased gradually, until towards the end of their Putney stay just about every punk band had been through their doors and demanded gigs. By necessity in fact, because at a time when punk and new rebel music was rejecting the dry ice and 2,000-seat hall approach and picking up on the tails of pub-rock by playing in small, smoky, licensed dives throughout the country – where you paid under a quid at the door and got your ears damaged irreversibly – Albion virtually had a monopoly on all the small key venues. If your band clicked with the Albion Agency, you were in; five gigs a week, maybe six, in places such as those Nashville Rooms, the Red Cow in Hammersmith, the Hope and Anchor in Islington, the Newlands Tavern in Putney, the Rock Garden in Covent Garden, and more.

One of the earliest bands through their doors had been The Stranglers, at that time an incompetent, mildly psychedelic sixties-style four-piece. Albion sent them on a six-week tour of RAF camps and offered a management and publishing deal on their return. They also promised them a virtually unlimited run at their own venues – enough, they said, to break the band and get them a major record deal. The Stranglers jumped at the chance.

The wait was longer than expected, but they were finally signed by United Artists Records (UA), a US-owned middle-sized set-up that had operated as a fairly insignificant arm of its film empire and was best known for its soundtrack releases.

The punk/r'n'b band 999 also signed to UA after a similar link with Albion. At the time, Davies and Savage felt that they were unable to sign any bands to a label they might operate themselves. Early attempts by others had mostly failed.

But the success of Stiff Records, run by one of Davies's old colleagues, as well as that of other independents around them, and the trouble they had had to get The Stranglers a deal, later forced a change of mind. Maybe they could run a label themselves. They reasoned that they had spotted talent successfully thus far, and it had only been farmed off to others. A flourishing label, they believed, might earn them a small fortune.

So a deal was struck with United Artists: Albion would have semi-independence in that they would have their own label name, a budget to sign and record new acts, and in return a cut of the profits. But they were essentially a talent-spotting operation – UA would do all the pressing, packaging, marketing and distribution. The deal was for a minimum of one year with options for an extension. But the year went, and UA declined to take any up. Albion had consumed large amounts of money and had given them little that was successful.

Albion then struck a similar licensing deal with Arista, another relatively new mini-major in the UK, a division of the US Columbia Pictures Corp, and the pressure increased. On their move to Arista they knew they needed a major long-term signing and fast. They had to prove to their employers, if not to the rest of the industry, that they could sign a hit act. They had already enjoyed the success of a top-twenty US hit with Ian Gomm, one of the first Albion signings, but there was a high chance that he wouldn't be able to repeat it. They needed some sort of security. Hazel O'Connor, still unravelling her posters on their desk, was a long shot who might just pull through.

So as well as her desired gigs, O'Connor also got a one-single contract, and with that came the enlarged dream of success detailed earlier. But that single was pulled, interest seemed to wane, and that led to the switchboard work.

That, of course was all before the news of *Breaking Glass*. In the weeks that followed her audition, O'Connor talked often with Albion about the possibility of securing a longer-term recording and publishing deal. Both would offer her peace of mind; her ego and ambition would be massaged with perhaps a five-year contract and visions of appearing on 'Top Of The Pops' and on the cover of the music magazines; and her financial worries would be lightened by an advance payment on signing the contract, anything from a few thousand to maybe as much as £50,000.

O'Connor had received no advance on her previous single deal with the company, and the promise of only very small royalties. But, she figured, what the hell. It was such a short-term commitment. This new record contract would be for the standard five years – a firm deal perhaps to produce two albums a year.

Like most artists, she was keener to sign and start work than read the small print. Like most artists, too, O'Connor would learn the hard way. Not that she didn't have proper legal advice. Her first solicitor, James Ware, had advised her on early singing and dancing commitments since 1975, but had since moved into the industry proper to join Virgin as a legal troubleshooter. He recommended O'Connor to transfer to Iain Adam, a slightly less established music specialist in his early thirties who ran a small-scale operation from the front room of his house just off north London's Kilburn High Road, and had previously advised O'Connor's brother's band, The Flys, over their contract with EMI.

In plain terms, he explained to O'Connor that the deal offered by Albion stank: the advances were too low compared to what she might expect from any other interested companies (as yet there was none); the royalties were too low; the demands on her creative output were too high; the controls she might have over how her work was treated were too few. He advised her to hold off until the offer improved. She took his advice.

And at the same time, Albion's eagerness that she conclude the deal increased. Her following seemed to be growing after each gig, and it looked almost certain that she would soon hear that she had landed at least a small part in *Breaking Glass.* Albion didn't want to lose her to an acting career. Further, they felt, if they had agreed terms by the time she landed a role, a screen appearance could only boost the sales of her work – and it wouldn't cost them a penny in promotion. There was even talk of Albion managing her.

The longer O'Connor took Iain Adam's advice and held out for a better contract, the more her own financial state deteriorated. Her irregular concerts netted next to nothing, and any savings had been eaten up by rent on her small Swiss Cottage flat, as well as on food, fares and clothes. (Clothes, in fact, were the least of her worries; her flat had a nudist policy. If you weren't naked when you watched TV and cooked the dinner, it was argued, then you just weren't really at home.)

Her irregular concerts at the Nashville and the Rock Garden paid only £15 and £10 respectively, less 10 per cent Albion Agency commission. Albion refused to support her band, usually a four-piece featuring her flatmate Gary Tibbs, two members of punk band The Boys and brother Neil O'Connor who showed up when he wasn't playing with The Flys, and their split of the fee was barely enough to get them mildly drunk. Most nights they were billed as Hazel and the Unknown. The easiest rock journalists' jibe was that that was how they would remain.

But late in 1978 it was the rock press that pushed her nearer to a long-term deal. Both *Sounds* and *Melody Maker* gave her live act the thumbs-up and asked Albion for more information. This new interest in turn boosted Albion's desire that she record her first album, which she did, and the longer the finished master tapes lay on the shelf, the harder they pushed to conclude a record and publishing deal. Despite her lawyer's advice, it was the latter that again began to look far too good to resist. The current offer would get her a £2,080 advance at the rate of £40 a week for her first year. What she surrendered in return was relatively unimportant for her at this stage: what *was* important was that £40 a week would provide both minor security and a bit more fun in town at night. At present she was spending only £25 a week all in, and in mid March her bank account showed a credit of just £1.82. Her next monthly rent payment of £33 was due in three days, and there seemed to be only two options: one, sign the deal and sign away her copyrights; or two, find another job at once, almost certainly in a non-music field.

One incident in particular forced her hand. Band rehearsals were currently under way for a new run of upcoming gigs. Davies and Savage both disapproved of her amended group line-up; *she* was the attraction, they felt, and the band could only be detrimental to her progress. They had advised her to ditch them before now, but strengthened their case when her bassist claimed that his contribution on one song in particular merited a writer's credit. O'Connor said no, arguing that it was an integral part of the arrangements that the whole group had worked on. But tempers flared, and other similarly minor issues niggled at O'Connor's resistance. She collapsed into tears and chased up Davies and Savage for advice.

Still tearful, she explained the argument and told them that the band were waiting in reception for a settlement. According to O'Connor a day later, the Albion directors insisted that she needed a guiding hand, a form of protection against anyone's attempt to muscle in. The record and publishing deals would give her that security. They were already fully drawn up in their files. All she had to do was sign. She signed.

Her lawyer Iain Adam had categorically warned her against signing anything in his absence, and O'Connor phoned him directly afterwards, clearly still emotionally distraught. 'It was all my own stupid fault!' she bawled. Adam was furious and promised he'd write to Albion at once. The subsequent letter requested copies of the contracts and closed by saying, 'Whilst I hope that Albion's relationship with Hazel will be a cordial and successful one, I must point out that you and David Gentle [Albion's lawyer] were aware that I had not gone through the recording agreement with her, and accordingly her rights are reserved . . .'.

The problem was, they weren't. For while Iain Adam knew that an artist who had not received independent legal advice may have the contracts nullified in the courts, O'Connor had just entered into a bargain that was as legally binding as any. She was old enough to decide her own destiny. She had just signed herself into a long-term commitment, and if either she or her lawyer didn't like it, then too bad. After all, they were not in the courts, but in the real world – the music industry. And, Albion told O'Connor, welcome to it.

The two freshly signed agreements, both dated 30 March 1979, seemed to embody all of her solicitor's worst fears. He read them aghast: not only were the payments due to O'Connor exceptionally small, but her commitment to Albion was extensive and vigorously demanding. Moreover, even her artistic and creative output seemed to be subject to the most stringent of company controls.

The recording agreement specified:

1 She was required to record exclusively for Albion, and to deliver two singles and one album during the first year. At Albion's request she could also be bound to record up to two albums per year for four additional option years, making a possible nine albums in all. It meant that while O'Connor had taken twenty-three years to come up with her first album's worth of material, she might now have to come up with double that amount each year until 1984.

2 She would receive no advance on signing, and only £2,000 on or before the delivery of her first album in the first option period. This however was the only album to carry any contractual advance, and given that royalties may often take up to a year to be paid, it was quite insufficient to maintain even the most frugal standard of living.

3 Royalty rates were set at 5 per cent of the retail price of all releases in the UK and US, and at 4 per cent in the rest of the world. This too, of course, was an alarmingly low rate for the time. It wouldn't have been unreasonable for Iain Adam to have hoped for a royalty of at least 4 or 5 per cent more. That amount, he knew, could mean the difference between O'Connor earning thousands and hundreds of thousands. It was his protestations at the low rates that resulted in an additional clause being tagged to the agreement some weeks later. It increased the royalty by 1 per cent on each album that sold more than 75,000 copies in the UK; by a further 1 per cent on albums that sold more than 150,000 copies in the UK; and another 1 per cent on albums selling in excess of 400,000. It was only very rarely that a newly signed artist ever sold 75,000. At the same time it was quite feasible that if a Hazel O'Connor album reached the top ten, it might still have sold less than 75,000 and she could have been earning only a 5 per cent royalty on one of the biggest-selling records in the UK. The big names in the same chart could easily have been on 12 or 14 per cent.

4 The royalties due to O'Connor would only be calculated on 90 per cent of the recommended retail price of albums sold. That clause, too, could mean that for a hit album O'Connor received several thousand pounds less than a royalty rate calculated at the full selling price.

5 A packaging clause further reduced her royalty. It stated, as above, that while calculation would be made on the basis of 90 per cent of the recommended retail selling price, any packaging costs (apart from plain single sleeves) would cut the 90 per cent down to

(a) $83\frac{1}{2}$ per cent in the case of singles with a picture sleeve
(b) $83\frac{1}{2}$ per cent in the case of picture-sleeve albums
(c) 80 per cent in the case of gate-fold sleeve albums ('special' album covers)
(d) 78 per cent in the case of cassettes.

Since (b) and (d) were all-essential to the sale of O'Connor's work, the further reductions meant another considerable loss of possible income. These last two clauses were not uncommon in other recording agreements of the day, but for O'Connor they only served to confuse; her mental calculations were still based on what she might earn on 100 per cent of the retail price of her records.

6 The first album under the agreement had to be 'commercially satisfactory' to Albion, the contents of which would be specified by Albion 'in consultation' with O'Connor. Subsequent albums had to be 'of comparable quality'. It was a wide clause: in theory Albion could reject O'Connor's work *ad infinitum* and retain the exclusive right provided by another clause to prevent her from recording elsewhere. There were several requirements regarding the artist's delivery deadlines too, none requiring the company to release her work by a set date.

7 Albion had the power to choose recording studios, producers, accompaniment, and arrangement. O'Connor was to be consulted, but the final say in whom she worked with and where was not hers.

8 Albion were to advance all recording costs within an agreed budget but these would be subtracted prior to O'Connor receiving royalties resulting from these recordings.

9 The first year's recording budgets were set at a maximum of £500 per single and £10,000 per album all in, which was also mean for the time. A more usual average budget stood at perhaps three or four times that amount for a new artist.

10 Albion agreed to consult O'Connor over the release of any record or press or promotional material, but it was understood that a failure to do so should not be regarded as a fundamental breach of agreement.

11 There were provisions for O'Connor to insist on an independent royalty audit if she so wished, but this would be at her own expense unless major errors were found.

12 In the event of an attempted breach of the contract by either side, it was formally agreed that it would be appropriate for the offended party to seek a court injunction to prohibit that breach.

O'Connor thought this a superfluous clause, like many of the others. Who the hell thought of the courts at a time like this?

The publishing deal, judged against similar contracts of the day, was also strikingly poor. Under it, O'Connor agreed to submit all her work to be published exclusively by Albion Music in the next year, with possible extensions for up to four additional years.

She was signed to a world deal at a 60:40 split, increasing to 70:30 in the fourth and fifth years. Albion got the rights not only to all the material O'Connor was to write under the contract period, but also all the songs she had already composed in past years that had not been assigned to another company. Her advance, fully recoupable by the company against her first royalty income of course, would be that £40 a week paid in monthly instalments, total £2,080. Each accepted option would provide her with an advance of £1,000. As with the recording deal, the meagre advances and royalties may have reflected Albion's lack of confidence in O'Connor's ability to come up with the hit goods. Alternatively, Albion may just have been playing it mean out of greed.

The eight tracks O'Connor had recorded in the last few months could now be released at last, and Dai Davies and Derek Savage turned their minds to the album sleeve and the promotional work required to launch a new act into the charts. The record would be distributed and marketed by Arista Records, so at least that problem wasn't theirs. O'Connor herself looked forward to the release – the finished master tapes, produced by Vic Maile after his success with Dr Feelgood and Tom Robinson, were not amazing affairs even to O'Connor's ears, but it meant a record in the shops and something to show her friends. Moreover, she felt, it was one record down. She was continually learning, and since the work was an infinite improvement on her first aborted single, the next release would also, no doubt, be a step up.

A few days later – about a week after O'Connor had signed those recording and publishing deals – the *Breaking Glass* production office telephoned again, apparently with news of her bit part. In fact, they were considering her for the lead. The script had been rewritten, the original big-screen 'Rock Follies' idea had been ditched along with Brian Gibson's original plan to have a male lead, and a strong female singing role had emerged in its place. It was between O'Connor and the Stiff Records singer Lene Lovich.

It would be a live contest: neither Gibson nor producers Belling and Parsons, nor, more importantly, the film's backers United Artists, had actually seen O'Connor performing live, and the lead's rise to fame was provisionally scripted as one of hard, grafting gigging.

Dai Davies and Derek Savage were initially thrilled at the prospect – a film star on their label wasn't a bad catch after less than two years of signing acts. Even better if she was to be in a musical – no way that couldn't boost her record sales. Better still as it looked like being an all-stops big-budget affair with a massive promotional campaign built in. It would, they hoped, not only take care of all the advertising for them, but maybe do it ten times over.

O'Connor's group had just been disbanded on Albion's advice (they had signed a solo deal with O'Connor and made it clear they were unprepared to support the upkeep of a band), but it was now hastily reformed so that the singer could impress the film people. Albion set her up at the Nashville for several nights, and on the third Gibson showed up and raved. A further gig was arranged for the UA crowd and more of the *Breaking Glass* crew. The lead was hers within two weeks.

And within a month the full soundtrack had been offered to her as well. The original plan, albeit a vague one, was to piece together a soundtrack from several artists, and possibly release it as an album on its own merits. (This had been done with *That Summer*, a film Belling and Parsons had only recently completed. But the film had bombed at the box office, and the double album soundtrack, a cobbled old mesh which included Elvis Costello, the Boomtown Rats and Ian Dury, had fared little better.) O'Connor, however, had not only impressed them live, but also persuaded them that she could write and perform all the movie's music herself. Undoubtedly someone who would be as closely involved as she could be invaluable if new songs were needed at the last minute or if a verse needed amendment, she argued, and tailor-made material could thus be woven around the plot and vice versa. So far, she admitted, most of her material would probably be unsuitable.

But she told Brian Gibson she was currently writing as never before. She was, she felt, a singer–songwriter first, and an actress second. She was on an up; they had to let her have a shot.

Then the backing collapsed. UA had already committed themselves heavily to Michael Cimino's epic *Heaven's Gate*, and it was running horrendously over budget; it would have had to do massive box office business even to break even. So with their resources already heavily over-committed, UA had little option but to ditch *Breaking Glass*.

Belling and Parsons were at the Cannes Film Festival in May when the news came through – in effect the ideal place to find other money. A new deal was eventually struck with Dodi Fayed of Allied Stars, a 26-year-old Egyptian with a background in commerce and shipping, and a nephew of billionaire Adnan Kashoggi. *Breaking Glass* was to be Allied Stars' first film, and Fayed hoped that a £10 million investment in the company would be recouped in one swipe with its profits.

That at least was the dream. For while O'Connor got the new company's thumbs-up, there remained several financial reservations. The film was to have one of the biggest 'British' budgets that year – an estimated £1½ million. It was modest enough by Hollywood standards, but it wouldn't have Hollywood appeal; there were no bankable stars; the rock rise-and-fall subject matter looked either clichéd or risqué depending on your age; and as yet it didn't have either a UK or a US distribution deal.

In short, Allied Stars needed at least a little security, and they began to look towards the soundtrack. They asked Albion for £70,000, arguing that O'Connor would sell a warehouseful, that the film would do wonders for her career, and that she would be boosted to the skies with no promotional costs at all.

Dai Davies and Derek Savage knew the advantages well enough, but they could not meet the asking price. They struck a deal: they agreed to let the soundtrack appear on the label of another interested and wealthier company so long as

1 Albion received a cut from the album's profits, and
2 Allied Stars would give Arista, Albion's distributors and financiers, first refusal to take it for the same fixed price; Davies and Savage were still trying to provide them with a big seller.

Agreed, but Arista turned the album down: not enough security, too much cash. It was picked up at last by A&M Records, the UK

wing of the 17-year-old American company set up by horn player
Herb Alpert that had achieved remarkable success in the sixties,
largely through Alpert's own hits with his Tijuana Brass. Their current
biggest UK act was The Police, and they were also enjoying success
with Squeeze and Joe Jackson, the latter still published by Albion.

Albion in turn drew up a deal with O'Connor by which they let her
go to A&M for the one album, and she accepted a 50 per cent royalty
cut. Hence, for each album sold she received just $2\frac{1}{2}$ per cent of retail
sales. Her publishing income was unaffected as Albion retained
exclusive rights, but the recording royalty reduction meant that while
her own income would be halved, Albion would receive a large
windfall just for letting her record elsewhere. It was just reward, they
argued, for helping her land the part.

For a man about to embark on the final script and direction of a major
full-length film on the subject, Brian Gibson still knew relatively little
about the music industry. A small part of what he had learnt had
come from the lips of Dai Davies, and it was a peculiar irony of the
film that it gradually took on the shape, if not the course, of Hazel
O'Connor's own experiences. Her dealings with a booking agency,
closely modelled on Albion, for instance, had already entered Gibson's
script, and the record producer in the film quickly took the form of
Tony Visconti, the real-life producer of the *Breaking Glass* soundtrack.

Visconti was O'Connor's idea. She knew a great producer could
transform a song, and she hadn't worked with one yet; Visconti was
simply the most famous she had heard of. O'Connor was a long-term
fan of David Bowie, and Visconti had produced or co-produced a whole
heap of Bowie's million-selling records. He had developed Marc Bolan's
talents since 1968, and produced him until his death. He had scored
with Mary Hopkin, The Strawbs, Thin Lizzy, Iggy Pop and many others.
Visconti, by contrast, had never heard of O'Connor. A New Yorker of
Italian descent, with blow-dried light brown hair, seemingly permanent
tan and nothing but black clothes over a powerful build, he was every
inch a young and imposing Svengali, and he charged impressive fees. He
was not the sort of producer a new and unknown artist could usually
afford. He had a phone in his Soho, London, recording studios that had
a built-in calculator; he was fond of using it to calculate transatlantic

deals. Films, however, remained an area he had never touched, and he longed for the call-up. He had seen an early *Breaking Glass* synopsis and it looked sketchy and unconvincing, but he was intrigued that O'Connor had been able to get him a trial.

Brian Gibson and producer Parsons filled him in further in Parsons's front room a couple of days after he had first heard of the project. It was to be about 'youthful self-expression' and 'vibrant energy' said Parsons. Visconti mused that it had a fairly high potential for disaster.

O'Connor arrived half an hour after Visconti. Parsons and Gibson had told him of her intangible 'spark' and drive, and he too saw it within minutes. Then he heard some early recordings, rough cuts of her first proposed Albion album, and he changed his mind again. They were uncertain, squeaky little songs, quite the opposite of what was required. The film needed a belter, and these were whispers.

Things swung round again when O'Connor put on a new backing cassette and walked around the room singing a song called 'Will You' at full pelt – again not a belter, but a reflective, well-observed ballad. Visconti was taken with her gutsy conviction and even gutsier voice. It wasn't a beautiful voice, he thought, and there was no hint of perfect pitch. But then it wasn't that sort of musical. He thought he could work with it well, and was confident that if the film bombed they would at least have a great soundtrack.

Visconti at this point was a man with two solicitors – a sure sign of someone whose trust in the music machine had dwindled to nothing. Already the victim of several bad deals, he was determined he wouldn't get bitten again. His early Bowie days still proved the most painful: in the late sixties, in the days when even name producers operated under the heavy wing of a management or publishing company, Visconti signed a deal engineered by Mercury Records and his agent David Platz, then still a young but vastly experienced publisher. He produced the bulk of the *Space Oddity* and *The Man Who Sold The World* albums on the basis of a 2 per cent royalty on sales – but the albums had to sell 50,000 in the first six months for the contract to be honoured. Unfortunately for Visconti they sold well under, and he received nothing. David Platz did well from the arrangement – he was one of Bowie's publishers – and Visconti still feels sick about it. Until he came on the scene, no other skilled producer had expressed much interest in working with the relatively unknown singer.

The two albums were repackaged and reissued when Bowie's *Ziggy Stardust* finally established him as a huge worldwide name. *Space Oddity* and *The Man Who Sold the World* subsequently sold over a million copies each and would have netted in the region of £250,000 for their producer. The six-month clause ensured that Visconti never saw any of it, and at the time of *Breaking Glass* those two Bowie gold discs hung opposite his studio desk to remind him of his folly. He has since noted to friends that the word 'ruthless' entered his vocabulary about the time of *Ziggy*, and at the end of 1979 he was using it with regularity.

His *Breaking Glass* contract specified that he was to receive a 3 per cent cut from A&M of all album sales, and a $\frac{1}{2}$ per cent cut of net box office profits from the film's backers. His solicitors insisted that he also received a full-screen solo credit for musical production and direction. ' "Produced by Tony Visconti" right across the screen – I don't share it with any other name,' he noted. 'I like stuff like that!'

Hazel O'Connor hit it off with him from the start. She spent a week with his wife and kids in their home in Wargrave-on-Thames near Henley. His wife at that time was Mary Hopkin, (dubbed by one keen critic as 'the girl who was too pure to have an asshole'), and O'Connor found the writing atmosphere as conducive as any she'd been in.

Brian Gibson telephoned most nights with new theme twists from his latest draft, and O'Connor wrote the bulk of the soundtrack within that week. For the recording, Visconti handpicked several sessionmen, including highly regarded sax player Wesley Magoogan, and he played a lot of the bass himself. It was a predictably laborious process; O'Connor missed notes and had trouble grappling with her new vocal style, but the final results enjoyed genuine all-round enthusiasm. O'Connor in particular learned a great amount, especially from Visconti's criticisms. It was, she felt, by far her best work yet.

With his shooting script still unfinished, Brian Gibson hung about in the studios for much of the recording, and often took verbatim notes of O'Connor's and Visconti's conversations. It became clear within weeks that, being slightly unsure of his ground, Gibson wanted real life; O'Connor's own career was the closest he had ever got to it.

Her young manager in the film, a role cast for the fresh-faced Phil Daniels shortly after his success in *Quadrophenia*, was also based closely on the young and fresh-faced figure who now handled her day-to-day business affairs in reality, Alan Edwards. Long before the film, and even before her first Albion deal, Alan Edwards was also part of O'Connor's Covent Garden scene and had previously turned her down for management on the grounds that he was too busy looking after The Damned. Their paths crossed again later, when during his employment as a part-time press consultant for Albion – principally to look after The Stranglers – he also had to deal with requests for information about O'Connor. But with the film looming and that first album set for release soon, he changed his mind and agreed to take her on. (As if to underline the incestuous nature of the independents, Edwards's management operation, soon to be called Modern Management, was established in partnership with another ex-Albion director, Ian Grant, who had taken on The Stranglers for management after their Albion rows.)

Though both still short of experience, O'Connor and Edwards believed they had now progressed a fair way from those Covent Garden days. Above all, they seemed good for each other. They spoke each other's language, they were roughly the same age, she felt she could trust him and approved of the acts he had previously been involved with. As for Edwards, he thought he might soon have a major film star on his books.

An agreement was eventually drawn up between them in September 1979. Under it, he was bound to handle her entire professional career for a minimum of four years at a cut of 20 per cent of all gross earnings (that is, an off-the-top cut irrespective of any expenses), and he was bound to account to her twice yearly. The 20 per cent cut also extended to the two years *after* the termination of the agreement, after which it was reduced to $12\frac{1}{2}$ per cent in perpetuity.

In all, the terms were fairly standard. As with every management relationship, the crucial factor could not be worded in sub-clauses at all; the intangibles were paramount – trust, respect, vision, gut feeling, those sorts of things. Often, the best you could hope for was that experience and good fortune would pull you through. O'Connor chose to ignore the fact that Alan Edwards was still remarkably short of experience.

By the time O'Connor next looked at the *Breaking Glass* script, the tale was still cliché-ridden, but it was also still youthfully exuberant and very loosely accurate. The music industry looked horribly monochromatic: harsh, corrupt and totally devoid of intelligence or a feel for music. As a microcosm of a world, it appeared unreal and unbelievable. But in some respects it was the bravest and most revealing industry *atmosphere* film yet attempted.

Shot over eleven weeks towards the end of 1979 at Cricklewood's Production Village, *Breaking Glass* had attracted an impressive cast. As well as Phil Daniels for Edwards, Jon Finch was recruited to play the Visconti role, and Jonathan Pryce was down to play a deaf, drug-pumped saxophonist. O'Connor just played herself to the power of four. She found the character's early struggles familiar enough, and the size of her ego permitted a credible shot at playing the big time. Also, she'd seen the onset of neurosis and drug abuse among friends, and anyway it was part of that great 'live fast, die young, have a great-looking corpse' fable that nutshelled a large chunk of the rock 'n' roll lifestyle. She worked hard for her £6,000 fee (the Equity minimum), and she felt sure she had done an impressive job.

Shooting concluded in February 1980, and in May it appeared out of competition in Cannes, three months prior to its scheduled UK release. A&M naturally planned to release the soundtrack just before its London première, even though O'Connor's thirteen songs were already in the can many months earlier. 'Why rush it?' thought A&M's marketing department and managing director Derek Green. It wasn't as if she was going to burn herself out or get over-exposed.

The problem was, A&M had reckoned without Albion. Dai Davies and Derek Savage reasoned that O'Connor was going to be hot in a few months, and the fact that they'd given away the soundtrack meant they'd receive only a fraction of A&M's earnings. They had signed a hit act, and they wouldn't get the credit. Moreover, they still wouldn't have the sort of turnover to keep their mother company, Arista, happy, and they still wouldn't be able to attract any widely headhunted acts to their label if it couldn't first prove itself in the charts.

One solution: release that old O'Connor album recorded back in mid 1978 and coast home on the wave of the movie. They already had eight tracks on hold, and their agreement with A&M made no mention of any restrictions on Albion's release schedule. Indeed Albion had already tested the water in August 1979 when they released a recut version of O'Connor's first aborted single, 'Ee-I-Adio'. It received little promotion, next to no airplay, and sold disastrously, but that was when she still had a relatively low profile.

O'Connor now had a far stronger image – a quasi-robotic, pierrot look, a face of even darker eyes and darker lips than before, topped with a frazzled pile of bleached hair – and her role in the film had already received much location publicity; the release of the Albion album now might just set the indie company up for good.

O'Connor was horrified at the prospect. Not only had her style of singing changed drastically on *Breaking Glass*, but the songs themselves and the Visconti production put any previous records to certain shame. Albion were begged to release nothing until the soundtrack appeared or until she had time to record new material for the label. A&M too rallied fiercely against Albion's plans. Sure, they said, they would affect sales of the soundtrack and hence A&M's coffers, but that in turn would mean a smaller cut to Albion. Besides, it would confuse the paying customer, might swamp the market, and might eventually prove detrimental to O'Connor's career.

Savage and Davies both had doubts about the direction in which the film was taking her, foreseeing problems with the punkish image they feared she might never shake off, and doubting whether she'd be happy performing that sort of material once her chart boundaries had been locked tight (they claim they saw her, as she later saw herself, as more of a blues singer). But they relented all the same. They released no non-soundtrack material until four months after the release of the film. Deep inside, both Savage and Davies probably hoped to God that they had been wise in holding back, prayed O'Connor would still bring them the hits. They knew that their detractors had been looking at them with raised eyebrows for some time now.

The reaction to *Breaking Glass* at Cannes boosted Albion's hopes no end. The film got a far better reception than even some connected with it had hoped for, although Brian Gibson for one was aware that the public preview theatres represented little more than a *claque*. The truly testing arenas were scattered throughout the UK.

O'Connor, by contrast, was bowled over. Not only was her work acclaimed, but she became this peculiarly English spectacle – a natural in an atmosphere of calculated pose and glamour – and the truly hot discovery of the Festival. Her hair, in tight blonde plaits especially for the occasion, became an instant media focus along with what the press saw as her forthright, ballsy approach to life in general and men in particular. A large crew of paparazzi, led by her old friend Richard Young, pursued her by the coachload throughout the Festival, which was fine for about a day, but was already becoming too much when, four days in, a clutch of photographers asked O'Connor to throw a pair of handcuffs on to Roman Polanski's dinner table next to hers in the Carlton Hotel. Polanski was dining with his current flame and young star of *Tess*, Nastassia Kinski, and the snappers reasoned that the publicity shot would do all three careers a power of good. O'Connor, aware of Polanski's notorious involvement in the Manson case, refused to do it. The photographers chucked the handcuffs towards Polanski themselves, widened their angles and began clicking, at which point Polanski went wild, threw his food everywhere and stormed out with Kinski in tow. O'Connor was pursued back to her apartment and collapsed on the bed in tears.

'Is this what it's like?' she bawled to Jon Finch on the phone. 'I thought acting a megastar would prepare me for this, but I feel just like a performing monkey here. I want success, but I don't want this! How long can you fight them? How long before you become just like the rest?'

Finch, a former lover and confidant, had provided similar moral support two months earlier when an excerpt of *Breaking Glass* was used in the Royal Film Première to illustrate the stumbling development of Great British Musicals – a support to the main event of *Kramer-vs-Kramer*. The plan was that the stars should meet the Queen. Dustin Hoffman, Meryl Streep and a gang of others said yes please. O'Connor, in a rash moment, first thought of the kick the event would give her mum, then thought she would somehow be betraying her new-wave fans if she accepted the honour, and so refused. 'It was nothing against the Queen,' she explained, 'I just felt that we didn't have much in common at that point in time.' The press hammered, and Finch consoled her.

But Cannes, she wept, was much worse. Not only had she not expected the attention (she had only recently returned from a quiet writing holiday in Italy with The Stranglers' singer Hugh Cornwell), but she had no idea how to cope with the dilemmas it presented. She knew hers was an age-old problem: she wanted the acclaim, but begged to retain her privacy. Neither did she want isolation – she wanted a normal life. She told Finch that she was now sharing her Cannes flat with a completely unknown woman – an ex-girlfriend of manager Alan Edwards, who had now taken flight – and that she thought she might be going a little 'nutty'.

She recovered in London for the next two months, writing and trying out new material for her first official Albion album. Most weeks she made frequent trips to a hypnotist in an attempt to regain her voice and rid herself of a sore bout of eczema, both direct effects of her stay in Cannes. Each session with the hypnotist ended in tears. There was also a certain amount of promotion work to be done following the moderate success of the first single released from the *Breaking Glass* soundtrack. But unlike the anarchic flush of Cannes, the pace now presented few problems.

The A&M press office arranged for several TV appearances, press interviews and photo sessions, and other departments liaised with her over sleeve design and future album promotion. This, she felt, was how it ought to be: no rush, regular creative confidence boosts, first-class star treatment, limousines to pick you up in the mornings. For a company a fraction of A&M's size, Albion treated her the best they considered they could. But as thoughts turned towards the new album, *Sons and Lovers*, O'Connor wondered whether she wouldn't be better off with a major. Although pleased that Albion had shelved their plans to release any pre-*Breaking Glass* material, she remained uncertain about the independent's fire power – about its ability to repeat her A&M treatment. She told them she would be less concerned if she could at least work with Tony Visconti again, but Davies and Savage checked back and told her he wouldn't do it.

At the time she wouldn't believe it; they had so far worked so well together. Moreover, it looked like they would have a huge hit album on their hands within weeks. She only found out more some months later: he was keen as hell, but felt he couldn't afford the risk. Albion were unable to guarantee him the minimum of £25,000 he regarded as his very cheapest per-album rate, and he distrusted their ability as a company to earn him at least that through his 3 or 4 per cent royalty cut: for Bowie he now demanded perhaps double that advance. To receive less than £2,000 per track for O'Connor would almost have cost *him* money, he argued. His main worries concerned Albion's poor history and distribution arrangements.

Davies's and Savage's manufacturing and distribution relationship with Arista, struck in March 1979, had deteriorated rapidly because of a lack of Albion hits and an abundance of Arista staff changes, and it was over within nine months.

The obvious new outlet seemed A&M, who were indeed keen to handle O'Connor, and could promise Albion the run of all their resources in international distribution through the massive CBS network. Yet O'Connor was all A&M were interested in, and when Albion said take their whole roster or nothing, the deal was off.

Other outlets, too, expressed interest in O'Connor, but both Davies and Savage found no major takers for the entire Albion package. One option remained: they were an independent company, so why not go through an independent distributor? A deal was struck with Spartan, the most established and successful indie enterprise that had flourished by handling much of the small DIY punk boom of three years earlier. They had already proved they could handle big hits, but had yet to build up a reputation to rival the majors, and Visconti doubted whether the Albion/Spartan twinning would get O'Connor the success she would have with A&M. Hence, if Albion refused to allay his fears by giving him his minimum guarantee, he was out – and so it proved.

Albion's own choice of producer was Nigel Gray, a man who had enjoyed but a fraction of Visconti's experience or success, and was best known for his engineering and co-production work on The Police's first two hit A&M albums *Outlandos d'Amour* and *Regatta de Blanc*. He would find *Breaking Glass* a tough act to follow.

Released three weeks before the film, the album and simultaneous single release of 'Eighth Day' both reached number five in their respective charts within a month, the album going gold (sales of 100,000 plus) and remaining in the top 100 grid for twenty-six weeks. A second single from the soundtrack, 'Give Me An Inch', also charted high two months later.

The film faired altogether less well. Distributed by GTO Films, a small company run by former Rolling Stones' business accountant and all-round production entrepreneur, Laurence Myers, the movie 'just didn't open', to use the Hollywoodese.

Myers spent £150,000 acquiring the UK rights and around £600,000 on prints and TV, poster and newspaper advertising, and concluded some months after the première that only 'Hazel went to see it, her mum went to see it, my kids went and about seven other people went – that was it.' In fact it opened at seven West End cinemas and did a very average £18,000 of net business in its first week. 'But it's a kids' film and many of them can't afford West End prices', said GTO marketing director, Jocelyn Towns, at the time. 'We expect the film will really take off in the suburbs and provinces.' Not so – it stiffed in the sticks as well. One of the GTO companies was bankrupted as a result, and Myers's office affectionately dubbed it *Breaking Disaster*. What's more, he couldn't understand its failure – he had seen the daily rushes since the fifth day of production and approved with few reservations. He was especially taken with O'Connor's performance, and the two got on swimmingly. Myers soon became one of her closest business confidants.

And many of the critics echoed his enthusiasm. The *Guardian* compared its energy to Bob Fosse's *All That Jazz* and regarded O'Connor as a 'talent both as singer and actress, with a tiny touch of the Midler's'. The *Observer* suggested that the current music business was both more interesting and complex than the film suggested, even though 'it would be difficult to exaggerate the ruthlessness and corruption' to be found in it. The *Guardian* offered the premise that *Breaking Glass* 'will certainly encourage O'Connor to think that life sometimes imitates art'.

Its failure at the box office disappointed O'Connor relatively little – in fact for a long period she was told that business was fairly buoyant. It was almost enough for her that she starred in a film at all and that during their time together Visconti had introduced her to her adolescent hero, David Bowie, and that Bowie himself professed that he liked the film. He was flattered that his Ziggy Stardust period had provided at least some of the inspiration, and, says O'Connor, asked: 'Did you take the name of the film from my song too?' O'Connor, embarrassed, confessed that she had never heard of the title elsewhere. Bowie put her at ease and said he had heard she had cut Visconti's hair – would she do his? She considered the whole affair quite a wheeze. She could deal with this guy as an equal. She wasn't just a fan any more.

The next logical step was to bring her bank balance into line with her ego. Her face had appeared on billboards eighteen feet high, on the cover of many music weeklies and on 'Top of the Pops' several times – a pop star by anyone's term of reference – and she was still actually considering charging Bowie for his snip. By the end of 1980 her fee for the film had already long disappeared and O'Connor became increasingly disturbed at her lack of recording income.

By December 1980, with the *Breaking Glass* soundtrack already on sale for three months, estimates suggested that the album would sell in the region of just under 300,000 copies. The singles would jointly sell

about the same. Under a standard deal she could have hoped to gross
about £100,000. Under the deal that Albion had arranged with A&M,
and which she had approved, she was set to receive only 50 per cent
of her royalties, the other half siphoned off by Albion. Add to that the
fact that, now she was a chart act, the recording royalty was at least 4
or 5 per cent below what she might reasonably expect to receive
against her high volume of sales elsewhere, and O'Connor felt she had
a raw deal. And when her recording statement arrived some months
later, totalled at £34,470, she was informed that she would see none of
it. It was to be retained entirely by Albion against unrecouped
advances and earlier recording costs. Her main income was to come
from publishing, but the payment of advances, VAT, Alan Edwards's
20 per cent cut and debts and other expenses left her with barely
£5,000.

But O'Connor's main gripes against Albion were less concerned
with cash than they were with the way they treated her; after the
luxury of the pampered film treatment and the cushioning of A&M,
their small Oxford Street operation seemed particularly low-rent,
almost seedy. Her ego found it hard to come to terms with the fact
that she had to retain £1.50 cab-fare receipts and cassette battery
packages. In short, she doubted Albion's ability to develop her career.
Hence she happily signed a licensing deal Albion had arranged with
A&M for her future US releases in the hope that at least the task of
pushing her in America would fall into experienced hands, even
though she received no share of the $150,000 advance Albion received
from A&M in return.

As far as the cash was concerned, she convinced herself that her
existing deal wasn't *that* bad, especially compared to some of the
horror stories she had heard – artists receiving 2 per cent royalties on
hit albums and the like. It may have been slightly mean, she was
advised, but it was fully enforceable. If she did break the agreement
on financial grounds, she was told that the courts would show her
little sympathy. Far stronger, perhaps, would have been the argument
that she had signed under duress: young girl, first contract,
insufficient legal advice, signing in tears . . .

O'Connor, acting on the whim and gut feeling that now seemed
regularly to characterize her actions, expressed an eagerness to fight
herself free of Albion through the courts if necessary. Alan Edwards,
significantly more cautious, advised her instead to renegotiate. He had

approached Queen's Counsel for advice and was told that a court case instigated now would take a minimum of a year (if not two or three) to conclude. He held several hastily arranged clandestine meetings with O'Connor and A&M managing director Derek Green, the latter as keen to sign O'Connor as she was to engineer a break with Albion. Several 'buying out' sums were discussed and put to Davies and Savage: both stood firm, preferring to see the long-term rewards of their signing. Out of all the acts with whom they had a recording agreement, O'Connor was the only one to bear fruit, and they weren't prepared to let her go lightly now.

Edwards won through, and the renegotiated recording and publishing contracts were signed early in December 1980. Clearly, Albion were pleased with the new deals; like Edwards, they wanted anything but a lengthy court battle. And O'Connor knew that she certainly couldn't argue that they were signed under duress. In fact, they looked as watertight as you could get.

Under the deals, O'Connor's recording royalties increased from 5 per cent to $12\frac{1}{2}$ per cent in the UK, and to 9 per cent in the US and $10\frac{1}{2}$ per cent in the rest of the world. The UK figure would increase by a further 1 per cent in the (extraordinary) event that sales of a particular album exceeded 400,000 copies. It would have been extraordinary mostly because the contract specified that this only applied to albums other than *Breaking Glass*.

Advances were also provided, unlike her first agreement, but still remained relatively low for a hit act. She would receive £15,000 on signing and a further £15,000 two months later. The contract outlined three extra option periods, each yielding an advance of £12,500 on acceptance and the same amount again on delivery of the first album in each period. In all, O'Connor could be asked to produce a possible seven albums in the next four years.

As before, all advances could be fully recouped by Albion before paying out royalties, and all recording costs would also be deducted from advances. This last point actually meant that O'Connor would receive little money to call her own – high recording costs could even leave her in debt. Especially so as the new contract expressly omitted the provision contained in the previous agreement which stated that Albion would be responsible for paying all producers' royalties and advances. Thus, if Tony Visconti again demanded a £25,000 advance guarantee, then this would come from O'Connor's advance. If he demanded a 4 per cent royalty, this would cut O'Connor's earnings from $12\frac{1}{2}$ per cent to $8\frac{1}{2}$ per cent. It was a small omission, easily glossed over. In practice it could mean the difference between O'Connor's profit and loss.

Remarkably, the new publishing agreement decreased O'Connor's earnings. Her split, previously pegged low at 60:40, decreased to 50:50. At this point in her career this figure was now absurdly small: 70:30, the current average for a hit act, would have been far more realistic. Worse, the sub-publishing agreements Albion had fixed up with overseas companies such as Mushroom Music in Australia, Clouseau Music in France and Chappell International for most of the rest of Europe, yielded a total UK income of 80 per cent, the rest remaining with the respective companies. Hence O'Connor only received 40 per cent of her publishing income from abroad.

O'Connor's net income from live performances was also low. Although a major UK tour ran over the 1980–1 Christmas period, playing to 2,000-seat venues and climaxing at a sold-out show at the London Tottenham Court Road Dominion, a nightly average income of £1,500 was more than offset by high wages, heavy hiring fees and other expenses. O'Connor's band, Megahype (a purposely ironic reaction to the music-press criticism that O'Connor's success was due simply to the hype of the film), demanded an off-the-top cut, as did Alan Edwards, as did the VAT man. Albion provided tour support – the odd £3,000 to buy a new synthesizer, and £5,000 to cover the lighting fees – but of course it was all added to O'Connor's slate and deducted from royalties. Album sales benefited indirectly from the tour, but as yet only *Breaking Glass* was available.

The largest non-returnable lump-sum tour income in fact came from the support group, Duran Duran. Still unknown and newly down from their native Birmingham, they had paid a few thousand to 'buy on' to the tour – a regular ploy to play larger venues and reach bigger audiences than they might otherwise at that stage in their career. The last night at the Dominion saw Duran singer Simon Le Bon joining O'Connor for her final encore of Bowie's 'Suffragette City'.

Sons and Lovers, produced as planned by Nigel Gray, was released early in 1981. A single, 'Time', which also appeared on the album and was the first to be released by Albion after her success with A&M, was both a major disappointment for O'Connor and a disaster for the label: it bottomed out at number 150, and received next to no airplay or TV attention, and this despite the fact that it even had a relatively costly accompanying video, O'Connor's first for Albion. O'Connor blamed Nigel Gray's production and the lack of Albion promotion, and she laid heavily into Spartan's distribution service. She moaned too that neither she nor Alan Edwards had been consulted about its release. Albion backed up Spartan and blamed the song.

In February O'Connor put a £2,500 deposit on a new £25,000 flat in Kilburn and arranged for a monthly £294 mortgage repayment. In part the move was in celebration of what she saw as a rare act of creative Albion good sense: they agreed that Visconti should re-produce a single, 'D-Days', that Nigel Gray had previously produced for the album. The single cut needed more urgency. It got it, and began to chart in mid March. Albion were clearly delighted – their first biggie at last. And just as well considering that up to £30,000 of their advances to O'Connor had still not been recouped in royalties.

O'Connor's first cross-coast US tour had been fully scheduled to begin two weeks later. It was the same harshly shaved budget affair that most British bands in Megahype's position have to suffer: the crowded, stinking Spacevan rattling through a thousand highways, each inspiring a progressively jaded version of 'Route 66', in an impossibly scheduled run from half-empty rock club to motel to road to half-empty rock club to motel . . .

The end of March found them in Chicago for one day. According to O'Connor, the phone rang at their motel at five in the morning: Derek Savage calling from the Albion offices: ' "D-Days" is at number ten! "Top of the Pops" wants you on this week – you record tomorrow – get the first plane back – will pay you back at once . . .' O'Connor and Edwards discussed what might happen if they pulled out of the tour now. They figured that even three dates missed would probably mean the US agency and promotion mafia would see they never worked in America again, and there were still three weeks of dates to run.

'Why don't you send a video crew over here to string something together?' said O'Connor.

'Not enough time, too expensive . . .' said Savage.

They argued at length before O'Connor and Edwards hung up, furious. They couldn't rush home. Albion would have to make do as best they could.

In all, the tour was that Great American Adventure the band had read about, but it proved gruelling way beyond their worst fears. O'Connor's ego took another harsh pounding. She could cope with smaller audiences, she told Alan Edwards, 'But where the hell's the support from Albion? Why don't we have enough money? What *are* they doing back there?' Edwards explained he'd tried to get a bigger budget but that this was all they could afford: 'Never forget that they're not a big company.'

'They won't let me forget!' yelped O'Connor.

Things improved slightly in New York. Though *Breaking Glass* had failed to get a major theatre release (a try-out in North Carolina had not augured well), it opened in downtown Manhattan to a small but enthusiastic crowd of rock clones who had already read much about its star in the airmailed British music press. O'Connor herself believed there was even a risk of being mobbed at nightclubs and other artists' concerts, and took delight in the prospect of disguising herself. McCartney had once done it so well that he fooled Brian Epstein, and sure enough she succeeded in conning Alan Edwards.

The money had now become a major problem, and she began missing meals. 'We've been on the breadline for weeks,' she told the New York correspondent of the British *Daily Star*. 'I'm still in debt. Actually everybody thinks I'm rich, but I've made very little money. Though I know I will eventually.'

In New York she received a batch of letters from her fan club in Coventry. 'Let us club together and pay next month's rent,' ran one, collectively signed by the members of the KHHC – the Keep Hazel Happy Club. It came with the news that after two weeks at number ten, and with no live appearance on 'Top of the Pop', 'D-Days' was going down.

O'Connor's previous US trip with Alan Edwards in August 1980 had been a more leisurely, luxurious affair. An executive at Paramount Films had seen a mass of potential in *Breaking Glass* and struck a deal with the two of them: flight to America and $100 a day each for a month in return for the first refusal on any ideas for future films. Peanuts for the film company of course, and a great holiday for

O'Connor and Edwards. The month was spent largely around Pennsylvania in search of the puritanical Amish sect, and their relationship bonded and flourished as it had had little opportunity to do before. They didn't sleep together, but the professional relationship that had been toughened previously by constant talk of career and finances turned into a close, laughing friendship again. Here was a certain ally, she thought. Far more than a manager. Someone on whom she could really depend when the going got rough.

Shortly after the band returned to London, A&M released the fourth single from *Breaking Glass*, 'Will You'. One of the first full-length songs that O'Connor ever wrote, the same song she first performed for Visconti in Clive Parsons's front room, and the track that had since been recorded with a lush and dreamy sax solo from Wesley Magoogan, it peaked at number five in June. It was further proof, thought O'Connor, of the one common denominator in her hits: the Visconti production. The success further strengthened her bullish resolve: she insisted that her next Albion album, *Cover Plus*, would be recorded on her own terms. She had no control over Albion's promotion and distribution, but she did still have a contractual say over the choice of producer. She wanted Visconti again. After all, she argued, it was Visconti who had remixed 'D-Days' and got Albion their biggest hit yet. Dai Davies and Derek Savage again said he'd be great, if only they could afford him. Again Visconti demanded a minimum guarantee of £25,000; he was ever more doubtful of Albion's ability to sell enough records even to reach this break-even point. He understood that the Nigel-Gray-produced *Sons and Lovers* had sold about 60,000; *Cover Plus* would have to sell twice as many before his royalties exceeded his minimum demand (working from the premise that he was to receive a 4 per cent cut off a £4-retail album).

A deal was struck: he received his £25,000, but it would be deducted directly from the royalties due to O'Connor under her publishing agreement. This way Albion couldn't lose, and they'd get the ideal producer. And since the new recording agreement implied that O'Connor would have to pay for producer's royalties anyway, she regarded the minimum payment guarantee as a statement of intent;

the intent was at least to break even with Visconti and sell over 100,000 copies.

Cover Plus came out in July 1981 and sold only about 60,000 again. Rarely questioning her own talent or the quality of the album, O'Connor again cursed the day she signed to Albion: 'They simply can't handle a star!' she told Alan Edwards repeatedly.

She believed that the history of the first single off the album – the title track – proved her point beyond doubt. It rose to number forty-two, and she did 'Top of the Pops'. Or at least she showed up – to be told that there were so many new chart entries that week that they would have no time to broadcast her own three minutes' worth. But would she mind doing a post-production (that is, taping the song now for broadcast when the single went up further next week)?

The post-production was recorded as suggested, but next week the single went down a place and the recording was never shown. A 'lost' appearance on 'Top of the Pops', still the most sales-generating three minutes on TV, O'Connor regarded as unforgivable. That single should never have been allowed to drop: Albion's distribution and promotion, the same old problems, had let her down again, she felt.

A major UK tour was already booked for October–November when the album's second single, 'Hanging Around', was released, and all parties acknowledged the need for a hit to sell the remaining concert tickets and further boost album sales. This too peaked in the high forties when the call from 'Top of the Pops' came through. Again, too many acts necessitated post-production. Again, it seemed only feasible that the single would rise next week. O'Connor, too, believed that Albion must have learned their lesson by now – it was their profit too, after all. But next week the single dropped a place.

The British tour climaxed at the prestigious Hammersmith Odeon, and O'Connor still drew a packed house. Her live audiences had increased considerably since her last dates, and crowds averaged 3,000 nationwide. Her gross per-concert income averaged around £2,000, but heavy debts, expenses and management and agency cut-offs meant that she was still short of money on a day-to-day basis. Her band also frequently found themselves out of pocket. Alan Edwards, too, was increasingly concerned about his own income and its effect on his management firm and on Modern Publicity, his public relations company, and he appealed to Albion for more financial support. He was told that Albion was doing all it could; it was already running flat out on the O'Connor budget. In all, the British tour lost (and hence would cost O'Connor) in the region of £20,000. Some of the loss, albeit not an amount of that magnitude, was at least half anticipated by both Edwards and O'Connor, and there had been direct contingency plans. Edwards had arranged a set of Fleet Street interviews to promote the tour, with the *News of the World* offering special terms: they'd pay £15,000 for some juiced up kiss-and-tell. In short, they wanted the details of her entanglements with Hugh Cornwell, Jon Finch and Midge Ure, her thoughts on sleeping around, her views on drugs, that sort of thing. Eager for the cash and publicity, and aware that her gingerly exaggerated autobiography, *Uncovered Plus*, would appear anyway before the end of the year, O'Connor agreed. (The book was in fact ghosted by an old friend, Judith Simons, who had written about her for the last two years in the *Daily Express*.) The problem was that O'Connor was unaware of the exclusivity of her *News of the World* contract, and told most of the same yarns to any other interested papers too. Whereupon the *News of the World* duly cancelled and refused to pay.

As the band prepared for dates in Ireland, Germany and then France, O'Connor learnt of Albion's intentions to take up their first option and extend the recording contract until at least September 1982. Both good and bad news, this; it did mean another year and possibly two albums with Albion, but it also meant the prospect of an immediate advance of £12,500, needed now more than ever. But by the time she played Germany some weeks later, again to packed houses, the money had still not been paid.

Albion had retained the £12,500 advance against the sums still owing from unrecouped previous advances, and this despite the fact that, in O'Connor's estimation, they had been expressly prohibited from this 'cross-collateralizing' by a clause in the renegotiated recording contract.

Albion wrote to Alan Edwards requesting an acknowledgement of their accepted option and the receipt of the £12,500, making no specific reference to the cross-collateralization of the advances. Edwards acknowledged both points on behalf of O'Connor – that is, he acknowledged the receipt of the 'advance' even though it was a payment that merely went to lessen O'Connor's debt.

Matters came to a head in France, *en route* to a large rock festival at which O'Connor had top billing. A break in the journey allowed for a snack in a local café. Out of money themselves, the band asked their road manager for their daily allowances. The road manager explained that he hadn't received enough from Alan Edwards. Edwards's defence was that he had received insufficient funds for the trip from Albion. The band turned on O'Connor. She hadn't talked to them for the last few days of the tour, and even her brother, Neil, now a permanent member, hadn't been able to communicate with her. The band approached her *en masse*: 'Where's the fucking money, Hazel? How come there's never any fucking money?'

In the next couple of weeks, at the very end of 1981 and during what appeared to be her first real break from work in two years, O'Connor met Alan Edwards several times. Typically these days, the talk focused on money. There was cash due, he explained, principally publishing royalties, but it was likely to be directly recouped by Albion in return for previous advances, tour loans and other expenses. Edwards estimated that the amount Hazel O'Connor Limited still owed Albion and others was now alarmingly high, not to mention the amount soon to be due in tax payments. A total figure of £30,000 would have been conservative. On top of that, Edwards's income from his Modern Publicity firm was insufficient to clear his personal debt – he still owed his landlord many weeks' back rent. He explained that the offer of the lead in a kids TV series, 'Jangles', would bring her in a few thousand, but that the lengthy filming in Bristol would create further pressure on the honouring of her recently optioned recording commitments. He also acknowledged Albion's desire to disband her group on the grounds of insufficient cash; the French concert had been their last. Worst of all, there was no clear way forward. They had already signed a renegotiated settlement. They could attempt a further renegotiation, but they couldn't simply break the existing contract at will, no matter how badly things were going.

O'Connor then put her case; she wanted out. She had had enough of Albion, of the pressures, the recent lack of success, the continued lack of money, the escalating debt. She was geared up for a fight in the courts, and she was convinced she had a strong case: she was sure that no court would sympathize with a company that made an artist sign under duress, as she believed they had; convinced that much money that was owing – like that £12,500 advance – would never be paid unless she fought; convinced that Albion were nose-diving her career. The course was clear, she felt; she would leave Albion, fight if necessary, and win through eventually.

Edwards thought otherwise; by careful negotiation they could possibly either get her more money or get her off the label. He had already had talks with Cliff Busby, the head of EMI Records, about the possibility of buying her out from Albion. A figure of £250,000 had been mentioned, and surely this would be sufficient to tempt Albion to part with any hit act, especially as the company's relationship with O'Connor – never good at the best of times – had progressively soured over the last year.

O'Connor, however, doubted Edwards's ability to pull off the EMI deal. Things had already gone on too long, and she reckoned that if she really was worth £250,000 to any company, then she really had talent worth fighting for. Above all, she recognized that Edwards was not the fighter she felt she now needed – too good-natured, she reckoned, too faithful to his old friends at Albion, hardly a high-powered troubleshooter.

She turned for independent advice to Midge Ure, the successful singer with Ultravox and an old friend who had been through similarly tough industry experiences in his early days. He further boosted her resolve, and O'Connor thought increasingly of the option of fighting Albion without Edwards.

And in her eyes things then went from bad to worse. By chance she was told that without either her knowledge or permission Edwards had authorized the use of her *Hanging Around* promo film in a pornographic *Electric Blue* video. The *Electric Blue* manufacturers had requested its use, in return for a nominal payment of £500, to act as the 'now' half of a 'then and now' feature they were planning on O'Connor. They had already bought the rights to the X-rated erotic comedy *Girls Come First* that she had made under the name of Charlotte Hayes in 1972, and which incorporated nude modelling and a simulated foreplay scene in a bath. Understandably it was a departure that O'Connor wished forgotten.

That Albion should approve the use of the clip in a package that she felt could conceivably only damage her career, she considered to be typical of their lack of concern for her future and proof of the breakdown in their relationship. (Dai Davies defended his action with the claim that he believed the new clip would be used anyway; the inclusion of the music video might help to present a fairer picture, he felt.)

That her manager should also approve its use (a fact that he disputed), O'Connor found both astonishing and unforgivable. She found it hard to believe that this was the man with whom she had once toured America for a month in the same hired car. Besides, O'Connor herself received only half of the £500 fee: the rest was retained by Albion.

Information from her accountant, Peter Lawrence of Lawrence Grant, alerted her to the fact that while Edwards's claim for management commission for the period 1 August 1979 to 30 June 1981 came to £23,500, her own net income was not expected to exceed £7,500.

Peter Lawrence wasn't slow in pointing out similar discrepancies and numerous accounting errors or oversights. All pointed to total mismanagement, she believed, and all swiftly severed what remained of her clinging emotional ties. In mid January 1982 she phoned Edwards to inform him he was no longer her manager. Her reasons centred not primarily on finances or the *Electric Blue* incident, but on his unwillingness to take on Albion. '*Everything* has gone wrong,' she told Midge Ure the following week, again close to tears. 'Alan was naïve about management and he won't fight. He means well, but he just doesn't have the power. It looks like I'm going to have to take them all on at once.'

The next week she informed Albion and other business concerns that as from 1 February she was no longer to be considered under Edwards's management, and instructed all payments and correspondence to be sent to her direct, care of Peter Lawrence's accountancy firm.

The same period saw O'Connor receive a large pile of outstanding debts from Edwards's office, including a damages claim from a truck accident in Germany, hire fees for the use of lighting rigs and public address systems, and wage bills for the last tour – some £30,000 in all. She called Peter Lawrence to check on the Hazel O'Connor Limited bank balance: only £700 in the black.

Tearful and uncertain at what was to come, but sure that whatever did come would only result from months of cool-headed aggression, she told Peter Lawrence she needed time to draw up a plan of attack. She would be back in two weeks, she said, and the campaign would begin. Until then she'd ignore the £30,000 debts and blow all but £20 of her remaining earnings on a trip to Morocco.

Away from it all, certainly, but not the sort of place in which O'Connor found it easy to relax. Two points occupied her thoughts almost exclusively: one, she *was* doing the right thing – the only way ever to push on again; and two, if she was to battle on without (and against) Edwards, then she needed a new, high-powered, partisan business adviser. She'd learned with Edwards that while trust, loyalty and friendliness were attributes that made a manager easy to deal with, it was really only half the requirement. The other half demanded a level of hard industry realism and experience that Edwards lacked, and O'Connor only knew one person who might prove suitable.

She approached Laurence Myers on her return. The ex-Rolling Stones accountant who had moved into business management, TV record promotion and movie distribution with his own company, GTO Films, Myers was the man who met O'Connor on the set of *Breaking Glass* and struck up that instant mutual admiration and rapport. Still a definite biz dandy in his mid forties, with backswept, light brown thinning hair, weeping moustache and heavy cheeks that gave his face a somewhat owl-like appearance, he dressed his avocado-shaped body in a mixture of fashionable silks and cotton, and presented a grand caricature of an ageing, plumping rock fan – every inch seemingly cuddly, lovable and harmless.

In fact, he had won a reputation as an industry hard man, and a succession of successful litigations and prime deals for the likes of the Stones, The Animals, David Bowie, Gary Glitter, Mott the Hoople, The New Seekers, Iggy Pop and many others had set him up in many eyes as the British answer to Allen Klein. Myers and Klein had indeed done business together and had become good friends. Like Klein, Myers was keen on telling his artists that 'The great thing about being a professional gunfighter is that you never actually have to draw your gun.' Things didn't always work out that way, he explained, but it was worth a shot: 'In my first negotiations I used to grunt a lot – people said, "What do you think of 12 per cent?" and I'd go, "Grunt", and they'd go, "All right then, 13 per cent." '

O'Connor approached him first for personal management, to be told that he considered himself 'too old to deal with phone calls at four in the morning from artists saying, "I'm in Huddersfield and my van's broken down."' 'But you have to help me,' pleaded O'Connor. 'It's just not Alan Edwards's forte to be a fighter. He's a real sweetie and you really have to fight. These people need to be really beaten up in the courts for what they do.'

He offered to become her business manager and to find her another personal manager in due course. But he warned that battling against Albion could take years, exactly how long depending on the company's obstinacy and the strength of their case – another favoured Myers' phrase was that, 'There's always three sides – his, hers and the truth.' If she really was committed to a fight to the death, then she had also better get some heavy-duty industry solicitors, he suggested. Her personal lawyer, Iain Adam, was by now out of the frame. The highly regarded firm, Clintons, with whom O'Connor had become familiar since the commencement of Alan Edwards's management and who were now advising Edwards, could clearly be used no longer. Instead, Myers suggested he introduce her to Russells. It was hoped that legal aid would cover the costs of any litigation.

Although by March 1982 O'Connor's relationship with Dai Davies and Derek Savage had already deteriorated to a point where, in practical terms, neither party found that they could work together creatively any longer, Russells' first work for O'Connor centred not on Albion but on Alan Edwards. She was indignant that despite what she regarded as a termination of his contract two months earlier, he continued to approach Albion and her live booking agencies in the capacity of her manager. Towards the end of March, Russells wrote to cancel his engagement formally and advised him that he should never contact O'Connor directly again. The six-page letter, every paragraph a damning attack on his management and accounting abilities, shocked Edwards rigid.

In what was claimed to be merely a few examples of a 'non-exhaustive list' of Edwards's misconduct, the majority arising not from the evidence of her accountant, Peter Lawrence, but from O'Connor's own recollections and records, Russells stated that

Edwards seemed not to have O'Connor's best interests at heart, that bookkeeping had too often been quite inadequate, and that surely something was wrong with figures that suggested that at a time when O'Connor netted £7,500, Edwards had claimed a cut of £23,500. The letter closed with the reiteration that O'Connor was now a free agent no longer bound by the terms of their old management contract.

Edwards presented the indictment to his solicitors, Clintons, with disbelief, and far from simply denying the many complaints, went on fierce counter-attack himself. The two-way legal flak, increasingly bellicose with each letter, culminated in a writ issued by Clintons in June 1982.

It detailed Edwards's version of the events and requested a swift resolving of two central claims: an injunction specifying that Edwards was still bound to receive all fees and commission as detailed in the original management agreement; and an order that payment of the £20,947 – the amount of commission already owing – be paid at once.

But after this, a strange silence. Edwards prepared an affidavit, but O'Connor was put under no immediate pressure to issue her defence – indeed Clintons agreed to give O'Connor fourteen days' notice to deliver it. But no date was set for a court judgment, and the outcome thus remained open ended. No way of telling how long it would remain so, either.

Which didn't do much for O'Connor's security but did something to lessen Russells' immediate workload. For Dai Davies and Derek Savage had to be dealt with too, and the record company dispute was rapidly taking centre stage. The Albion conflict was in fact far more important: the long-term significance for both parties looked that much greater, the cash involved was that much fatter, and the eventual settlement was likely to be much more complex. Also, Laurence Myers was far more worried about the outcome, and that counted for a lot.

But that wasn't all. The disputes just kept on coming: Wesley Magoogan, O'Connor's sax player, had been talking to his CBS publishing wing, April Music, and through them had decided to stake a claim in all royalties resulting from 'Will You', the hit he claimed he co-wrote. A sizeable claim which O'Connor and Russells refuted from the outset. Magoogan refuted their refutation, and the case refused to go away. The harsh irony was that April Music was headed by James Ware, O'Connor's first solicitor.

The first exchange of those lengthy O'Connor/Edwards accusations and counter-accusations back in March contained a series of figures that made O'Connor increasingly suspicious of the way she had been handled by Albion. How could a gross credit of £140,000 from Albion Records and Albion Music (including her cut from *Breaking Glass*) in the August 1979 to June 1981 period have resulted in a *net* income of only £6,500 and a current Hazel O'Connor Ltd bank credit of only £700? The simplest answer was that her total expenditure on recording and touring (including all the Albion clawbacks for packaging, promotion and production) had almost totally cancelled out her income. (It was there, but only on paper, because although Albion credited £140,000 to O'Connor's account, little of this was ever seen by her bank. Rather, all third-party costs – recording studios, tour transport and the rest – were paid for by Albion and then summarily deducted from the recording and publishing royalties they owed O'Connor in each accounting period.)

Even with this reasoning, O'Connor suspected foul play and inaccurate accounting on Albion's part. 'There's just got to be *loads* more than that,' she cried at her Russells solicitor Brian Howard. For a start, there was the £12,500 she considered due the day Albion picked up their first one-year option last September; she professed to have no knowledge of any modifying arrangements under which the advance could be justly held back. In mid April she telexed Albion personally asking for the payment, and a few weeks earlier Russells had expressed their own complaints to David Gentle of Albion's solicitors Gentle Mathias, concluding with a demand for a royalty audit.

> I'd join the dole if I could [O'Connor was quoted as saying in the *Daily Mirror* in March]. I can't even afford the fare to Ireland for my cousin's wedding next week. Don't ask me where it's gone. Did I buy the big house, the flash car, the expensive clothes? No. All I wanted was a band, and now that's gone too. I loved that band. All the money I made from *Breaking Glass* went into paying their wages. Big Mamma Haze – that was me. Too modest. Too easy and too eager to please. I was famous. A star. And the record company had me travelling round the country on a second-class train ticket with people staring and shouting, 'Sign here Haze!' What a bloody joke.

The new firm of accountants appointed for the royalty audit on O'Connor's behalf sifted through the Albion accounts and found that under the recording agreement alone O'Connor was due around £108,000. They admitted that £55,000 of this could be accounted for by inadequate documentation on Albion's part, and would indeed be found not to be due if this documentation came to light. The remaining £53,000 centred primarily on the £25,000 that had been guaranteed from O'Connor's royalties to Tony Visconti and the £12,500 option advance that was currently proving such a tough bone of contention.

Albion appointed different accountants for the same job. They found they owed O'Connor only £44. The fever of mistrust (and what both sides considered to be plain deceit) continued through most of April and early May 1982. The period also saw O'Connor and Edwards – although still at fierce loggerheads – both trying to engineer another buy-out deal, this time with WEA Records, another giant US-owned multinational that had expressed keen interest in the songs she had composed for 'Jangles'. Again the talks broke down. O'Connor and Edwards blamed Albion's selfish obstinacy and greed; Dai Davies and Derek Savage blamed inadequate remuneration.

On 7 May the Albion directors received the letter that both parties must have regarded as inevitable for some while. O'Connor, acting through Russells, terminated her Albion recording contract. She had not been paid her £12,500 advance, due eight months ago, and she now interpreted it as her company's intention no longer to be bound by their agreement. She, of course, had accepted their intention (with glee).

Davies and Savage, increasingly distraught at how much time O'Connor was consuming each week, of course saw things rather differently, and in the two weeks that followed spent many hours talking with Gentle Mathias. The case might well now take up all their time for months, they understood, but they were determined not to lose O'Connor at her whim – especially over a technical point they argued they were fully justified in making anyway. Their remedy seemed to be to seek an immediate court injunction preventing O'Connor from signing a recording deal with another company.

It was a contingency measure: they may have hoped to retain O'Connor as a recording artist for years to come – to bind her to Albion by their annual acceptance of their option – but if she won't record, she won't record. Hence it was likely that even if Albion won the court injunction, another, much lengthier, trial would be necessary to rule on the validity of their respective cases, decide on damages and costs, and settle their differences once and for all. That might take years, of course. Even the outcome of the injunction proceedings would take a good few months.

An *interim* injunction was granted swiftly at the end of May, Albion successfully preventing O'Connor from entering into any other agreements until a full hearing could consider both sides of the dispute in detail.

A judge's order of 12 July set the full day's hearing of the interlocutory injunction in early August, but also made a significant amendment to the interim injunction as it stood: the new Order permitted O'Connor to make new master recordings with whomever she wished, provided they weren't delivered to a new company before the outcome of the full hearing of the injunction request became known. In other words, any company could now offer her an immediate deal and even begin work with her, but it would all be undone if the final judgment ruled that Albion had a stronger case and should thereby retain her exclusive services. And with the outcome still so uncertain, no record company considered the risk worth taking.

The four weeks preceding the August hearing was finger-chewing and ulcer time, with both sides gathering evidence furiously. Twenty-three affidavits in all, in fact, twelve for Albion, eleven for O'Connor and a bundle of documentary evidence almost a foot high, all finally brought before Mr Justice Beldan on one of the hottest days of the year. The real guts of the battle came, as expected, from three affidavits from Derek Savage, one from Dai Davies, and two from O'Connor, each amplifying their case as before and refuting each other's allegations in turn. But along with the bulk of the remaining oaths, which included those of accountants, agents, promoters, and Alan Edwards, the strongest new line of attack centred on O'Connor's ability to survive and prosper while still tied to Albion, and Albion's ability to flourish without its most successful act.

Dai Davies's statement led with the claim that Albion and he in particular had done far more to land O'Connor the role in *Breaking Glass* – and thus launch her career – than she herself might suggest. Without Albion's organization of those trial pub gigs for the film executives, for instance, he doubted whether she would have got the lead role. He reasoned that this boost in itself should be sufficient to prevent her just upping and offing now.

And Albion's other arguments for a preservation of the status quo held several further trumps. Derek Savage reasoned that with almost all his company's major foreign deals, licensees had made specific reference to the inclusion of their Hazel O'Connor catalogue and he provided evidence to show that certain contracts would only be renewed if this remained so. Without her, he argued, they'd be sunk. He stressed also that O'Connor's recent television work, incorporating 'Jangles' and frequent appearances as a guest critic on 'Granada Reports', had shown her well able to make a good living outside of her recording work, and therefore she wouldn't be much affected if she was unable to record with another company for the time being.

Alan Edwards, siding firmly against his former client, weighed in on similar lines. 'My own involvement with Hazel as her manager deteriorated at the beginning of 1982, principally because of her concern to develop in areas other than music,' he swore. He also outlined several TV appearances she had recently turned down, including the prestigious Saturday morning kids' show, 'TizWas'; more proof, he argued, that she could survive merrily without a new record deal. Pace Posters, and the merchandising firm Concessions, both provided her with substantial royalties, he argued, and live work too would continue to provide a large source of income.

Concert promoter Nick Leigh repeated the claim that she'd earn at least £1,500 per night for live work, as did Richard Hermitage, general manager of O'Connor's agency, International Talent Booking. Leigh now worked for the Derek Block Organization. Previously he'd been a director of the Albion Agency. David Thomas, director of Spartan Entertainments, Albion's independent record distributors, took a more defensive line in his consideration of what might happen to Albion if the injunction was lifted:

> In the event it became known in the music industry that Hazel O'Connor were able to walk away from her contractual commitment, serious and unquantifiable damage would be suffered by Albion . . . In the future one cannot estimate what would be lost by way of Albion's inability to sign new artists . . .'

Thomas went on specifically to praise Albion's past treatment of O'Connor:

> . . . (a new) company would not be able to provide a similar degree of personal attention which I know Albion Records

supplied ... major record companies tend to produce and promote artists in a slightly stereotyped and bland manner rather than carefully nurture and develop artists as Albion have done ...

He parted with a shot that presented as strong a case for the retention of O'Connor for the well-being of his own company as it did for Albion: If she was allowed to desert, then, '... the ability of my company to promote other artists of Albion Records would be prejudiced. On approaching record shops, it is obviously an advantage for salesmen to sell records of lesser known artists at the same time as the more famous ...'

The O'Connor battery pounded with equal conviction. Personally, she swore that she would not be able to support herself unless she made further records, provided of course they weren't for Albion. The debts of Hazel O'Connor Ltd, the company she formed on the advice of her accountant to reap the benefit of VAT, now stood at £20,000 – and she made it clear that she saw her departure from Albion as the only way of avoiding bankruptcy. 'I fear I am on the brink of obscurity,' she pleaded.

But debts of an even greater magnitude – £63,270 – were, she revealed, visible on Albion Records' balance sheets as at 30 June 1980. She claimed that more recent documents had not been forthcoming despite frequent requests by Russells, and that she doubted whether Albion's position had materially altered since. Not a company in healthy financial repair, she suggested, reasoning that they might not even be able to afford to retain her and pay her damages, if that in fact turned out to be the court's judgment.

Her accountant Peter Lawrence of course echoed her sentiments fully, but calculated the debts of Hazel O'Connor Ltd to stand at £11,000 excluding the £20,000 claimed by Edwards for unpaid commission. He also revealed that as at the end of March 1982 O'Connor's royalty earnings had still not paid off £5,316 of her advances from Albion, and explained that she had never received actual royalty payments from Albion, only advances, and these advances were mostly used by Alan Edwards to pay off expenses. He concluded that if the interim injunction was upheld and extended, Hazel O'Connor Ltd would be forced into liquidation and O'Connor herself would face bankruptcy. The only way out? Make a new recording agreement with another company ...

Next up was Sharon Hamper, another of O'Connor's agents, who swore a different agent's tale from those heard previously: in her opinion O'Connor could not survive without continued and successful recording work. That was the only way she could guarantee future engagements of a *non*-recording nature.

In an attempt to discredit Albion further, Russells even brought in a summary of a telephone conversation that one of their articled clerks had had with *Breaking Glass* director Brian Gibson two weeks earlier, describing his first meeting with Dai Davies (whom he regarded as O'Connor's manager) and his first acquaintance with O'Connor: 'Nothing (Davies) said or did at this meeting or subsequently influenced my choice in casting Hazel. I am normally polite to managers. However, I normally ignore the things they say.'

In his judgment, Mr Justice Beldan's first observation concerned what he considered to be a quite inconsiderate mass of superfluous evidence: 'If every such application were to be pursued in this fashion, the ability of the courts to provide this most necessary remedy would be gravely impaired.' Further, he expressed distaste at the prevalence of 'lunge, parry, thrust and riposte of almost every conceivable aspect of the dealings . . .'

The bare facts of the case he found altogether less astonishing, and considered it favourable to maintain the status quo. No, O'Connor could not sign with another company, and yes, her loss would be too great an infliction to impose on Albion, especially as he considered it unfair to release her at a time when she still owed unrecouped advances. On O'Connor's side he acknowledged that her ties to a company in which she had lost all confidence and which held considerable control over her income was 'a serious matter' which should be reviewed speedily at full trial. He considered the existing affidavits ably suited to serve as pleadings and saw that, 'It is in the interest of both parties that this trial should take place as soon as possible.'

In fact it was in the interest of both parties that there should never be a trial at all. Far better a negotiated settlement favoured by both sides, far better that both sides' dirty laundry wasn't washed in public. The costs, too, were another heavy minus – Russells estimated the shock to the loser to be at least £25,000, and that didn't even account for damages.

The main problem, of course, was that the loser was by no means a foregone conclusion. From O'Connor's angle, she could win her claim that she was still owed an advance of £12,500 for that first option, but lose out on the big one – her struggle to get off Albion Records. For even if the trial judge ruled against granting the final injunction (an injunction which at this stage would mean that O'Connor would either have to resign herself to Albion or give up recording altogether), a court ruling only partially in Albion's favour could mean that no other record company would dare offer her a new contract for fear of being sued for interference with her obligations to Albion.

Russells sought Counsel's advice in September, and its verdict on O'Connor's chances of ultimate success was far from rosy. Her best chance would be over the £12,500 advance. If she won that, and it could be shown that Albion's refusal to pay it constituted a breach of their agreement, then that would be the end of it – O'Connor would be free. (Then again, if Albion convinced the court that their withholding of the £12,500 was only proper and as agreed, they could argue that O'Connor's refusal to record the required album would constitute a breach on her part, and thus merit the injunction.)

On three other points, Counsel was less confident. The question of Albion's poor accounting was particularly weak and hardly substantiated in their audit report. The matter of Albion failing in its contractual duties to O'Connor (excepting the £12,500 affair) was of course hotly disputed by Albion, and anyway would probably be insufficient to repudiate the contract by itself.

There was also the question of who was responsible for the payment of the producer's royalty and whether O'Connor herself should really be made to foot the bill, but this too looked shaky for the singer, not least because Russells had yet to contend with the evidence of John Cohen at Clintons, the man who had advised her at the time of signing the contract and therefore knew what both parties intended. At that time, of course, O'Connor was close to Alan Edwards' solicitors – the firm now committed to showing Edwards in the best possible light against his former client.

Whatever O'Connor's chances of success, it was clear that even up to mid November Russells were gearing up for the eventuality of another court battle. Accordingly, O'Connor's legal aid had to be extended to cover possible costs (the current position was that it would cover 85 per cent of all of Russells' and the court's fees, the remainder being made up by O'Connor herself), and Mark Cran, a barrister with considerable experience of the music industry, thus prepared an opinion for the Law Society as to the validity of fighting the case and the chances of victory. He regarded O'Connor's prospects of partial success as 'very high' and those of total success as 'fair'. On 16 November, presumably in a bid to keep all options open, he wrote that, 'It is of very great importance to the defendant if her career is not to die, that the contractual position with Albion is determined by the court.'

But on 3 December 1982 the entire feud was over. A deed of settlement was drawn up by both parties, and on the surface it looked as if neither party had lost out. There were no real winners either, but at least it detailed a brighter future for O'Connor and some financial remuneration for her record company. It meant both parties could again revert to the artistic pursuits at which each had once flourished.

The deed of settlement outlined the following:

1 Each party was now freed of all chains and claims of the other. In other words, O'Connor could now sign a new recording agreement with whom she wished and Albion lost their prime possession.

2 Albion however recorded a considerable financial victory:

(a) for the next six albums made by O'Connor, her former company were contracted to receive a 3 per cent royalty override of the retail price of all UK sales. This dropped to 2 per cent once UK sales exceeded £100,000 and for all non-UK sales. Alternatively, they could receive one-third of total royalties received by O'Connor, whichever was the lesser.

(b) Albion were also now entitled to a cut of $22\frac{1}{2}$ per cent of all O'Connor's future advances, also on her next six albums. This would serve as an advance against all the royalties due from O'Connor.

(c) There were provisions too to ensure that Albion received a copy of all future O'Connor contracts before they were signed, and that any new record company would account directly to Albion.

3 The above applied to the next six albums with one condition, namely that O'Connor's new company would provide Albion with the masters of her first new-label album in order that Albion could fulfil their prearranged licensing deals and license the album to Germany, Austria and Switzerland. This would apply for one album only and only to those countries named (but it was a significant concession as O'Connor was still most popular in those markets).

4 Hazel O'Connor Ltd would receive a cheque for £2,384, this being the agreed amount found owing after O'Connor's demand for a full audit in April – £1,490 of this being underpaid royalties. This was deemed to have been credited as at 30 June 1982 in order to leave O'Connor's company in credit with Albion at that date to the tune of £361.

5 Hazel O'Connor Ltd was ordered to pay Albion £10,000 costs in this action, less the sum of £361 above.

Although he had helped to construct it, Laurence Myers saw the settlement as a messy, demeaning document, far from favourable to his client and friend. With the problems regarding Alan Edwards's court action, and the dispute with saxophonist Wesley Magoogan over the writers' credits and royalties of 'Will You' as yet unsettled, he feared it wouldn't be the last. But the next battle was clear enough: get her a new record company and get her working again, a matter he was relieved was now no longer his principal responsibility.

Three months earlier she had taken on a new personal manager, Alan Seifert, to pick up where, pre-litigation, Alan Edwards had left off, so let *him* do it, thought Myers. Myers was only on a commission of 5 per cent, and his central job – to get O'Connor off Albion with the assistance of Russells – was now over; Seifert was just beginning with her and he wanted at least a five-year deal at a rate of 15 per cent . . .

Highest on the list of Alan Seifert's selling points was that, as a man in his early forties who had been employed in the music industry for the last sixteen years, he had about eight times the experience of Alan Edwards. He had worked first in contract liaison at EMI in the late sixties, a job which also entailed close contact with Brian Epstein and The Beatles. He moved on to CBS Television and later to Warner Brothers, negotiating contracts with US lawyers. Disenchantment, not least with the fact that he was doing his end of things for a flat monthly salary while the US lawyers he was dealing with were earning a huge percentage commission, led to the formation of his own management consultancy and soon to personal management. His clients have almost all been women: Elkie Brooks, Elaine Paige, Marianne Faithfull, Toyah Wilcox and now Hazel O'Connor.

All I can offer you I think is honesty [he told her at an early meeting in his cramped Chelsea studio-office]. If it's not going to work, I'll tell you. I can pick up a phone and get through to people, but I can't ever guarantee you a record deal. I'm always a very bad negotiator of deals. I can offer you expert guidance in avoiding the pitfalls. I know when a thing is wrong, but I'm not creative – I wouldn't sit down with you and tell you how to perform or how to write music. But I'd have to be your manager for about six months before we'd really know if it was working.

Though in appearance quite the opposite of Laurence Myers (Seifert was tall, angular and bony, and had a full head of curly dark hair that made him look not unlike a swarthy old-style Hollywood film star in swashbuckling mode), the two managers did share an admiration for O'Connor's talents, and that, thought Myers, was the best starting point of all.

Seifert's contract, only finalized in April 1983 after nine months of stop-start negotiations, detailed that he'd provide O'Connor with day-to-day management but leave further troubleshooting, should there be any, to Myers. Generally speaking, it was a fairly standard affair: the term was agreed at five years, and he was to receive 15 per cent on all O'Connor's earnings, including royalties earned on all records before his term except *Breaking Glass*. It was also established that certain commissions, such as those from live performances, would only be paid if based on a net profit rather than a gross income – thereby eradicating the possibility of Seifert receiving more than his client.

Although nothing had been heard of the Alan Edwards affair for several months (and it now appeared that nothing more would be heard again), O'Connor's new management contract expressly refused to provide any warranty that she was currently free to enter into new agreements with Seifert or Myers. In practice this could mean two things: if Edwards reappeared to press his claim, Seifert might suffer a loss of commission (possibly 5 per cent) for a limited period; and that if Myers or Seifert lost out as a result of an Edwards claim, they couldn't then turn on O'Connor and insist that she make it up. Both considered it a risk worth taking.

Seifert urgently needed to seal a new record deal to make that risk worthwhile, and it's likely that even he underestimated the problems involved. Not only was he unable to offer Germany, Austria and Switzerland as part of the package on the first album, but he was faced with the difficulty of handling an artist who was now considered to be distinctly less than a hot property. Fans could be awfully fickle, Seifert realized, and O'Connor was no evergreen superstar. Besides, the dragging litigation may well have carried a creative price too; she may have lost that competitive spark that had initially fired her early success. Also, it would have to be a substantial deal to make it worth O'Connor's while: she was already committed to paying a considerable amount of advances and royalties to Albion, and now another 20 per cent of total income to her management. On top of it all, she still had large debts.

In April 1983, four months after the settlement, Russells had again disputed Albion's underpayment of royalties, and this time with some success. But O'Connor used the large majority of the resultant recording cheque of £16,696 and the publishing cheque for £5,586, to pay off fees and yellowing bills – in fact the new cash couldn't be deposited by Peter Lawrence quickly enough. The Albion publishing cheque was still light to the tune of £785, an amount withheld along with many hundreds of pounds from other sources by the Performing Right Society, as a result of the prolonged dispute over 'Will You'. The sax solo had by now also been lifted from the single as a theme song for the television programme 'Ennals Point', and Wesley Magoogan was still claiming a share of the single's royalties and the full amount of the 'Ennals Point' earnings. His case was being argued not only by James Ware of April Music but also now by Alan Edwards, who claimed a cut through Magoogan's association with his own company Mainly Modern Music.

Up until April 1983 there were still no court proceedings and still only four parties involved – O'Connor, Magoogan, April Music and Mainly Modern Music. But with the arrival of that underpaid royalty cheque from Albion's solicitor David Gentle, came the news that there was to be a fifth: Albion Music was joining the fray and would soon issue a claim against all four. The dispute had frozen Albion's cut of the royalty, argued Davies and Savage, and it was their copyright ever since O'Connor signed her publishing deal in March 1979.

Claim was followed by defence and counter-claim, with the four defendants claiming and counter-claiming against themselves as well as Albion. From the outset it looked to be a battle that might last years. Albion were also pressing for damages against O'Connor, and Russells doubted whether either their fees or a possible court showdown would be covered by legal aid now that her main tussle with Albion had been resolved and her finances had gradually improved. All the more important, therefore, to conclude a new record deal as swiftly as possible.

Early interest from Richard Branson's Virgin Records tailed off because of the loss of the German market, and several other companies, including RCA, expressed doubts over her ability to come back charting as before. But towards the end of 1983, RCA managing director David Betteridge heard a rough tape O'Connor had recorded with voguish producer Martin Rushent and interest revived. If that partnership worked, Betteridge reckoned, they could have an unexpected monster on their hands, and the contract was drawn up accordingly. Signed at the end of November, it was to cover a minimum of one year and one album, after which RCA had the option of asking for two more albums each year for two years, followed by one album in the final year (a possible six albums in four years). O'Connor bagged a £20,000 first-year advance on signature and a further £65,000 on delivery of the album, minus that album's recording costs. UK album and single royalties were set high at 15 per cent and 14 per cent, and that was even on 100 per cent of sales, not on 90 per cent as with Albion. Royalties for sales in the rest of the world decreased by 1 per cent, which was also generous, and agreed presumably with the knowledge that a sizeable cut would go automatically to Albion.

Happy faces all round. O'Connor's royalties did, however, include Martin Rushent's producer's cut of 4 per cent – understandably high for a man who had built his own thriving recording studios, Genetic Sound, in Berkshire, on the back of a string of hits with The Buzzcocks, The Stranglers and The Human League.

The resulting album, *Smile*, produced also in part by O'Connor's brother Neil, who was now working at Genetic full time, appeared in October 1984. And did very little. It was treated as low priority by RCA and received little push. David Betteridge, who had by now left to form his own company, was known to be less than thrilled with the result: they were very average, synthesizer-based mixed-tempo pop songs and it was far from the remarkable album he had hoped for. This would all have been instantly forgivable if it had sold, but it stiffed. RCA declined to take up their next option and cancelled their contract, leaving O'Connor not only without a deal, but now more than three years on from her last success and saddled with the knowledge that she'd already had a shot at the chart comeback and failed. Recording costs and other rake-offs had taken their toll, and she emerged only with around £2,000. Once again, she began to rethink her choice of manager.

A sold-out two-week run at Ronnie Scott's jazz club in Soho and some successful shows abroad early in 1985 suggested continued live popularity, and irregular television appearances in drama serials and light entertainment shows also boosted her small income. But by mid February she had informed Alan Seifert that their partnership was over: 'I felt that we were just no longer seeing eye to eye any more, and I felt that he was getting a bit tired,' she said at the time.

The next few months were split between further TV shows and the hunt for a replacement for Seifert. She had talks with John Hade, the Thompson Twins manager, and with John Reid, the manager of Elton John and Billy Connolly, but both came to little.

The 'Will You'/Wesley Magoogan affair had dragged on through 1984 and was still unresolved.

In April 1985, O'Connor learned that Derek Savage had recently· taken up a new job in Wigmore Street, the same address, in fact, where Alan Edwards worked. In August she read that they had formed a new publishing company together.

In May she wrote and recorded 'Push and Shove', a benefit single for Greenpeace, which she recognized wouldn't make her any money but hoped would at least land her a sizeable hit – she could then at least negotiate a new long-term deal from a position of strength. She hoped for a top forty entry in the first week, and was crushed to learn that it peaked at number 186.

Even in early 1985, more than three years after her last chart success, Hazel O'Connor had her hair done free by Trevor Sorbie, a leading London stylist. After many flirtations with various shapes and punk dyes, it was now full blonde again, and long, curly and ribboned over a smooth-skinned, but always drawn face that's ever pushing back the makings of a double chin. Her clothes and image are both slightly affected baby-chic, with those red ribbons and adult-sized romper suit making her look not unlike a savagely well-developed 3-year-old.

She's sitting in Manna, a heady and cramped vegetarian restaurant in London's Primrose Hill, right opposite old friend Kit Hain, once of the pop duo Marshall-Hain, and someone who, like O'Connor, has seen little success in recent years. The talk runs to future plans: Hain is off to America in ten days to live with her producer/boyfriend, and hopefully to find that winning formula again. She too has gone through a whole batch of managers, even Alan Seifert was a candidate at one point, she says.

O'Connor talks of her hopes for future management and record company deals too, intermittently fending off rumours about her having an affair with Wham!'s George Michael or being about to join the Hare Krishna movement. Albion, Edwards and the court cases inevitably feature heavily too. 'It's really very sad,' she offers coolly. 'But even now there's no real regret. Some of it's very funny if you think about it.'

Her comments are peppered with a certain sardonic astonishment –was this really me? – but there's still some anger and resentment in there too. Speaking about the whole affair again three months later, her attitude is little different. Even thinking about it is a learning process, she says, another lesson in not being fooled again.

I've learnt so much [she says at one point, blinking back the tears]. It's such a shame I had to be educated like that.

I'm just a bit of a mixed-up person who probably came into the music business with a bit of an idealist's dreamy approach and found that in fact it was a bit like going into hospital and having shock therapy – finding that it's going to shock you all over the place. I just decided I don't want any more shock treatment. And the only way to stop getting shock treatment is to stand up for yourself. It was like a tumour or something. You had to cut the whole lot out – even if your arm was attached to the tumour.

Albion just didn't have the facility to deal with a star, and that was it, full stop. And they didn't make the star – the star was made by herself and other people. But the battles dragged on and on because I don't think their pride could ever admit that. We were working against their egos. It got to the point where judge's clerks used to come to our front door all of the time with writs. They'd be these kindly gentlemen going: 'Hazel O'Connor? I'm awfully sorry but...' And I'd go 'Oh, thank you, I wonder who this is from!' There were millions – and of course it's still not over. In fact I'm still thinking of maybe suing the *Daily Mirror* for something they wrote which made it look like me and my flatmate were lesbians... and after all those stories about how many hundreds of men I was supposed to have had!

I think I'm kind of an established star, even if I have money or don't have money. I'm kind of a name that a cab driver knows or a little girl in Tokyo knows and your fundamental responsibility is to the people who are your fans. You have to remember that when you get sucked into the business. And all pop stars do get sucked into the game, even when we try not to play it. Until you wise up. It's like being a little puppet dancing up and down, whether it's us that are pulling our own strings or somebody else. Everything seems to be a game within a game. You think you're pulling your own strings and that you know what you're doing, but you're always going to be scratching somebody else's back.

I know that I'm a bit nutty and I've got funny problems in some ways in dealing with people, but this whole thing is the most enriching experience I've ever had in my whole life. And I wouldn't have missed it for the world. It's like taking a trip to Disneyland and seeing all these people, and all these scenarios. You should think that you're lucky to be able to sing and write and that if we have ego problems, then that's the price we have to pay.

Some people just don't understand it because they operate in a world where you discard your business at the end of each day. But I am that business. I wear it all the time – it's something that I can't just put away in the cupboard like a suit. And that is probably what makes stars. Toy stars are generally the people who put it on and then put it away again. Real stars are nutty, eccentric, all right people... They perform in life and people go, 'Wow! wish that was me!'

Whenever I get really pissed off, I just look at that [very favourable] *Music Week* review [from an 1984 Ronnie Scott's show] and think that somebody saw what I was projecting and thinking of me as a Piaf or Billie Holiday figure. I don't, but I know that's the sort of person I am. And that's what people will eventually realize. People in the business always look at 'Will You' as a classic standard. Because I've done that once, they know that the chances are I'll do it again.

As far as the *Breaking Glass* syndrome and the fame is concerned, I've come to the conclusion that there are two ways that I could have done it. I could have got tough, nasty managers and not have had any ideals and put on the sort of frocks they wanted – but I have this sneaking suspicion that that just wouldn't have worked anyway. And the other choice is to struggle. And when you give up struggling, you compromise, and that's called growing old.

Last week I was going to meet John Reid. The plan was I'd go round to his house for a meeting in the afternoon and then he was going to take me on to Elton's party that night. When I got there, feeling matchstick height at the door of this mansion, he wasn't in. His housekeeper said he hadn't been home and was going straight on to the party. I started to drive home and I wanted to cry. I felt so lousy. And then I stopped. I thought, 'Don't be silly!' Because he's forgotten, it doesn't mean that you're tiny and minuscule and that people don't love you or care. I had to look at things like a grown person. He was right to put me last on his list. I wasn't making him any money.

February 1985 found a streamlined Albion Records in a new airy building just off an industrial estate in the rundown Latimer Road area of west London. From Dai Davies's office window you can see the beginnings of a new state-of-the-art recording studio (not Albion's) and a peeling giant cut-out of the head of Wham!'s George Michael, recently trashed by Wham!'s lighting company next door. In Albion's own office hang the same metal discs as hung in Oxford Street: a few from their Stranglers and Joe Jackson publishing deals, and a few, of course, from O'Connor. Dai Davies still presents a fine advertisement for the budding, slightly bumbling, amateur. Rich anecdotes are delivered in a soft Welsh brogue still unspoilt by all those London pub nights, and the look of black foppish hair over a plump and slightly puffy face, and blue jeans tugging gently against beer belly, all add to the picture. He's *not* an amateur of course, but it would always be hard to imagine him as the pounding hard man. Clearly too, he's still a diehard rock fanatic.

A few months before he joined Alan Edwards, Derek Savage was also in jeans and woolly jumper but spoke with more suspicion, more reserve and more economy than Davies. His light brown curly hair has thinned further since he first met O'Connor, and his brown and grey beard has probably grown slightly in mass and length, extending the length of his face. He too would look more at home against a rural landscape than the shimmer of metallic records, and certainly he doesn't like to see himself as part of the machine.

Their largest current venture is to swing the deal that will land Albion the soundtrack of *Porky's Revenge,* the latest sequel in that seemingly endless churn of American high school movies.* They both talk of their experiences with O'Connor with extremely little emotion. Each occasionally sniggers at the thought of one of her demands, but the whole episode is not something they admit to having thought of at length. That is, the details were significant, but the saga is now insignificant. An attitude of *c'est la guerre*, in fact.

'None of it [the split and court case] was about cash,' asserts Dai Davies. 'Basically she wanted to be with another label, and we didn't mind her being on another label but we wanted a sort of reward.'

'It just got a bit confused and a bit silly in one crazy moment,' continues Derek Savage, 'and her caretaker manager said we'll take you to court. We said, "What for?" and they said, "We don't think the contract's right." We said, "That's nonsense," and the court agreed with us. So we then compromised.

Davies:

The film wasn't an error for Hazel – it was a golden opportunity that nobody would ever turn down. [But] it's an odd thing to do to a human being – to take a struggling musician off, make them into a film star for nine months, and then dump them back to where they were before. She viewed the short period as a film star as the high spot in her life and viewed her return to being a normal recording artist on a small label and selling a respectable but not-that-large number of records as being a great comedown. And it's very daunting to feel that it was only really the event of being in the film that caused those sales and it wasn't really you – it's really tough. It was remarkable

---

*They didn't get it.

actually, because you would have thought that anybody with the perception to make that film and see this story about that [rise and fall] process would actually be aware that it might be happening to them as well.

Savage:

So aware that you'd never fall for it. I never thought she'd actually fall for it – she seemed like a very down-to-earth person. It just crept in.

Davies:

She just became very, very, very confused. She didn't know what she wanted to do. She was looking round at other scripts and thinking maybe she should be an actress. She really missed the trappings that went with the film – the limos and stuff like that. All that stuff we felt very strongly against because the artist always gets charged for those sorts of things. She wasn't particularly well managed either. The guy who was managing her was a bright guy and very good at a lot of things . . . but at the time he didn't really have any experience of that sort of thing.

In London's Gaylord Indian restaurant, a short walk from his Wigmore Street management and PR office, Alan Edwards now talks of O'Connor as a small and relatively unimportant notch on his career summary. He understates ('We don't really get on . . . I wouldn't say Hazel and I were very close'), and overplays ('She's worth about 40 pence now'), and she is clearly not a person who turns his thoughts a lot these days.

His PR firm is now in the big league: with his old friend and co-director Ian Grant he now looks after the press of Bowie, The Stones and Bryan Ferry. With Big Country and The Cult his management roster is on the up too, and he's now even in a position to turn down acts.

Now in his early thirties, the last three years have seemingly taken little toll on his inner idealism or outward show of hip: he still talks and dresses in a smooth, well-measured street style that would endear him to rebel guitarists and company vice-presidents alike. He, too, is clearly still a rock fan, a closet upholder of the rock 'n' roll myth – perhaps quite beyond his better judgement.

Two months before Derek Savage moved into his offices, Edwards spoke as if the severing of his O'Connor ties had meant that his Albion links had also been broken for good. Further, he seemed glad about it. His trust in the company seemed to be waning as early as the late seventies:

Dai and Derek really seemed to doublecross us [Edwards and Ian Grant]. They started this Albion Records thing and they offered me and Ian both to be directors, and they offered us a percentage of the company and they didn't realize just how thick [close] Ian and I were. When we went home that evening and checked the deals we were offered, the deal seemed to add up to more than 100 per cent. We'd both been offered 70 per cent of the company or something. So around this time we began to feel that perhaps this wasn't our future . . .

The real reason I fell out with Hazel O'Connor was because I didn't get her off Albion, and she thought she was being ripped off by them. She never ever accused me of ripping her off – in the end she ripped me off. I was left with all the debts when she walked out on me . . . about £35,000 . . . and I've only just finished paying them off, all these years down the line. I was very resentful about it – I never got a penny . . . About two or three years ago Ian and I were maybe about £100,000 in debt. I lost thirty-five grand on The Members when they broke up, we lost thirty-five grand with Hazel, maybe ten grand with The Passions at the stage when they got dropped from the record company. I can't explain to anyone the pressure of being all that money in debt. Every morning you walk in, you're depressed, the bailiffs are there ready to clear you out, they're knocking on the door. It's enough to bring you to a nervous breakdown. It really fucks you up.

Also, [Hazel] wasn't straight with me. I've had arguments with other artists, and they've said: 'I don't want you to manage me, so here's a grand and fuck off.' It's all been face to face, and I'm not a bad man in that way, in so far as I wouldn't spend my life suing an artist. She did it all behind my back. She brought someone else in. Laurence Myers was a middle-aged accountant who said to her, 'I can get you in films,' – that was his line. I think he talked her into doing this thing of breaking away from me. And that's why I was bitter, because not only was it all done slyly and they said, 'We'll give you money,' and they never gave me anything, but the thing was that the manager that took her away really was a multimillionaire who lived in this amazing mansion up on the hill in Hampstead and had money coming out of his ears. I could have done with even £500 just to pay off my landlord.

Laurence Myers is clearly less of the tycoon-cum-ogre than Alan Edwards would have people believe. Rather, he is typical of that dying breed: a fast-talking, severely jocular, instinctive entertainment entrepreneur who seems equally boastful about his failed shots as his successful ones, and who still jolts with infectious buzz whenever he connects with a hit. And since his early days as one of the first rock business managers in 1969, the definition of hit has expanded from chart records to major contractual and court victories to cramming people into cinemas and video shops. He remains, with his hair thinning and gut thickening, midway between groupie and city gent. He plays tennis with Gary Glitter, but they talk tax afterwards.

From his GTO/GEM office, unrivalled in its view across London's green Soho Square to the CBS building opposite, Myers now enthuses about the new Julie Walters/Ian Charleson film he'll be distributing, *Car Trouble*. After a run of pulp and schlock movies, it's the first legit name project he's been involved in for a while, and it may be more than accident that there is a small part in it for Hazel O'Connor.

Myers remains one of the few industry figures that O'Connor feels has stuck with her through the decline. And clearly he still holds a soft spot for her talents. His sentiments, however, are cooled by experience and realism, not emotion, and there's little resentment or bitterness in his voice. Little doubt either.

Alan Edwards just wasn't keen on a fight. It wasn't a love of Albion, but he liked the quiet life – he wasn't a professional gunfighter. And Albion were very difficult because there was just like tunnel vision, and I think they were stupid. It was mostly a case of holding on to what they had. Obstinacy is a sign of weakness and the guys at Albion were obstinate out of insecurity.

Their intransigence cost Hazel a vital, vital year and maybe in the long run her career. Because that was the time when she should have had product out, and she didn't, and she went off the boil. Hazel has the ability to actually do wonderful things. She was seen because of *Breaking Glass* as a punk-orientated artist, but at the time when she should have been making records and wasn't, she could have grown out and on from that, as lots of artists have. She's basically a blues singer – she's got a wonderful voice – and that's the tragedy.

Although he helped to find and approve Alan Seifert as O'Connor's personal manager, Laurence Myers 'nevertheless felt that he was uncomfortable with her' well before their split. And despite Seifert's long and hard-won experience of handling women artists, if not because of it, O'Connor too soon found a certain lack of dynamism, a failure perhaps to speak the same language.

'I do not exploit my artists. They exploit me, and that's the difference,' counters Seifert from his cramped and ill-fitting Chelsea studio. Two weeks before their split there's already a marked detachment, even coldness, in his appraisal of his work with O'Connor.

It was always so-so about her career. She was never really home and dry.

I thought it would be easy to get her a record deal after the court case, but of course it wasn't, because after two years people didn't want to know. No one wants to get involved in that sort of thing unless it's a band like Wham! where you take a chance because the profit will be so enormous. Also, people think she's difficult. In fact, she's no more difficult than any other girl I've ever known, but she's not had that international success that makes it worthwhile to keep on fighting for her.

She sold hardly any records in the time she was with RCA, and purely on commercial reasons I understand why they dropped her. But I think it was the wrong company – she needs a more creative, smaller unit than a corporation that does things in triplicate. I now think it's going to be quite hard to find another record company.

She's an irritating artist actually. She's so close to being wonderful, but I don't think she's a perfectionist, and to be a really big star you have to be one. All the big stars will say, 'Forget it, let's do it again, again, again,' whereas Hazel will say, 'All right, that'll do.' With Hazel I think she tends to have too many other things getting into her head – like at the very big shows she'd be pining for the boyfriend.

She could come back if she had a really good song . . . you can't say that if you stop for two years, you can never come back. If Shirley Bassey stopped, she'd still come back to her adoring fans. Hazel just didn't have enough adoring fans to rely on. In her heyday she had a fan club of 4,000, but by the time the court case was over, it was down to forty. But she'll probably persevere, and who knows? By the time she's forty, she may well be huge again.

Crowded by yet more shiny metal discs hammered into the three sides of a Swedish-style wood-panelled cabin in his own Good Earth Studios in London's Dean Street, Tony Visconti takes an ambivalent stand on the affair. Her own stupid fault for signing, he feels, particularly after legal advice, but then he knows that many artists would have done the same. And it was hardly her fault that she was handled so poorly by Albion, he says. He too still rates her talent highly, and there are distant chances that he may work with her again soon. 'I will do something to help her, but I don't know what it is. I hope she doesn't sign a stupid contract with me . . .'

He has less sympathy for Albion:

They had a star handed to them on a silver platter. They had a star who'd made a film, who had hit records, and they fucked it. Hazel and I worked as a team, but they were still not too pleased to bring us together, because apparently I cost them too much money. Dai Davies has been around a long time, he's got no excuse. If I was Albion, I would have taken out a second and a third mortgage on my house and I would have made that (second) album work. There was no reason why it shouldn't have worked, except that there was no money spent on it and it did not get promoted after it was made . . . they just fucked it.

Now divorced from Mary Hopkin, divorced from his past all-black uniform, and with a new project for a cassette-only label in the offing, these days Visconti presents a roundly self-assured figure of a control freak. New-found confidence has been formed largely by a recent completion of an ego-boosting Exegesis course. You can't afford to be too loyal in this industry, he says, and the Visconti watchword is still 'ruthless'. 'You get very few friends in this business. You have to get what you want first, and then make sure that what you want works for everybody.' O'Connor, he feels, still has the wrong approach.

> I think she's created this mess. There's some kind of quirk in her make-up where she feels loyalty to people, but her loyalty is to the wrong people at the wrong time. Like she's always felt loyal to Alan Edwards and he's just turned around and completely disowned her. She's really put her faith in a lot of creeps.
>
> She likes to be everyone's little darling, but it never works out – it's better to be controversial. She's lost that if anything, and that's what got her off in the first place; she *was* controversy, she was radical. But as soon as she started going around and meeting a lot of people, she just wanted to be everybody's friend, and unfortunately she did this in the world of contracts and business where that doesn't go. In fact, she's more powerful than she thinks she is. A lot of people don't really understand just how powerful they are, just how much they're wanted.

David Betteridge, the man who signed O'Connor to RCA but subsequently had little further involvement with her, possibly had the least to lose by her lack of success. And perhaps more than anyone, his comments seem to carry real compassion.

> At the end of the day, Hazel didn't come through. As far as RCA was concerned, Martin Rushent was going through a difficult situation and didn't deliver the album we hoped, and therefore neither Hazel nor Albion finished up as the winner, because nobody actually sold any records. Which is a pity really – I think it's hard now for her to come through. We are in the pop business and the pop business is a young business and maybe Hazel's time has passed. I hope I'm wrong, but I think I'm right. I think that may well be it for her.

9
'Don't play golf
with Richard Branson . . .'

The music industry has never been short of the opinionated. It is one of the attractions of the business that everybody thinks they *know* – know what will chart, know how to make money, know how to avoid getting shafted – and it's one of the truths that only very few ever prove themselves right.

What follows is a collection of quotes on the industry from insiders. The majority are culled from interviews conducted personally in 1984 and 1985, although a few are pinched from newspapers and magazines. As far as I'm aware, the quotes were not prompted by alcohol or drugs.

The ignorance

Mistakes? Sure we made huge mistakes! But we were 18-year-old boys who knew nothing about it. Everyone makes mistakes like that. The rip-off is the age-old story, isn't it? It's always going to happen. It's the story of middle-aged businessmen whose product comes from young boys and girls who don't know what they're doing. It's always going to be the same. So it's going to carry on happening.

George Michael, Wham!, 1984

Unless they have proper representation, and even then you need money – they don't want to know unless you've got money.

Andrew Ridgeley, Wham!, 1984

My nature is to be very trusting. I was just convinced that we wouldn't get fucked – I don't know why. And I would be today, too, if I hadn't learnt so many awful lessons about this industry.

Pete Townshend, 1985

Every major contract that I've ever signed I think has been done in a dressing room or I've signed it when I was drunk. Along would come the contracts, and they'd wheel them out and . . . scribble . . . signing things all the time. I still see things all the time now bearing my signature and I don't remember anything about them. I don't have any legal documents that I can attach to them from my files. I can't remember having any independent advice on them. Can you imagine actually trying to sit down in the middle of a tour and explain a very complex bit of tax law to somebody as stoned as Keith and I used to be most of the time, or as thick as Roger used to make himself out to be?

Pete Townshend, 1985

Nobody really comes into a publishing company knowing all that much about what goes on. At least they know no more than how a record company works – and there's no real reason why they should.

Richard Thomas,
managing director of CBS Songs, 1985

I don't think anyone understands how a record company works unless they work in a record company. I managed various bands for ten years, and it's embarrassing to think of the kind of conversations I used to have with record company personnel, because I really didn't know how it functioned or what it was about. I was discussing a fantasy world. When I started running a record company, it was a total revelation to me.

> Dave Robinson,
> (then) managing director of Island Records
> and Stiff Records, 1984

I'm increasingly aware that a lot of my clients are very young, and some of them are more excited about having a single out next week and having their picture in *New Musical Express* than anything else.

> David Gentle,
> specialist music business solicitor, 1985

In the early days we made a lot of errors – you find that record companies are saying one thing and doing another a lot, but when you're out there and having a good time you don't tend to think of things like that, that people are playing these little tricks behind you. The companies do their business, and they don't want you to know *how* they do it. They want you to be The Star.

> Paul Young, 1985

We had management problems that you wouldn't believe . . . really it's like them playing tiddlywinks with you. They just have all these plans that you don't know about. I could do it now, I suppose, I could completely take a young band to the cleaners. Just on what I know, so these guys who study law . . . they're probably laughing up their sleeves.

> Dave Stewart, Eurythmics, on his days in The Tourists, 1985

We weren't represented when we signed, and had a pretty poor deal. Let me put it this way: if we had been represented like an act is represented now, we would have made three, four, five times as much money as we ever did, easy.

Q But before they seek representation, how much do artists now know about the sort of deals you're offering them?
A The artists and 80 per cent of their managers still have no idea whatsoever.

Muff Winwood,
once of the Spencer Davis Group,
now senior director A and R, CBS, 1985

The talent source

Being an A and R man is rather like being a man in the front line going over the trenches in the First World War. Not many survive for any great length of time. It's a very tough, and very rough business. They have to be bright, they have to be extremely hard-working, they work very unsocial hours, they have to be sober, they have to have great taste, they have to have imagination and they also have to be stupid. You can't believe that anybody would actually want a job like that. They get well paid and if they actually balance out the value of the business to them, if they get three good years under their belt, and they sign perhaps one and a half internationally successful acts, they should then go and get themselves a record deal and start their own company.

I can just about measure on two hands the number of A and R men I respect in this country. It's very easy to sign an act – there are fifty to sixty bands playing in this town every night, no problem. But to actually sign an act on the right deal and then get the marketing money, and then find the right producer and break it through – doing all those things becomes very hard. It's a great ego boost to sign an act and drive a deal through. You say, 'I just signed this act, it's the greatest thing since The Beatles . . .,' but most A and R guys don't know what to do with it after that – only eight or ten of them do. And that's not even to say that every time these people sign an act that it's successful – that's not so. None of us have done that, anyway, ever. At the end of the day, we all lose our butts.

David Betteridge,
co-founder Island Records,
ex-managing director CBS, ex-managing director RCA,
currently founder and managing director
of the Virgin-linked Siren Records, 1985

People who work in the UK majors are careerists, opinionated and in most cases very talented. They're taken in by the same things as you or I. They're taken in by hypes, they follow the leaders, they go with the band the buzz is about, and they're human and frail. They've got a bad image, they're all supposed to go round stuffing coke up their noses and some of them do, but I think the ones that survive are the ones with talent. But the people who care about the artists they sign are not the ones who make the corporate decisions. They're not the MDs or financial advisors, they're the A and R team and below.

Theo Chalmers,
managing director of independent music publishers,
Complete Music (formerly Cherry Red Music), 1985

About seven years ago, myself and my partner, Ian Grant, had a record deal called Modern Records, and we had a deal with a big major. There was quite a bit of money – we were paid ten grand a record or something. I remember going in to see this major company's head of A and R, a big executive, at four in the afternoon for a meeting. His secretary said: 'You can't go in there, you can't go in there – he's in conference!' So after a while we got really bored, and either myself or Ian just opened the door a bit, and he was asleep on the floor, still pissed from his lunch! And that's the head of A and R!

Alan Edwards,
director, Modern Publicity
and Modern Management, 1985

For a few years around the time of punk, the situation did improve immensely. You could go in with a new act and the A and R guy would listen to it and really take an interest – you got a fair hearing. Now it's worse than it was before punk. It's very, very bad. You now ring up an A and R guy, and these are even A and R guys that I know and have taken acts to over the years, and they're too busy, or they're at lunch, or they can never be bothered to see the act. The only things that end up getting signed are people that are signed through favours. The bad old days are back where most of the record-company guys, with notable exceptions, are more interested in getting drunk and stoned and getting home early. One A and R guy I know has a yearly pay packet of supposedly £120,000. To me that sort of figure is incalculable. And this guy probably spends a good part of his time with a biro tube up his nose.

Alan Edwards, 1985

Today's music business is: 'Leave a cassette with us – we'll let you know.' And then every time you get something back that says, 'Thank you very much, but we're going to pass on it . . .'

Larry Page,
ex-fifties pop star,
ex manager of Sonny and Cher,
current manager of The Kinks, 1985

[My dog] Charlie is as much a part of this outfit as I am. He helps show artists and managers what a wonderful, decent, likeable human being I really am. And how can any superstar's agent come to see me with venom in his voice when Charlie climbs up on his lap and licks his ear? Charlie has a seat at my board meetings and he's a real watchdog in the sense that, when he gets restless, I look at my watch and realize that the meeting has been going on too long. In the office, he either gets up and pads across to meet a new client, or he growls and circles round them. I don't base my decisions on his responses, but we do act in accord sometimes. There was one punk band that came to see me last year, and he walked right out of the office. He didn't like the look of those characters and neither did I. The deal fell through.

Maurice Oberstein, (then) chairman, CBS Records, 1979

The crooks and the machine

There are stupid-bad cowboys and clever-bad cowboys, and the clever-bad cowboys are big companies. They dress up their deals in such a way that they're not susceptible to legal action. The stupid ones are, and they probably won't survive. But there are large publishing companies who don't act honorably, and certainly don't act in the writer's interests, who fail to account on time, lose sales, do sneaky deals with their sub-publishers in foreign territories, all sorts of things.

Theo Chalmers, 1985

The entire business is run on bullshit . . . But you don't have to fucking go up to your neck and eat it as well. With a bit of thought, you can sort of paddle across it. And if you're really gonna be a media Jesus, actually walking on the bullshit is the ultimate challenge.

Billy Bragg in *Spin* magazine, 1985

There are so many people in the industry trying to trip you up and push you over and catch you out and unveil you. The industry is just rife with jealousy and hatred. Everybody in it is a failed bassist. Everybody wants to be on the stage – they all want to be you. It's just really awash with jealousy and sourness and bitterness. When you as a band are trying to lay down the rules and break rules, you're actually spoiling things for so many middle-aged mediocrities who control the whole sphere of popular music.

Morrissey, The Smiths, 1985

There's a feeling when you start out that a record company is this thing that comes along and gives you a big bag of money and you go off and be a rock star for the rest of your life. You trade an awful lot for that. We see other groups around us and they always seem to get worse, don't they? One good album and then it starts getting worse and their music gets more and more diluted and homogenized. You really have to define your own territory in these things, or otherwise you're robbed. It's all taken slowly down the line, and you end up with nothing to give or communicate.

Bono, U2, 1984

There are some very corrupt rogues in the industry, and there are also some very decent people who've got a great love of music and want to go out and pass on their enjoyment to millions of people throughout the world – you've just got to tread your way between the two. I don't think the major companies are corrupt – I don't think they're *inherently* corrupt. They're too big as businesses nowadays to be corrupt.

Alexis Grower,
specialist music business solicitor, 1985

Clearly the industry's exploitative. Of that there's no question. But it's less exploitative than it was. It has become very much more professional in the last few years and the areas of exploitation have been restricted and limited.

David Ravden,
specialist music business accountant, 1985

Corruption? Yes, of course there's corruption. And yes, there are some sharks. To a certain extent a lot of people get caught out fairly quickly. Some people are sharp, rather than sharks. I've occasionally come across situations that I've turned against – you have to maintain honesty in your own business. Some of the things that I find the worst are lack of integrity and lack of intelligence . . . Bands that have been destroyed by bad managers or bad agents or bad record companies. That's a crime in itself.

But I get pissed off that people in the industry are often more interested in that level of the business than other levels. We all start throwing shit at each other and complain about each other's motives maybe too often.

David Betteridge, 1985

There are always people who will be there ready to take an act away from another smaller company. They'll say, 'Well, now you're number one in the charts, what are you getting? Six points? Oh, we can get you twelve.' The music business now is run by marketing people, by lawyers and by accountants.

Larry Page, 1985

We've found that the people that we've ended up wanting to work with in the music business are the people who play fair. And those people stand out a mile. If you take your policy as being, 'Get in there quick before anybody else does – screw before anyone else screws,' and use it with your artists as well as with the other people in the business, then you're going to get a bad name and lose out. You don't have to thank people for trying to make money out of you when they're not letting you make any money out of yourself.

George Michael, 1984

When Wham! first began, their first 'Wham! Rap' record was in everybody's top five at the *New Musical Express* and they were considered to be quite subversive . . . street kids who weren't going to be part of the system; kids who weren't going to take a job; kids who were saying, 'Tell 'em all to fuck off, it's all a load of shit.' And now what are they? They're actually completely integrated into the machine. And that's how we felt in the last days of The Who. We looked around, and we thought, 'Fucking hell – we're part of the American business machine'. This was

considered by a lot of people to be a denial or refutation of all
the things that we stood for in the past . . .

Pete Townshend, 1985

About ten years ago, bands loved the element of surprise and
risk in their work and lifestyle – they lived their music. Today
it's a job, it has a certain time factor involved and people read
their contracts to find how many videos they can make.
Where's the risk in that? Where's the fun in that?

Years ago you never considered yourself to be part of the
industry. Today, a group is constantly thinking of themselves as
a business every inch of the way. From the moment they start
recording in the studio to the moment they finish recording
their video, it's all a very well protected, schemed and worked-
out project. Before, you went into a recording studio and you
never knew if you were going to come out alive. I don't believe
that any great records in those days were thought up before
they went into those studios. Now, because of the nature of the
creative accounting and because everyone's in the business, the
records all tend to sound the same. Very colourless. You don't
hear an element of danger. Now it's all so packaged. Then, you
could hear that there was always a risk that the singer might
knock something or someone over.

Groups these days have become real executives – they're all
yuppies. It used to be a case of Johnny Rotten putting his fag
ends out in his beer. Now it's The Cult, supposedly a rebellious
band, spending time perusing fucking hotel wine lists! Those
kids may have been rebels in some respects, but they soon
became yuppies. It's Margaret Thatcher who created Spandau
Ballet and the rest of the boat that they sail in.

I don't know what's going to happen next, but I do feel I'm
not alone in my views. I met a kid in Newcastle last week who
said that one of his main pleasures is going round churches,
throwing bricks through stained-glass windows. On the brick
he writes a little message, and the message reads: 'Magic's back!'

Malcolm McLaren,
ex-manager of The Sex Pistols,
fashion designer, pioneering plunderer,
pop polymath, and now screenwriter, 1985

The cynicism and the realism

Q Have things got back to normal after Christmas yet?
A Aw, I don't know. It's really the same thing no matter what
month it is. Every month it's still the same old shit.

Maurice Oberstein,
three months before retirement
as chairman of CBS Records, 1985

It makes me hysterical when people get formal about pop, when
people give pop a history. It's so pompous. I think pop music's
funny. People ask me how important is the Frankie album in
the history of pop. Don't make me laugh! How important do
you think the *history of pop* is? And pop hasn't changed that
much in twenty years. When they say most records are bought
by people aged 12 to 25, I'm not surprised – you *have* to have a
new generation if you're still dishing up the same old thing, still
serving up hamburgers. Personally, I'm sick of hamburgers.

Trevor Horn,
star record producer and co-founder
of ZTT Records, 1984

I really don't enjoy going to live gigs any more. And out of the
250 or so albums that CBS and Epic put out each year, only
very few of them ever find their way on to my shelf at home . . .
Even fifteen minutes of fame seems too long these days.

Jonathan Morrish,
head of press at CBS subsidiary
Epic Records, 1985

I'm kind of cynical about bands, having had to deal with them
for twenty years now. You try and tell them it's a new world
and you want them to try and perform in a new kind of way,
but they inevitably do the same things as the last band. My kind

of interest in life is selling records, I've never considered a record company as being a huge artform per se. I don't sit down and say, 'This is great, this is not'. If I have an artist, then I'm selling the product.

Dave Robinson, 1984

A lot of us executives are walking around physically ill – needing to pretend that we're creating something artistically worthy . . . But since we're all capitalist enterprises, we have to capture the lowest common denominator. What's wrong is that we have to cater to the rancid, infantile, pubescent tastes of the public.

Jerry Wexler,
senior vice-president of Warner Brothers (US),
date uncertain

I don't think there are any record companies now in the real sense of the word. We're all in the fashion business. You used to be able to sell records purely on music and musicianship. Now it's packaging, media, television and video.

Chris Blackwell,
co-founder and owner of
Island Records, 1984

Video was so good for the majors because it put them in a position that they could afford to make them – they had enough money in the bank. But those small little independent companies that were having a laugh were buried by video. And then if a major's band gets a hit, that band wonders where its money has gone . . .

Larry Page, 1985

Promotion is what a record company is about. And absorption. That's what a major does – it sits around and it absorbs. Anyone that has a good idea, the majors will quickly absorb it.

Independents say: 'We are the only one, we are the reality', but they're absorbed in no time at all.

Dave Robinson, 1984

The big companies aren't interested in profit as much as market share, and the company's market share is what the real fighting's about. CBS, being an American company, are in it for their shareholders – and it's really names like Neil Diamond and Barbra Streisand that these shareholders understand. The proof, if you like, is that next to the gold discs in the CBS reception in Soho Square there are almost as many certificates celebrating their big market shares. All they have to do is to keep a hold of that market share to keep investors happy. The more money they start spending on new acts, that's not too clever, and CBS in this country are far better off really just boosting the big American acts. The advances they're paid over here might be vast in UK terms, but not in worldwide terms. I'd say that what they paid for Sade would be peanuts, not vast, and I'd say the same for Alison Moyet . . . the CBS deals are crap, they really are.

Larry Page, 1985

Decca are supposed to be making records, but they might just as easily be making baked beans. A record to them is just a piece of plastic, and what's on there doesn't really matter.
I'd rather the Mafia than Decca.

Keith Richards,
The Rolling Stones,
date uncertain

The jobs and the workers

Publishers don't do anything for artists. They just sit there collecting money – they're bankers. They collect in the money, take off a cut, and hand you over the rest. Their risk is whether you are going to be successful or not. Lawyers have come along and pointed out to writers how much money they're losing to publishers, and said that successful artists might as well go round the world and make their own publishing deals.

Alexis Grower, 1985

Some lawyers are virtually acting as publishing houses on behalf of their clients, and they are doing deals themselves for their clients in every territory of the world, territory by territory, and getting them an advance for each. But he would charge by the hour and for a job fee, job by job, and who is to say whether his fees are fair? He might argue that his client must have an 80:20 deal in each territory at source, and you might think, 'Wonderful! What a great guy!' But it will look different when his fee comes in, and he probably hasn't even done his job . . . One lawyer recently charged his clients fees that were higher than the advance he had negotiated for them. One even said to me, 'I don't think that ought to be the single.' I said, 'I don't give a fuck what you think – you're the fucking lawyer!'

Theo Chalmers, 1985

It hasn't worked out very well for lawyers who move into prominent positions in the music industry. Paul Russell at CBS, who I used to use as a lawyer, is I think the only lawyer running a record company in this country, and I know of at least two who moved into positions of power and failed miserably because they couldn't feel for it. When the business became more complicated and when contracts became more difficult to interpret, the lawyers looked in and said, 'Why is that man in that position? I know more than him, I should be there.' Because at that time the business was, and still is to some extent, run by amateur creative people – people like Dave Robinson and Richard Branson – and what is their qualification? Some of them were expelled from school! But they just have a gut feel for the business and they are good because of it. The lawyers thought they could outsmart these people, and of course they couldn't. You could easily buy your financial director and your marketing director, but if you are running a record company you have got to have some sort of taste for the music. And if you think you can bullshit your way through intellectually, you've had it.

David Betteridge, 1985

When I was [first] at Stiff, we shared a sales force with Virgin. We had a clause in our contract which said that Richard Branson couldn't attract anybody else into it without our agreement. Which is essential, because Richard is always building an empire even when he is standing at the bus stop – he'll probably have incorporated three or four people into the company before the bus comes.

[Another company did eventually enter into the agreement on Branson's suggestion, but a failure to resolve the details satisfactorily with Stiff led to Stiff's departure.] There were a few legal mutterings, but nothing actually happened. A year later, I played a game of golf with Richard, and on the fourteenth hole, he took about nine shots to get out of the rough and he was really uptight and he said, 'I remember the sales-force thing with you!' And he sued me. I got a writ the following week. I was thinking of putting a thing in *Music Week* saying: 'Don't play golf with Richard Branson – you get a writ!'

Dave Robinson, 1985

Yes, it's true about my bee factory. Bees are so much more productive than the people in the record industry. They are wonderful workers . . . they don't take holidays.

Chris Blackwell, 1984

The pressure

There's a terrible, weird complicity in the industry – in the industry's belief in the power of a name and in a belief in that name's ability to regenerate money. When I made my solo contract I made a three-album deal with Atlantic and I had a five-album Who deal with Warner Brothers. We are talking about eight hit albums, each one with advances well in excess of $1 million, for which I was solely responsible for the writing, and I sincerely believed that I was capable of coming up with all those songs. I was swept along by the dream. Meanwhile my wife is telling me, 'Listen, you are going to kill yourself, you are going to break up our marriage.' And I'm saying, 'Yeah, I'm sure it's going to be all right.' What it actually led to was alcoholism, drug addiction, financial collapse, the end of The Who, and practically my death.

In the case of The Who it led to Warners withdrawing the contract and suing the group, and us settling for a repayment of $1.7 million. I am now two and a half years late with my solo album – I just can't work any faster than I am working now.

The pressure is introduced in the form of contractual delivery dates with large amounts of money attached to them. I hate that part of the system that will sign up a band like The Roaring Boys for £200,000 and land them with this enormous load. And I see it with bands like Duran Duran. Great that they get big advances and all the rest of it, but what a load to put on these young kids.

Pete Townshend, 1985

The record companies in this country are too sophisticated. All of our talent-spotting techniques are so together and organized now that we see artists too early. It's no good saying, 'Oh, this guy is 19 and he has got a lot of talent and in three years' time he'll be really big, so we'll wait.' Somebody's going to sign him now, and they could destroy his career. You just can't tell how he's going to handle it. And there is no way of getting out of that, it's just part of the screwing ourselves slowly but surely into the ground with more and more momentum.

Muff Winwood, 1985

The Americans

You can eat off our industry compared to the industry in America. There is no doubt about it. Our industry is pretty good, actually. And that is saying something because it is also so appalling. So if we are good, you can imagine what the Americans are like.

Barry McKay,
music business consultant, 1985

I don't think I had a particularly happy time as managing director of RCA (UK) – most of it was because RCA records over here is such a small cog in such a huge corporate machine. I once had to go to the US to ask for $15 million to buy a new distribution depot. I thought the only thing they would understand was a presentation that said, 'This is what CBS UK do, and this is also what RCA (UK) should do.' So I arranged for someone to go around secretly and take a lot of pictures of CBS installations – their plants, their offices, their salesmen going into shops – and then I had a lot of pictures of our people running things on Victorian lines.

This RCA Inc committee used to meet once a month to hear people's pleas for money from all over the world. I was sitting in this waiting room on the fifty-sixth floor of this bloody building, waiting to give my presentation and there was this guy next to me who was the financial director of a carpet factory that RCA owned somewhere in the Mid-west – he had come in to ask for $50 million. The guy on the other side of me was from an RCA operation called Globcom, and this guy was asking for Christ knows how many billion to get the next satellite up. My $15 million was a piss in the bucket really, but I went in and did my piece in front of twenty-six guys, and I am sure none of them had any real idea about the record industry . . . [He didn't get the money.]

Geoff Hannington,
ex-managing director RCA (UK);
managing director of independent Logo Records, 1985

The foundation of the American music industry is built
absolutely on corruption and deceit and a lack of creative and
artistic instinct.

Morrissey, 1985

I've just been talking to the manager of a band with a current
top-five hit who just got back from the States. He met this
young, naïve record plugger who was saying how he got on
when he went to Boston. The young kid said he'd been round
to this radio station with the group's new record, walked right
in, saw the DJ straight away. The DJ picked the record up,
removed it from the sleeve, held the sleeve up in the air, shook
it, peered inside it, turned round to the young kid and said:
'Son, there's nothing in it, this record's not a hit.' The kid
walked away and couldn't understand it, but the fact is you
don't give records to these guys unless they've got money or
cocaine in them, and more often it's coke. They all run it like
that.

It's a science. I've sat in a meeting often in America where
they go: 'Right, your record is going to be at number 125 this
week, then we're going to get up to number fifty-six, then next
week we'll take it to thirty-two.' And I promise you this
happens. I know the head of radio promotion at one of the
major companies in America, a very big corporation, who left
recently. I don't know if he was fired or just quit. But he left
amongst pretty messy circumstances. After he left, bills came in
to the tune of $1 million in his name. Nearly all the debts were
from DJs, who said he owed them money for deals here and
deals there. Nearly all of them supposedly revolved around
coke.

I remember being in that guy's office not so long ago when
the manager of a very big act came in and said: 'I hope the
record's going to do well, and by the way, here's a couple of air
tickets for you and your wife to spend the weekend in the
Bahamas . . .'

Alan Edwards, 1985

The prejudice

A lot of the industry is just not prepared to make deals with me, just because I'm black. I've always had to make deals that were over the odds just to sort of compensate – I've got to pay them more than white guys, and that goes for both agents and artists. And it's difficult for a black person to get any kind of sense of history in the music business. I found that the only way to do an apprenticeship is in your own company. I can't imagine myself knocking on any record company's door and them giving me a job even in the postroom. I would love to be able to walk into a record company and meet a black person sitting there and talk to him about his band, and at a level where he is actually going to look at what I have got to offer for real – we can talk about the shows I want to organize! – and didn't look at me as a black man. I go into any record company now and I feel like a foreigner. You are always the outsider. White people there always think: 'He's trying to come into our thing.' Only Island are a little bit better.

Wilf Walker, concert promoter, 1985

I know a girl who was the head of the international department of a very major record company, and she wanted to go higher still, but was told by the MD that she'd *never* be made a director and that the board would never have it. Just because she was a woman. So she left and went into management.

When I was at Charisma we were handled by Phonogram International, which was all accountants. I used to go over and had to keep quiet and let the men tell them whatever was happening – and that was a joke because I would have to previously explain everything to these men anyway. These accountants just wouldn't take it from a woman. It was only when I left, and Charisma nearly went bust, that they thought, maybe she knew what she was talking about all the time.

Virgin have seventeen people in their international department and they are all girls, and it's the best-run international department there is. But there was one girl there who wanted to become an agent and knocked on the door of every single agency in London. Not one of them would take her, saying, 'There just aren't really any female agents.' And there is only really one woman promoter – and that is because I gave her Peter Gabriel when no one else would give her a chance.

And I still have a lot of trouble with secretaries when I call up and say I'm Peter Gabriel's manager – they immediately assume that I'm the secretary too. I still go to stage doors and say, 'I'm his manager.' And they go, 'Oh yeah, sure.' They assume I'm a fan trying to get in, aged 38. I then start to shout, and they say, 'Oh dear, she's another hysterical woman . . .'

Gail Colson,
co-founder Charisma Records
and personal manager, 1985

The fixing

Is hyping going on? Yes, of course it's going on. What is actually happening is that we all have teams, and there is an 'aggressive marketing' policy – nothing wrong in that. There is no difference if you are selling Mars Bars or Duckham's oil – you have an aggressive policy to get your position in the shop. But there still is manipulation as well, and every managing director thinks that he's smart enough to get away with it.

David Betteridge, 1985

I don't like to see groups reduced to the level of soap powder, where they are pushed in and faked up the chart. There's a good deal of records in the charts now which shouldn't be there . . . Records that have a lot of promotion and money behind them.

Alan Edwards, 1985

The injustice

The music business is always vulnerable. I remember in the old days there used to be talk that the jukeboxes were in the hands of the gangsters. There was always this kind of thing because it's a glamorous business and success is easy – and people can't believe that that kind of success doesn't come from some kind of crookedness. That always happens when people are successful easily. The music business is always in the foreground of contemporary ideas, and if there is any resentment against the popular or youth-orientated culture, it manifests itself as an attack on the record business . . . We are blamed for everything.

Goddard Lieberson,
as president of CBS/Columbia Records in 1973*

The music industry is often misunderstood by people outside it, and that's why a lot of people inside it aren't keen to talk about it. I'm not a violent person, but on two occasions I nearly punched guys out for what they said about the music industry.

David Betteridge, 1985

This is the fastest market in the world. The record comes out and six weeks later you've either done it or you haven't done it. The group are either blaming you for fucking up their career, or they're saying what a good record it was anyway and that anyone could have broken it.

Dave Robinson, 1984

---

*He said this a few weeks after Clive Davis had been fired from CBS Records Inc charged with $94,000 worth of expense account violations and writing off his son's barmitzvah reception against the company. Clive Davis was later under federal indictment for income tax evasion. (He pleaded guilty to the tax evasion and to irregular travel expense claims, and was exonerated from the barmitzvah charges. The same period saw widespread press allegations of drugola and payola scandals throughout the US industry.)

The injustice, part 2

David has been robbed blind. There were millions, but other people got them, not us ... David has taken people to court, but in the end he found it too unbearable to get involved at that sort of game – it simply puts you on their level.

Angie Bowie, 1977

Many companies have not paid me yet. They tore my toes and my fingers. I didn't have nothing to crawl with. I'm amazed, all these hit records – everybody done sung them but my grandmama. And everybody was rich but me. That's not fair. In fact they didn't pay a lot of black entertainers back at that time. A lot of companies are built on the blood of those black entertainers – blood and guts. That's why I worked all the time. And everybody said: 'Oh, you look so healthy!' I better had when I had no bacon on the table. And these companies sit there like they're legit business people – so sophisticated, so dignified.

Little Richard, 1985

I don't think the industry gives a shit about artists. They really don't. Artists, they are the scum, the product. They come, they go. We love you, you're number one. When was your last hit record? They hate you, you know, today's flavour of the day is tomorrow's castaway. And that in a way is fair enough I suppose, but do the castaways who have had hits end up with any money?

Barry McKay, 1985

The accountants

I have no use for bodyguards, but I have very specific use for two highly trained certified public accountants.

Elvis Presley, date uncertain

I know that we are very feared by a lot of record companies. We have a major superstar client who had a dispute with his publisher . . . They settled, and the settlement documents recited that the artist could retain a right of audit for a certain number of years so long as our firm were not instructed to carry out the work. We will find on average at least 15 or 20 per cent under-accounted, and as much as 100 per cent in some cases – in other words an artist has only been paid half. Which is astronomical, a terrifying percentage. To an artist who is earning £40,000 a year it's another £40,000, and to him that's a fortune.

David Ravden, 1985

The complexity

What's happened is that the three-page contract has turned into the sixty-two-page contract, and when you go through one you think it's unbelievable that two sets of people have actually gone to this length, to the extent that it makes the leasehold contract on a property look like a piece of paper that Rupert Bear has written. It's become a very suspicious business.

David Betteridge, 1985

When I've seen non-music lawyers look at music contracts they don't know what they're doing . . . There are now an increasing number of ways of exploiting an artist's work. Twenty years ago they didn't have videos, cable TV, satellite TV, pop songs used in adverts, jingle-writing, compact discs, cassettes, the 12-inch market, merchandising, and they didn't have TV advertising to sell records. The contracts have become more complicated because the whole industry has become more complicated, and you want to make sure that your client gets the benefit of it all.

Alexis Grower, 1985

The large record companies refuse to accept that anything could possibly go wrong with their system, and the people that you negotiate with, when you're negotiating the settlement of a major order, actually don't know how the hell the system works. You are sitting there at CBS talking to the business-affairs people, and they have no idea what actually happens on the floor of the (pressing) plant in Aylesbury. I find that incredible – the right hand doesn't know what the left hand is doing. To a large extent, the same could be said of all the majors.

David Ravden, 1985

The T-shirts

Bruce Springsteen, whatever his rock idealism is about, is not a musician any more. It's not his concerts that make any money, it's his T-shirt sales and his programme sales. They're making $25 to $27 in America for T-shirts, and the ticket prices are $12.50. So the saint of rock 'n' roll goes out and keeps the ticket prices low, but meanwhile he's taking $25 off everybody that comes in for a T-shirt. OK, so he looks at it and so it says 'Brucey Baby' and he says, 'Oh yeah, I like that, that's good.' That's really rock 'n' roll that T-shirt. Bullshit!

Pete Townshend, 1985

The baseball players

I've got a baseball bat on the wall behind my desk because I'm attacked from time to time – people come in and threaten me with violence. I've found the best way to deal with them is to smash their elbows or something. I have from time to time had to deal with people who were going to kill me.

Dave Robinson, 1984

The mashers

The music business is about 99 per cent no-talent losers who can't stand a winner in their midst. I'm a winner, and if they want to sour grape my success by calling me names, let them. I don't give a shit.

Q Would you lie?
A Oh, sure.
Q Would you steal?
A Probably.

Look, you have to survive, you do whatever it takes, because if you don't stay alive in this business you can't help anybody. . . . There's only one thing that gives me an edge: I'm the best. I know more about this business than anybody else . . .

It's really like chess, knowing all the moves. It's a game, for Chrissakes, and winning is everything. It's a shame it has to get nasty sometimes.

Allen Klein,
ex-business manager of The Rolling Stones,
ex-business manager of The Beatles,
talking to Playboy, 1971

An extremely experienced and ruthless negotiator who was accustomed to use the issue of a writ basically as a negotiating ploy rather than with any serious expectation that the action would be fought.

Mr Justice Walton on Allen Klein, 1984

The principle of management is that an artist allows somebody else to sign on their behalf – to decide how you're going to spend your time, to sign contracts for concerts and stuff like that which you don't see sight of. Having a manager is an enormous jump for an artist, and one which I think new artists tend to respond to with great desperation. They take what they can get and they hope that they can clear things up later on. And it's not just naïvety – there's a certain kind of calculated blindness about it.

But as far as I'm concerned, I still hate to feel that I'm arguing over money. I like to think that it doesn't concern me, and yet at the same time I hate the idea that somebody is scowling in the background feeling that they have made a killing because of my stupidity.

Pete Townshend, 1985

The backhanders

When I was a journalist on *Record Mirror*, I remember going to a gig organized by a company which was part of Warner Brothers. I remember getting off the coach with about ten other journalists and the PR guy was standing there, and he was giving out cash to all the journalists. He was saying: 'Here's some cash to get you home.' It was a few fivers, and you only needed 20p to get home on the tube in those days. I suppose that was bribery. I can't even remember if I took it or not – I probably did if I had any sense! Those things happen all the time.

Alan Edwards, 1985

The attitude

Eddie Kassner [an old-time music publisher] had a good phrase
about the industry. It was: 'They're all fucking animals!'

Larry Page, 1985

If you don't go for as much money as you can possibly get, then
I think you're stupid.

Mick Jagger, date uncertain

Hits Before Kids – CBS Records Policy Decision 7th September
1984.

Plaque presented by (then) CBS managing director,
Paul Russell to (then) CBS A & R Gordon Charlton
and Deirdre Rutkowski, member of CBS group Sunset Gun,
on their marriage in 1984.

I was never interested in being polite like other managers before
me. I didn't give a damn about the future or the royalties. 'You
can keep the royalties,' I used to say. 'Give me the money now!'
I thought royalties were a very abstract phenomenon to do with
creative accounting – like something you might never see. I
never believed what they promised, and I always thought they
were all crooks – and that's a fact: they are. I never thought of
selling millions of records and ploughing through accounts of
record companies to retrieve certain monies. You don't think of
that in the beginning. In those days I just thought to get as
much money up front as possible. You never know, they may
hate you tomorrow and throw you out. The group may never
sell a single record. Who knows?

I never intended The Sex Pistols to sell records – it was never
a significant point in their adventures. It was getting on stage
now and again and creating havoc and demonstrating their
whole sexual and political prowess, and it was getting money

from it from an industry which sorely wanted The Sex Pistols as part of their tame machine. That was the excitement of it all. If you sold records, then that was the icing on the cake. Perhaps the ideas behind The Great Rock 'n' Roll Swindle were too sophisticated – a lot of people didn't get it. John Rotten didn't get it. Really. He is still suing me – he still don't get it!*

Malcolm McLaren, 1985

What most people don't realize is that the whole thing is about getting as much money as possible in as short a time as possible with as much style as possible.

Malcolm McLaren, 1976

*In January 1986, however, John Lydon (Johnny Rotten) claimed to have had the last laugh. He and the other members of The Sex Pistols were jointly awarded almost £1 million in a tussle with McLaren over earnings that had been in receivership since the band's demise.

Index